The Galloping Ghost

The Galloping Ghost

The Extraordinary Life of Submarine Legend Eugene Fluckey

Carl LaVO

NAVAL INSTITUTE PRESS
Annapolis, Maryland

Naval Institute Press
291 Wood Road
Annapolis, MD 21402

This book has been brought to publication with the generous contribution from the
Paul Bechtner Foundation of Winnetka, Illinois.

Library of Congress Cataloging-in-Publication Data

LaVO, Carl, 1944-
  The galloping ghost : the extraordinary life of submarine legend
Eugene Fluckey / Carl LaVO.
      p. cm.
  Includes bibliographical references and index.
  ISBN-13: 978-1-59114-456-4 (alk. paper)
  ISBN-10: 1-59114-456-6 (alk. paper)
  1. Barb (Ship) 2. Fluckey, Eugene B., 1913- 3. World War,
1939-1945–Naval operations–Submarine. 4. World War, 1939-1945–Naval
operations, American. 5. World War, 1939-1945–Campaigns–Pacific
Ocean. 6. Admirals–United States–Biography. I. Title.
D783.5.B36L38 2007
940.54'51092–dc22
[B]

                                                    2006103510

Printed in the United States of America on acid-free paper ∞
13 12 11 10 09 08 07   8 7 6 5 4 3 2
First printing

In memory of my grandmother,
Ivy Lavon Canning LaVO,
a Utah pioneer
who gave me a love
of the printed word

Contents

Preface

Gene Fluckey was one of the great naval heroes of World War II. His exploits as captain of the submarine USS *Barb* revolutionized undersea warfare and laid the groundwork for the nuclear-powered ballistic missile submarine fleet that today is the primary deterrent and capability of the United States against nuclear attack by a foreign country.

At this writing, the retired rear admiral is the most decorated living American, having earned numerous presidential, congressional, and military honors in his lifetime. They include four Navy Crosses and the Medal of Honor, the nation's highest award for valor. In the war against Japan, he sank more tonnage than any other U.S. submarine captain, a total of eighty-five enemy vessels, including an aircraft carrier, a cruiser, a destroyer, and numerous cargo ships, and he also destroyed a troop train after landing submariners-turned-saboteurs on mainland Japan in 1945—the only invasion by the American military of the Japanese homeland during the war. In postwar years, he served with distinction in a variety of posts, including commander of all submarines in the Pacific, director of Naval Intelligence, and commander of NATO's Iberian Area operations based in Portugal. He knew every president from Franklin Delano Roosevelt to Bill Clinton and, even in retirement, participated in numerous national security briefings at the White House.

Admiral Fluckey's infectious, near spiritual optimism throughout his naval career had a transforming effect on the men who served with and under him. He loved people, from flag officers down to the most junior enlisted sailor. He devoted himself to veterans of the *Barb* and always credited them for his early success. And they returned that devotion to a skipper who raised them to greater heights without demeaning or treating them harshly. At the last ship's reunion with Admiral Fluckey in 2003, three crewmen broke down in tears while describing how the skipper had enriched their lives.

I met retired Admiral Fluckey for the first and only time at his home in the Baywood Retirement Center in Annapolis, Maryland, in the fall of 2004. At ninety-one years old, he seemed more like someone in his late fifties or early sixties with his full shock of hair, trim build, natty dress, and buoyant demeanor. I had just begun research into his career and thought he could clear up a few questions. Unfortunately, Alzheimer's disease had progressively robbed him of his recollections. He could recall moments from his childhood, his academy years, and his early service in World War II. However, he was at a loss in answering many of my questions. Still, even then, he displayed the dry wit that has characterized his life. When asked about an episode of his life he had long forgotten, he replied with a twinkle in his eyes and a hearty laugh, "I don't know. You tell me."

Through Admiral Fluckey's memoirs, Navy documents, relatives, shipmates, and friends, I took up his challenge. Here, then, is his story.

Carl LaVO
6 June 2006

Prologue

I know them and they know me to be determined
and unsidetrackable.

—EUGENE FLUCKEY, *NATO commander,*
on the eve of attempted assassination,
Lisbon, Portugal, 1971

The Bomb

Gene Fluckey stood before two thousand uniformed officers and sailors and Marines gathered on the flight deck of the nuclear supercarrier *Carl Vinson* (CVN-70) on the morning of 2 September 1995. Behind him in Pearl Harbor were the sunken remains of the USS *Arizona* (BB-39) and the battleship's entombed crew, killed on the first day of World War II. The retired rear admiral had come to Hawaii from his home in Annapolis to introduce President Bill Clinton on the occasion of the fiftieth anniversary of the end of the war. Fluckey, at age eighty-one, was a living reminder of the heroism that had galvanized the nation following the sinking of the *Arizona* and seven other battleships in Pearl Harbor in 1941. As a young lieutenant commander in the years following that attack, he was determined to win the war against Japan while facing nearly impossible odds. John H. Dalton, secretary of the navy, in introducing him, summarized his wartime feats. "Sailing in the tradition of John Paul Jones, Gene Fluckey carried the Navy's torch for a brief but critical period in the life of our nation. In five patrols as commanding officer of the submarine *Barb*, Gene Fluckey was awarded the Medal of Honor and four Navy Crosses—a remarkable achievement for a thirty-year-old submarine skipper."

Fluckey, in a navy-blue blazer pinned with medals, smiled broadly beneath the bill of a baseball cap denoting his service as a North Atlantic Treaty Organization (NATO) commander. Approaching the microphone to a thundering ovation, he provided the linkage between a fleet that was nearly decimated at the beginning of World War II and the powerful, unri-valed armada now at rest in Pearl Harbor. In 1941 diesel-powered subma-rines were among the few warships that could take the war to the enemy. Their weaponry—twenty-four often-defective torpedoes and a single large deck gun—would have to do. Fifty years later the *Carl Vinson* represented the most powerful single warship in the world, a floating citadel powered by two nuclear reactors, with a crew of 5,617 and ninety aircraft, including doz-ens of F/A-18 Hornet and F-14 Tomcat fighter jets. Nearby stood the con-ning towers of nuclear attack subs that could stay submerged for months at a time if necessary.

"World War II was the first time since the War of 1812 that our home soil was attacked," Fluckey began in a strong, patient voice. "Americans rose as one to win—and that we did. We won with persistence, determination, and bravery. The average age of the crewmen in the *Barb* was twenty-three. Their spirit and love of country kept us going forward, patrol after patrol. I've always believed luck is where you find it but, by God, you've got to get out there and find it. My experience in World War II gave me my philoso-phy in life: We don't have problems; we have solutions."

In his turn, the president acknowledged the admiral's "astonishing ser-vice" to his country while recalling the attack on the battleships in Pearl Harbor, the vicious and costly Pacific island fighting, and the hard-won naval battles.

Afterward the president and the First Lady dined with Admiral Fluckey and his wife in the carrier's wardroom. Inevitably the conversation drifted to world politics. It seemed to Clinton that success was within reach in a number of conflicts. In Bosnia a U.S.-led aerial bombardment had beaten back Serbian armed forces threatening to spark ethnic warfare through-out southeast Europe. In Northern Ireland a negotiated end to decades of internal strife had been achieved. And in Israel the government was about to grant Palestinians autonomy in a deal brokered by President Clinton and to be signed by Yassar Arafat and Yitzhak Rabin. Trouble percolated elsewhere, however—in Iraq, in North Korea, in Chechnya and Georgia in the old Soviet Union, along the India-Pakistan border, in Afghanistan, in Malaysia, and in the Philippines. The administration also had a grow-ing interest in the whereabouts and activities of a man named Osama bin Laden, a wealthy Saudi who had been expelled from his country in 1991. He was believed to be heading up a highly sophisticated and well-financed anti-American terrorist organization from bases in the Sudan. A 1993 car bombing that rattled the World Trade Center and a foiled attempt to blow up planes flying to the United States from the Philippines were believed to be bin Laden's handiwork.

At the luncheon Clinton wondered how the legendary submarine skipper might view the world situation. The president leaned toward the admiral. "What do you think, Gene, is the worst peril facing the United States?"

The answer came back quickly.

"Mr. President, in my opinion it's international terrorism. And I speak from personal experience."

No one anticipated an attack by men disguised as painters. No one suspected paint drums were packed with explosives and time-delay fuses. Nor was there any hint that their intent on the afternoon of 27 October 1971 was to blow up the new regional headquarters of NATO in Oeiras, Portugal—and kill Gene Fluckey.

The fifty-eight-year-old rear admiral had arrived earlier in the day to go over plans for the dedication of the new facility. For four years he had been involved in its planning and construction at the site of the long-abandoned Fort Gomes Freire. The eighteenth-century gunnery school, which guarded the mouth of the Targus River where it meets the Atlantic near Lisbon, was notable for its stone walls laid out in the shape of a pentagon. At a cost of $6.5 million, Portugal had erected a low-slung, two-story administrative headquarters just outside the perimeter of the fort. The building included VIP briefing rooms, offices, and a dining hall. Work continued on a subterranean communications, intelligence, and command network beneath the old fort. The entire complex, known as IBERLANT headquarters, was to be the nerve center for an expanded oversight of shipping lanes off the Iberian Peninsula, where 90 percent of western Europe's oil passed. The command also would be responsible for the security of the strategic Gibraltar Straits and its approaches from the Atlantic and the Mediterranean.

The imminent commissioning of the new headquarters was not only a symbol of NATO solidarity against external threats, but also represented much greater responsibility for Fluckey in the top post of commander (COMIBERLANT). From an initial force of 16, he would direct 41 officers from Portugal, England, and the United States, 159 enlisted men, 6 civilians, and a French liaison officer. Portugal contributed 40 naval vessels, including modern frigates and an antisubmarine squadron, augmenting a smaller detachment of British and American vessels that were occasionally joined by warships of 12 other NATO nations.

Fluckey had been keeping a wary eye on internal strife gnawing at Portugal. As a student of Portuguese history and politics, he had followed the nation's messy entanglement in Africa. Throughout the 1960s Portugal had struggled to put down rebellions in its colonies of Mozambique, Angola, and Guinea-Bissau. In twelve years more than 100,000 Portuguese soldiers had fought in Africa. Nearly 8,000 had lost their lives, while 26,000 returned home seriously maimed and injured. By the fall of 1971 much of Portugal was demoralized by a war that seemed endless and futile. Fluckey and many NATO officials believed Communists aligned with a dissident Catholic priest were taking advantage of the situation by fanning unrest against the dictatorial regime of Marcelo Caetano. Yet no one expected the dissent to manifest itself in an attempt to sabotage the new IBERLANT complex. Overt terrorism was all but unheard of in Portugal, where widespread censorship for forty years and a secret police force numbering twenty thousand made resistance difficult.

With the commissioning ceremony only two days off, Admiral Fluckey was inside his office attending to last-minute details. There would be a formal reception for the president of Portugal, followed by speeches by NATO's supreme Atlantic commander from the United States and the secretary general from the Netherlands. Portugal's minister of defense then would transfer the headquarters to NATO. Fluckey, in accepting the transfer, planned to frame his speech around the significance of IBERLANT to European security and to remind visitors that "the Russian wolf passes ever closer to our door." He viewed Africa as "a continent in confusion," particularly vulnerable to an unprecedented expansion of Soviet naval influence in the Mediterranean, the Red Sea, and the Indian and Atlantic oceans at a time when the U.S. Navy was shrinking. The cost of the Vietnam War had steadily drained the Navy's budget. Congress had forced the service to downsize its personnel by 10 percent—70,000 officers and enlisted men— plus deactivate 60 ships, 770 aircraft, and 8 aircraft carriers. The Soviet Navy, meanwhile, was dramatically more powerful than it had been ten years earlier and had new airfields south of Europe.

In Fluckey's view, the opening of IBERLANT was a step toward reversing the trend. But establishing the new command hadn't been easy. For months he had wrangled with a stubborn Portuguese bureaucracy, a lackadaisical workforce at the construction site, and even NATO allies. "There are contractor problems in training, equipment, and responsibility," he groused privately to U.S. Navy Vice Adm. Dick H. Guinn back in the States. "There are myriad problems with the Portuguese, tax-wise, legally, logistically, financially, messing, housing, teaching English, training, leading, and keeping strong and active in NATO. The way has been thorny, with much 'rug-from-under pulling' by highly placed officers of certain nationalities. I know them and they know me to be determined and unsidetrackable."

Such was the case when construction inexplicably slowed at the new headquarters. The admiral retaliated by ordering his entire command to occupy the building. It had the desired effect. "The minute we moved into our Topside Headquarters without water and lights, the contractor realized we meant business and seemed to have tripled his labor force."

A pre-dedication dinner fiasco, however, complicated matters. When a Portuguese caterer bowed out, Fluckey turned to IBERLANT staffers. But no one seemed to understand how to order the food or set up the affair. The admiral had no choice but to take charge himself, figure out the menu and the bar, order food, and hire cooks and waiters. At one point, he had gotten on the phone to Navy Secretary John H. Chafee in the United States to get him to bring over six cases of Campbell's Golden Mushroom Soup. Mixed with sherry, Fluckey believed it was quite delicious and perfect for the dinner.

The latest crisis was the British comptroller reneging on a promise to provide 150 place settings for the event. Fluckey had to scramble. He contacted a surplus yard at the U.S. naval air station in Rota, Spain, where he was known as the "King of the Junkyard." He had often combed it for discarded equipment that was still useful and donated it to Portugal to pad relations. This time he needed help—quick—and got it. Place settings were available at no charge but the admiral would have to arrange an emergency airlift. The tablecloths, glasses, plates, service settings, ashtrays, and serving dishes had just arrived.

It was this kind of dogged determination that made Fluckey a natural choice as COMIBERLANT.

He had served as naval attaché to Portugal for three years, from 1951 to 1954, during which time he achieved near fluency in Portuguese and French, and some Spanish and Italian. In a career spanning much of the Cold War between the United States and the Soviet Union, he had served in submarine operational commands and directed the Navy's intelligence division. He was known as a prolific writer and speaker with boundless "can do" enthusiasm, an officer who described himself as a "diehard winner." He was deceptively mild mannered but single-minded in achieving goals— and creative. The Central Intelligence Agency (CIA) once described him as "fearless and foresighted, a footnoter whose lone dissents of one year became majority view of the next." Fluckey, in fact, was never shy about his abilities and accomplishments though he seemed the most unlikely of warriors as a slightly built redhead, six feet tall with a disarmingly toothy smile and warm personality. His successes—especially in wartime—were astounding and a source of immense personal satisfaction.

As the afternoon faded at IBERLANT headquarters, the admiral thought of his days as a young attaché in Lisbon, the ancient capital city.

He pondered the happy irony that he would end his career there in less than a year. His wife Marjorie, in fragile health due to a lifelong battle with diabetes and other complications, suffered from extremes of heat and cold. Portugal, with its temperate climate most of the year, had been ideal for her and they were considering staying. The couple enjoyed their comfortable quinta, a farmette in the resort of Sintra about forty miles to the north. They also had many friends in Portugal and throughout Europe.

As far as the commissioning of the new headquarters was concerned, all seemed in order as a quiet confidence settled over Admiral Fluckey. But outside his office, Portuguese painters completed the job of positioning explosives where they might cause the most damage. The fuses were set. The workers announced to a guard that they were taking an early dinner break and would be back to finish up. They never returned. And it wasn't long before the bombs went off as planned. The shock wave shattered windows and blew out window frames on both floors. Doorways and office equipment were blown apart. Electrical control panels and overhead fixtures tumbled to the floor. Passageways crumbled in piles of mortared bricks and twisted metal. Underground, the new bunker and communications center suffered serious damage.

Stunned rescuers raced to the scene, wondering if Admiral Fluckey— the Navy's "Galloping Ghost"—was a casualty in the debris.

PART ONE

North Beach

Gene Fluckey learned at an early age the meaning of courage, self-control, and determination.

The year was 1922, and the great summer getaway for families like the Fluckeys was the new resort town of North Beach, Maryland, about an hour's drive south from the family home in Washington. Long before the Bay Bridge connected the Eastern Shore of the Chesapeake to the mainland and made Ocean City, Fenwick Island, and Bethany Beach on the Atlantic the favored haunts of capital families, North Beach on the Western Shore of the Chesapeake was the primary destination of those escaping the city heat. The resort was well known for its comfortable bayside cottages and two- and three-story Colonials along a seven-block waterfront. There a broad, sandy beach and a fishing pier jutting far out into the bay provided recreation for all. A trolley system made getting around easy. Restaurants and legalized gambling catered to vacationers.

The Fluckey family often made the trip from their brownstone Victorian in the Capitol Hill development where Gene Fluckey grew up as the second youngest of four children. He was born on 5 October 1913 in Washington to Justice Department lawyer Isaac Newton Fluckey and his wife, Louella Snowden Fluckey. In North Beach the Fluckeys rented a cottage on the edge of the bay where the kids could play at will.

It was that summer of '22 that Gene brought along Phil Greenwell, a neighborhood pal. Both loved the outdoors and were excellent swimmers.

The two dived in and swam about a quarter mile off the beach, when cramps suddenly overcame Greenwell. He yelled for help, unable to swim. Gene moved in, hooked an arm around his buddy's chin, and then started back to shore while urging Phil not to struggle. With great exertion Fluckey made the long swim, using a combination of floating backward and kicking and using his free arm to stroke the water while towing his friend and saving his life.

Gene's growing sense of confidence was reinforced a year later while he was dabbling with a radio set he had built. "I was tickling the crystal of my radio and picked up a station in Pittsburgh, Pennsylvania, just as our president, Calvin Coolidge, was starting a famous speech. Silent Cal did not speak often but when he did people listened," recalled Fluckey. What the president said was to have profound influence on the youngster: "Press on. Nothing in the world can take the place of persistence. Talent will not: nothing is more common than unsuccessful men with talent. Genius will not: unrewarded genius is almost a proverb. Education alone will not: the world is full of educated derelicts. Persistence and determination alone are omnipotent."

Fluckey was awestruck, scribbling down the president's message. He was so impressed that he named his first mongrel dog Calvin Coolidge. What the president said was more than fodder for a pet's name, however. It provided the young boy with a creed to live by: persistence and determination. Previously an average student, he now began to excel at his studies, enabling him to graduate early from grammar school. He refined the president's mantra later, recasting it in his own special way. "Put more into life than you expect to get out of it. Drive yourself and lead others."

With flaming red hair and blue eyes and so many freckles that he boasted of winning a freckle contest at age six, Fluckey was gregarious and inquisitive as a teenager and a dead-ringer for his father in both looks and personality. His infectious smile was so broad that when he was ten he noticed a sign advertising a smile contest near his home. He entered and won. He was a quick learner and very popular on the local sandlot as well as in school. In addition to swimming, he loved playing golf, riding horses, and playing tennis. He graduated from public grade school at eleven and at fifteen from Washington's prestigious Western High School. Alumni included Rear Adm. Husband E. Kimmel, who would command the U.S. Pacific Fleet in 1941.

As a student, Gene loved reading and writing and wanted to be a scientist or engineer. He also had one other consuming interest: military history. His ancestors had fought in every American war going all the way back to the founding of the nation, when the original Fluckey served on both sides of the American Revolution.

His name was Jorge Flocke. As the story goes, he was a single German in his twenties who happened to be riding his horse through Hesse in the German province of Alsace Lorraine on the border of France when he ran into Hessian soldiers, whose services had been purchased by Britain from the prince of Hesse for twenty-two dollars a head. They were among eight thousand mercenaries to join an expeditionary force of thirty thousand English troops in an attempt to put down a rebellion in colonial America. Flocke was conscripted on the spot, leaving him no time to even say good-bye to his family.

Arriving in New York City with the invasion force, Flocke became a foot soldier with orders to march south with the British to capture Philadelphia. En route he met a young Dutch woman, Margareth Stotz, who asked what he was fighting for. "Simple," replied Flocke. "I fight or get shot." Stotz was a secret agent for rebel Gen. George Washington, desperate to recruit replacement troops for an army of three thousand that had been overwhelmed by the British in New York and several skirmishes in New Jersey. Stotz convinced Flocke of the righteousness of the American cause. He subsequently defected by hiding in her beehive oven as the British and Hessians moved on and later adopted a new last name—Fluckey—to keep from being hung if captured by the British.

The newly minted Fluckey joined the Continental Army and quartered with Washington at Valley Forge in the bitter winter of 1776. Because he had been an apprentice tailor in Alsace, he made two uniforms for the general. He also was with Washington when he made his famous crossing of the Delaware River on Christmas Eve of 1776, in a surprise attack on nine hundred Hessian troops garrisoning Trenton. Washington's triumph was the turning point in the Revolution, handing the British their first major defeat.

George Fluckey survived the war, married Stotz, and moved to Philadelphia. He and his wife lived well into their nineties, giving birth to seven children whose descendants participated with Ohio Quakers in the Underground Railroad, smuggling fugitive slaves to freedom; fought in the Civil War on the Union side; staked out free land in the Oklahoma Land Rush; and laid claims in the California Gold Rush. One group of Fluckeys who reached the West Coast purchased author Robert Louis Stevenson's boat *Casco* and sailed for Siberia. There they were shipwrecked and lived with Eskimos until a U.S. revenue cutter located them and brought them home.

These stories regaled the Fluckey children, especially Gene, who hoped to serve in the military when he grew up. He found a mentor in the man next door.

Capt. Adolphus Staton was a real-life action hero. As a Navy lieutenant, Staton had earned the nation's highest award for valor, the Medal of Honor, for skillfully leading his battalion out of an ambush in Vera Cruz, Mexico, on 22 April 1914, during an incursion ordered by President Woodrow Wilson. Staton later earned a Navy Cross as the commander of the USS *Mount Vernon*, a troop transport delivering soldiers to the European war zone in World War I. The 29,650-ton ship was headed back to the United States on 5 September 1918 when it was torpedoed by a German U-boat two hundred miles off the French coast. Half the ship's boilers were lost to an explosion that killed thirty-six crewmen and injured thirteen. Damage control by Staton saved the ship, allowing it to return under its own power to Brest, France, where repairs were made.

Staton's sea stories inspired Fluckey, and the captain saw potential in his young neighbor. He encouraged him to get good grades and prepare for a career in the Navy.

Fluckey's interest in the outdoors and the military was further broadened by the fledgling Boy Scout movement, which incorporated many of the principles that were already driving Fluckey as a youth. The Boy Scouts of America provided a relatively new experience for youths in 1925, when Fluckey and his best pal, Stuart Fries, joined a local troop. The organization had been founded by W. D. Boyce, an Illinois publisher who in 1910 patterned it after a scouting organization in England that taught boys wilderness skills learned in the military. After obtaining a charter from the U.S. Congress in 1916, the Boy Scouts established a national headquarters in Washington. From the beginning, scouting stressed community service and basic scouting skills. Merit badges were awarded to those who successfully completed very specific and difficult goals. The ultimate goal was to become an Eagle Scout, achieved after gaining twenty-one merit badges—a sought-after aim for young Fluckey.

Scouting, however, wasn't Gene's only interest. Both he and Fries were members of their high school's officer training corps. Fries, on graduation, got an appointment to West Point and would years later lead a tank battalion ashore at Omaha Beach as a lieutenant colonel during the D-day invasion of France in World War II.

Fluckey, at age fifteen, was too young to follow. So he applied for a summer job as an office boy for the Atlantic Bitulithic Company in D.C. He was interviewed by phone and couldn't understand what the salary was because of the interrogator's Scottish brogue. Fluckey thought the offer was only fourteen dollars a month when it actually was forty dollars. Still unable to understand after a repeat offer, Fluckey balked. At that point the company treasurer upped the offer to fifty dollars a month. Fluckey accepted. He did so well the company offered him a permanent job. His father, however, wanted him to attend Princeton University, a dream that he had never realized himself but thought he might achieve through his kids. The elder Fluckey was a great believer in education, and his expectations for his children were quite high. Gene's older brother, Jim, was already enrolled on scholarship at Princeton and his younger brother, Ken, planned to follow.

At his father's behest, Gene enrolled in Mercersburg Academy, an academic preparatory school in Pennsylvania that fed the Ivy League. Fluckey did odd jobs to help pay his room and board. He proved to be an excellent student and soon gained notice. Mercersburg offered an annual award—the Original Math Prize—open to all students. Fluckey's professor, impressed with the student's aptitude, urged him to enter the strenuous, day-long exam. When Fluckey refused, the professor beseeched him, saying he had bet another professor fifty dollars that Gene would win. "Somebody believed in me. I couldn't let him down, so I entered," recalled Fluckey. "It was the toughest and most complex exam of my life. After eight hours, I had finished only one-and-a-half problems. I told my prof of my failure. He said what was more important was that I did my best. The results came out. I won. No one else had finished one problem."

Fluckey's academic credentials put him in perfect position for scholarships to Princeton, Yale, or even Harvard. Back home on summer break, Fluckey took a job selling Better Brushes door to door while he decided his future course. He did so well with his million-dollar smile that within two days he had enough profits to buy a used car to drive to work. Two weeks later he bought a second car, a jalopy, to be used for spare parts. His dad was so appalled at the looks of the vehicle that he offered his son five dollars not to park it in front of the house.

During the summer, Fluckey frequently talked to Captain Staton, who urged him to apply for the Naval Academy. "I saw the light," as Fluckey put it in a 1962 letter to a relative. Rather than Princeton, he now set his sights on Annapolis. It seemed to match perfectly his deep yearning for adventure and service to country.

Her son's making the U-turn to the Naval Academy from the road to Princeton couldn't have made Louella Fluckey happier. She was much in tune with his interest in history and the military and shared his enthusiasm for a Navy career.

As a former history teacher in Illinois, she resigned herself to follow her husband to Washington. He too was a teacher in rural Tower Hill, a coal mining district of south-central Illinois. Tired of squeaking by on a poor teacher's salary, he decided to pursue a paralegal career in the Justice Department while seeking a law degree. Mrs. Fluckey retained professional ambitions of her own. She studied oil painting at the prestigious Corcoran College of Art in the capital and started painting china, which she sold through the mail. She was active in the Capitol Hill History Club, serving for a time as its president. She also belonged to the Zonta Club, which worked to improve the status of women.

As parents of three boys and a girl, the Fluckeys were big believers in "feeding the soul," as one relative put it. Gene and his siblings got a steady diet of lectures, scholastic courses promoting critical thinking, and learning about all things. "Newt" Fluckey was known to be very demanding of his children and cranky at times, perhaps due to his inability to move up at the Justice Department, where his boss, who would later apologize for what he had done, blocked promotions in order to keep his brilliant assistant hard at work on the office caseload. The family didn't earn much money, making ends meet by renting rooms in their house, while Mrs. Fluckey gave art lessons, filled china orders, and cooked meals for boarders. She did so into her sixties, all the time nurturing her children with gentle kindness. Gene, who was quite close to her, noticed the strain and a growing fragility.

In terms of his son's future, Newt wasn't all that confident Gene would get into the Naval Academy because he lacked a congressional appointment. He thought his son was passing up a sure thing in Princeton and "time was wasting." Still, his son was determined he would succeed with the encouragement of his mother and the acquiescence of his dad. But there were difficult challenges ahead. Not only did Gene need someone in Congress to nominate him to the academy, but he would have to score well on a notoriously difficult and competitive entrance exam designed to weed out about two-thirds of the applicants. Each representative and senator annually could select five applicants for appointment to the nation's service academies. If Fluckey were lucky enough to secure one of them, he then could enroll in one of a handful of select prep schools that groomed applicants to take the entrance exams.

Young Fluckey was familiar with the Capitol, knew several lawmakers, and went right to work trying to line up support. For three weeks he knocked on doors. Yet he could not get a nomination; all available slots had been committed. It looked rather hopeless until he turned to Representative William T. Holaday, representing the 18th District in Illinois, where his parents had once lived. At first it was the same story: all the nominations were committed. Newt interceded on his son's behalf, stressing his family's Illinois roots—but even that didn't help. The representative, however, was impressed with the young man's passion to serve in the Navy, especially in view of the fact that he was willing to forgo an Ivy League education. So the representative pulled a few strings, getting special consideration for Gene to take both the academy entrance exam and the Illinois civil service test, a backdoor method to gain admission. If he did well, if enough other applicants were disqualified or dropped out, the reasoning went, Gene could slip through. Still, the deepening Great Depression made getting into the academy, with its free education, ever more precious and thus increasingly sought after.

With Holaday's endorsement in hand, Gene enrolled in Washington's rugged Columbian Preparatory School in September 1930. "Columbian in those days offered nothing but classes till 6:00 PM, six days a week, plus a tough German headmaster who batted anybody with a fifteen-foot pointer if you missed a question," Fluckey recalled years later. "As a result, I stood [number] one in the February examinations for the Naval Academy and one in the civil service exams from Illinois, which gave me my appointment."

The family was ecstatic. The experience also reinforced in Gene what President Coolidge had urged in that radio address: determination and perseverance triumphs over all. A test of that was just ahead—and it would take a near miracle for him to overcome the challenge.

20/20

The Naval Academy is a mere thirty miles east of Washington on hilly Route 50 but is a world all its own. The academy's massive, gray granite classroom buildings and single dormitory dominate a flat tidelands running out to the Chesapeake. It is sandwiched between the wide Severn River on one side and the historic seaport of Annapolis on the other. The academy's cathedral, an ornate domed shrine housing the crypt of naval hero John Paul Jones, dominates the center of campus with a crown of gold visible from all approaches to the school.

When Fluckey arrived in June 1931, his experiences in scouting and officer training corps in high school gave him an edge to succeed in this first, or "plebe," year and he adapted well. The academy's routine had a daily rhythm to it—up at 0630 and lights out at 2200 in Bancroft Hall, the world's largest dormitory housing all 2,400 midshipmen. Every minute of every day was covered by a precise schedule. Thus after awakening, the students would wash, shave, and eat breakfast before 0800, at which time they would march from the dormitory, upperclassmen in formation and plebes in double time. The men were organized into battalions and traveled from class to class with their group. First-year courses included marine engineering, naval construction, mathematics, English, and Spanish or French. Morning classes ended at 1215 for lunch and were back in session at 1320, continuing until 1520. What followed were military drills until 1730, when the midshipmen broke for dinner. Afterward they were expected to remain in their rooms studying until 2130. For plebes, custom demanded they keep their eyes fixed straight ahead in the presence of upperclassmen in the dorm, turn corners squarely, and eat sitting rigidly on the leading two inches of their chairs.

Organized sports, part of the afternoon curriculum, consisted of baseball, basketball, boxing, crew, fencing, football, gym, lacrosse, marksmanship, soccer, swimming, tennis, track, water polo, and wrestling. Fluckey went out for wrestling, football, and lacrosse. Eventually, he dropped lacrosse for crew, and wrestling for soccer.

Officially, the academy was an all-male, classless society. But in some ways it had social divisions akin to those of any college. Many midshipmen belonged to fraternities and dated debutantes, referred to on campus as "Four-0 debs." A good number of middies came from upper-crust naval families and called themselves "Our Set" and "blood." The typical midshipman like Fluckey had no such upbringing. Most came from small towns and farms or from the Fleet as enlisted men.

The midshipmen inherited a slang vocabulary unique to the academy. Among the descriptive nouns: grinds (students who studied too much), savoirs (especially brilliant students), bilgers (midshipmen expelled for academic or physical reasons), greasers (those that curried favor with higher ups), spooning (the practice of upperclassmen befriending a plebe, initiated by a handshake), crabs (local girls), snakes (midshipmen who were heavy daters), and drags (young ladies on dates with midshipmen). Middies were forbidden to drive cars on campus or anywhere in Annapolis. And smoking was prohibited except in dorm rooms and a designated recreation room at Bancroft Hall known as Smoke Hall. There a large brass bowl contained loose tobacco and cigarette papers and was kept under constant scrutiny. Smokers were held for the purpose of debating a posted topic of current interest.

Classes at the academy were in two-month segments. Middies were expected to study texts carefully and show up for class to solve problems and answer questions on the blackboard. But Rule No. 1, according to former Adm. James L. Holloway Jr., was not to appear to be too bright or eager. "I'll never forget when the instructor asked a question," said Holloway of his plebe year in 1915. "I put my hand up as one did in high school and quickly had it hauled down by a bilger, a friend of mine, who said, 'Don't do that!' So we learned never to volunteer any information, but to force the instructor to dig it out."

Most of the academy's professors had little formal scholastic training other than that received previously as midshipmen. "There was no lecturing; you'd get into class, and the instructor would say, 'Any questions, gentlemen? Man the boards,'" explained Slade Cutter, one of Fluckey's classmates. "You didn't dare ask any questions, because they couldn't answer most of them. So you manned the boards and the slips were made out by some Ph.D. assistant head of the department. And you would draw a slip, and if it covered material you knew, you would do all right that day."

Rear Adm. Robert W. McNitt, a brilliant high school student and academy graduate who was later to play a critical role as Fluckey's executive officer during World War II, wasn't all that impressed with the caliber of classes at Annapolis in the 1930s. "They were all interesting from a point of view of practicality, but it was a lot of 'sketch and describe.' We had foundry practice. We had mechanical drawing, inking drawings, for example, after you finished your pencil drawings. Electrical engineering was more a matter of plugging in DC motors and AC motors, and if it threw a big spark you got it in the wrong hole. There was an effort to bring you along to the point where you could understand the equipment of ships, but the principles behind it were not very well elucidated, or at least we never got them. . . . I think for its purposes in those days it was suitable and turned out fine fighting officers, but it didn't open your horizons to what the world's all about."

McNitt wrote of his mixed feelings in a letter to his father: "I enjoy the sports. I like the hops. I like the things we're studying. They're fun to do. I enjoy boilers and gunnery and everything that has to do with ships. But I don't think it's an education." His father wrote back, "Well, it's not supposed to be an education. This is not college. This is preparing you for a profession. If you don't like the Navy after you finish, then leave and leave quickly."

Academics aside, most midshipmen viewed their years at Annapolis as fulfilling and fortuitous, given such high unemployment during the Depression. There weren't many other options for young men at the time. Gene's older brother, Jim, at Princeton agreed in a letter: "You're lucky to be where you are for the present," he wrote. "I thought that Princeton would be the one and only refuge during the Depression, but even the University has been hit this year along with the students. No one is really broke, but there are a damn sight fewer weekends being taken and fewer girls brought down for the [football] games, though we can blame the team for that."

The highlight for midshipmen was the summer training cruise at the end of each school year. The voyage on Fleet battleships or cruisers normally was to distant ports in England, France, Spain, Italy, and Hawaii. It was a rite of passage, teaching midshipmen practical seamanship and emphasizing naval traditions as nothing else could. Fluckey's first such cruise in the summer of 1932 wasn't very exotic. Because of fuel costs, the Navy decided on a shorter voyage to Houston, Texas. Along the way, middies scrubbed decks and acted like seamen. They also enjoyed liberty along with the ship's company in ports of call. The cruise stressed the relationship between officers and enlisted men—with a touch of irony: the midshipmen took orders from petty officers although, in actuality, the midshipmen were senior to them. In successive years, summer cruises on the battleships *Wyoming* and *Arkansas* brought increased responsibility, like taking star sightings for navigation and learning communications and engineering at sea.

Fluckey was like a pea in a pod, so happy to be at the academy and doing well. He wasn't that much into dating, according to his roommate, but he loved to socialize and seemed perfectly suited to a naval career. Just when his dream was within reach in the fall of his third year, an unexpected problem threatened to ruin everything—the annual fall physical that every midshipman had to pass. The exam included a vision test that, if failed, would disqualify a midshipman. The academy would allow him to finish the year but then a forced resignation from the service was required, no exceptions. In 1933 about a hundred midshipmen flunked the test that required 20/20 vision or better. Fluckey was one of them. "Two examinations were held with no mercy," Fluckey recalled years later. "They used a box chart. If one could not read it immediately, a hand on your back pushed you forward until you could. One classmate, Sonny Christian, was so irritated with the pushing he walked forward and put his nose against the chart and said, 'Give me 0/20—that's what you want, isn't it?'"

Fluckey rated 11/20. He was nearsighted.

"The doctor assured me that my eyes would never get any better so I should accept my lot. Glasses would be provided. All the failures would be permitted to finish the year, then resign."

Fluckey called home, frazzled by the news. His parents consoled him as best as they could. His sister Lucy wrote to him: "It's just too damn bad and it really made me feel pretty bad, too—but cheer up—oh, gosh, Gene, the world's full of plenty else besides the U.S. Navy—maybe you could make the Japanese navy—they're about as good and don't tell me Japs have such wonderful eyesight."

Fluckey was despondent, so close to fulfilling his destiny only to be undone by an eye test. But he wasn't about to give up. He had seven months to find a solution. He requested and was granted permission to visit opticians, optometrists, and ophthalmologists in and around Annapolis. He was tested by ten of them. All but one agreed with Navy medics. But one wanted to experiment with a set of eye exercises. After a week, the best Gene could do on an eye chart was 12/20 vision. He gave up on the doctor, turning instead to Bernard McFadden's mail-order course of eye muscle workouts for weak eyes. Fluckey attacked "Sight Without Glasses" with religious fervor. By the time he finished the course, however, the midshipman's eyesight had regressed to 6/20 vision—much worse nearsightedness.

Fluckey was pondering what to do when an epiphany came over him. His body was in supreme physical shape from all the sports. "With that I obtained some books on eye muscles and studied while my roommate briefed me on current classroom homework. I put a pinhole in a piece of cardboard and could read 20/20 with each eye, so my problem was simple myopia." Fluckey read up on ciliary muscles that control the lens of the eye and ocular oblique muscles that control the shape of the eyeball. He concluded that in his case all the reading of textbooks had caused these muscles to become overly strong, elongating the eyeball and leading to nearsightedness. The answer to correcting this was to get eyeglasses that would force farsightedness by getting his eye muscles to relax. He wrote out three hyperoptic prescriptions for glasses that he intended to wear when he was up and around, looking at distant objects. One of the prescriptions was very mild, a second a bit stronger, and a third was what he called "a power house—*the bomb.*"

Convinced he had the answer and worried that time was running out, Fluckey scurried all over Annapolis looking for an optician who would fill the prescriptions. None would. So he telephoned his father who had a friend, an eye surgeon, who met with young Fluckey the next day. The midshipman explained his dilemma and how he had worked out a solution. The surgeon listened closely. "It just might work. It's never been tried before. Let me see your prescriptions."

Fluckey passed them to the doctor.

"His face was inscrutable. After a few moments of study with my heart standing still—my final hope—he smiled. 'I understand what you're planning to do, but take it easy and don't overtax yourself. If you start having headaches come in and we'll modify them. Let me know the results.'"

The surgeon signed the prescriptions just as the midshipman had drawn them up. "Good luck," said the doctor, adding a bit of advice. "Believe in them—it helps."

Fluckey began his daily regimen in his dorm room with the lowest-power glasses. His eyes improved slowly. There were no headaches, though he had to move around in a fog at times. Soon he shifted to the second set of lenses. Subsequent self-tests convinced him his eyesight had returned to 20/20 vision—and then surpassed that. He was confident near the end of March 1934. Then one afternoon he returned to his room from lacrosse practice to find terse orders awaiting him: "Report to the main office and sign your resignation tomorrow morning."

Rattled, he immediately sought out an eye doctor at Sick Bay in hopes his vision could be checked. Unfortunately, it was the same doctor who had flunked him. "Mr. Fluckey, it's a waste of your time and mine. Your vision will never come up above 11/20. I can understand you are desperate. I don't approve of these requirements, for I wear glasses, but I have no control. I'm sorry; I cannot help you."

The midshipman begged for reconsideration. "Doctor, my vision has improved. I believe you are afraid you might learn something."

Annoyed, the physician shot back, "Come on back!" The two went into a room with a vision chart.

"Read!" commanded the doctor cryptically.

To the physician's surprise, Fluckey reeled off the entire chart flawlessly.

"You've memorized the chart!" exploded the doctor. He reached for another chart and another. Through ten charts, Fluckey averaged no lower than 23/20 vision.

Perhaps he had been sick and that was the reason for improved vision. Fluckey denied it.

"Now what do I do?" he asked. "Sign my resignation?"

The doctor was baffled. He thought a moment, then sat down at his desk, pulled out a pad of paper, and began to write while addressing the midshipman. "Listen. Forget your resignation. I'll take care of that when I go off duty. There is a surgeon general's office in Washington in about two weeks for some ten midshipmen who have influential representatives. The bus will leave for the hospital and you will be notified. When you arrive, give this envelope to the doctor conducting the [eye] test."

The doctor wished Fluckey well.

The midshipman returned to the dorm, where he put on his most powerful glasses—*the bomb*—and stumbled around his room gleefully, joined by Al

Dinwiddie, who had read class texts and explained the content to Fluckey nightly to prepare him for his academic tests while Gene continued his eyeglass therapy.

Finally the day of the eye test arrived. Fluckey and the ten other midshipmen boarded the bus and rode in silence to Washington, where the representatives greeted them. The midshipmen sat on a long bench together, Fluckey on the tail end. Each was called into the examination, one at a time with his representative. A special consideration had been made at the behest of the lawmakers: as a perk, the required vision to remain at the academy had been lowered to 18/20.

Finally it was Fluckey's turn. The physician asked where his representative was. "I have none, only this envelope from the doctor," he replied.

The physician, who was wearing glasses, read the message, then led Fluckey into an office where he asked him to stand on a line. The doctor shone a light into the young man's eyes, assuring that his pupils would dilate and contract. He wanted to be sure Fluckey wasn't on any myopic drugs.

"Okay," ordered the physician, "start with the big letters and read down the chart."

Fluckey could clearly read the smallest letters. "Doctor, do you mind if I read the bottom line?" He did.

The physician walked toward the chart. "Well, read the line above it backward." Fluckey did, without a problem. The doctor thought Fluckey somehow had memorized the chart. So he retrieved a sealed pack of charts and pulled out one at random. After setting it up, Fluckey toed the line as the doctor ordered him to put a paddle over his right eye and read the next-to-the-bottom line forward, then the bottom line backward. The examination continued using different charts five more times, each time testing first the left, then the right eye.

During the exam, Adm. Perceval S. Rossiter, the Navy surgeon general, walked in to inquire about the results of all the tests. The doctor told him all had failed "as usual"—except Fluckey. "He is being dropped from the naval Academy as a myopic and is the most farsighted person I've ever encountered," he told Rossiter. "His medical record shows he had 11/20 on his annual physical with no improvement on two subsequent re-exams. Admiral, he's reading 36/20."

Both men were astonished.

At the doctor's orders, Fluckey demonstrated his remarkable new vision to the admiral. Rossiter took Fluckey aside, leading him to his office and having him sit down. The admiral studied Fluckey's health record for a moment. "Two of my doctors seemed to agree that your use of an opposite correction would have no effect. Yet obviously you have done something right to correct your vision, and more, by your own efforts.

"You do realize what you are?" he asked Fluckey, who guessed with a touch of humor, "First classman?"

"Not that," replied Rossiter. "You are an embarrassment to the naval medical profession."

The midshipman stammered that he didn't mean to, but the admiral cut him off. He wanted to make a deal with Fluckey. "If you permit me to write down for this re-examination 'Passed 20/20,' I will guarantee that, regardless of what happens to you physically during your first-class year, you will be found physically fit to become an ensign in the United States Navy."

Fluckey excitedly leaped to his feet. They shook hands. The admiral smiled. "My hearty congratulations on your accomplishment. Well done!"

Fluckey returned to the academy a new man, accomplishing what others thought was impossible. His family couldn't believe it either and were ecstatic. Now nothing seemed impossible or improbable in the budding career of Eugene Bennett Fluckey. His parents drove over to Annapolis, where he posed for a photo with his mom, who was beaming with pride in what her son had accomplished.

As a second classman, Fluckey approached his final year with renewed vigor, eager for his last summer training cruise to Europe at the end of May.

The middies would look back on the spring and summer of 1934 aboard the battleships *Wyoming* and *Arkansas* as the best ever. Happy omens seemed to follow the midshipmen everywhere. Fluckey was aboard the *Wyoming*, which also quartered the Navy's football team, considered a national powerhouse. The voyage was memorable for a number of reasons, as noted in the *Lucky Bag*, the academy's yearbook. First stop was England, where the midshipmen toured the sights, gawked at "long-haired haranguers" on soapboxes in Hyde Park, and attended a luncheon with Hollywood movie star Douglas Fairbanks and "a bevy of English beauties." The middies also shared tea with Lady Astor before the battleships set sail for the Mediterranean. The first stop was in Villefranche, where the middies enjoyed the glitz and glamour of Monte Carlo and Cannes. Next stop was Naples, where the ominous summit of Mount Vesuvius belched smoke. Then on to Rome, where the men from Annapolis gave a startled dictator Benito Mussolini a spirited "4N" cheer—"NnnnAaaaVvvvYyyy!"—vocalized in a quick stutter that echoed loudly through the Venetian Palace. They also visited Vatican City, where they had an audience with Pope Pious XI, who smiled benignly as the sailors greeted him with another 4N, after which he blessed them. On the return voyage, the battleships stopped in Gibraltar, allowing the middies to visit nearby Tangiers, which they described as "a Ripley-ish sort of place" for its camels and crosscurrent of Arab, Spanish, and British influences. A school of porpoises—a lucky omen—greeted the *Wyoming* off the Virginia capes as it re-crossed the Atlantic and followed them to Norfolk ("a whirl of dances, dinners, girls, touched with real Southern hospitality"). The ships continued north to the mouth of the Potomac River, where they anchored for three days, long enough for President Franklin D. Roosevelt to come aboard ("we greeted him with a 4N").

For Fluckey, the voyage would be remembered in quite a different way.

Unbeknownst to him, when his parents headed back to Annapolis after seeing their son a few months before the cruise, they were in an automobile crash caused by a drunken driver. Both suffered serious internal injuries. Newt recovered, leaving him with a permanent limp. Mrs. Fluckey also recovered but remained frail from the ordeal. The details of the crash and the full extent of the injuries were withheld by the family so Gene would not worry.

During the *Wyoming*'s fifteen-day transit to Plymouth, England, a Navy dispatch arrived with news from Fluckey's father: "DOCTOR ADVISES THAT MOTHER IS CRITICALLY ILL PNEUMONIA AND HEART TROUBLE COME HOME IF POSSIBLE I N FLUCKEY."

As much as he wanted to return, Gene thought that terminating the cruise would end his Navy career. Hope arrived the next day in another message, this time from his sister: "MOTHER STILL IN GRAVE CONDITION BUT HOLDING OWN WILL ADVISE DEVELOPMENTS LUCIELLE"

Two days later—on June 9—all hope was lost: "MIDSHIPMAN EUGENE FLUCKEY MOTHER PASSES AWAY SUDDENLY AT EIGHT FORTY FIVE THIS MORNING PERIOD EVERYTHING WAS DONE FIRST AND SHE FOUGHT COURAGEOUSLY THROUGHOUT BUT CONTINUOUS PNEUMONIA STRAIN WAS TOO MUCH FOR HEART PERIOD HOLD UP SON DAD."

Gene was heartsick.

From Washington, his sister wrote a long letter, explaining all that had happened, a letter that would eventually catch up to him on the French Riviera. She enclosed a lock of his mother's chestnut hair, snipped as a keepsake for each of the children. "I know it will be such a long, long time before you get this, but it's been so terribly hard up to now to sit down and let you know everything," wrote Lucy.

Gene read the letter despairingly. Too soon after the accident, he reasoned, his parents had taken a trip to visit his brother, Jim, who had taken a job in Ohio after graduation from Princeton. Along the way, Mrs. Fluckey contracted a bad sore throat and bronchitis. In her weakened condition from the accident, she returned to Washington, where the illness worsened. Pneumonia had set in, eventually taking her life at age sixty-one.

In her letter Lucy described how peaceful Mrs. Fluckey looked in repose in a flower-bedecked living room during the viewing. She was clothed in a pink dress with a locket and chain around her neck that Gene had given her. "She loved it so, and always wore it and told everyone about it," wrote Lucy. She recounted heroic efforts by two doctors to save Mrs. Fluckey from what was thought to be a heart attack. She had rebounded, even getting up out of bed a number of times. But the illness wouldn't loosen its grip. She took a turn for the worse because of pneumonia and died a week later. "I've felt so sorry for you having to hear about it way out there all alone, no one to comfort you," Lucy concluded. "Just be a good sailor and remember how mother worked and wanted you to stay at Annapolis. We're all glad you couldn't come home and spoil what mother'd worked so hard for. And take care of yourself dear; so that you can finish at the Academy."

By August, with his son still at sea, Newt Fluckey wrote for the first time since the funeral. He apologized to his son, noting that illness, the auto injuries, the stress of the funeral, and later trials had left him in weakened condition. "It is needless to say how greatly all miss Mom, and there is left only the holding of best memories. She loved her children more than they knew, but also had the satisfaction of knowing they genuinely appreciated the many, many things she had done in their behalf. She preferred to overlook errors in others—much more so than any general inclination."

It wasn't until 23 August that the midshipmen returned to the Severn on the battleship, and Fluckey finally returned home. The obituary in the *Washington Post* made no mention of the automobile crash. But the family henceforth would say Mrs. Fluckey had been killed in an auto accident. In fact, Gene bore deep bitterness toward the drunken driver who had caused the wreck. Mostly he internalized his grief. Lucy worried about that and later wrote to him, urging him to persevere at the academy. "Mother would be so pleased to know that you graduated from Annapolis."

That he did on 6 June 1935, with a commission as an ensign in the United States Navy. He finished 107th in a class of 464 graduates. Upon graduation, he received orders to join the battleship *Nevada* on the far side of the country, where worries about war with Japan were mounting.

Over and Under

Ensign Fluckey's great adventure as an officer in the U.S. Navy began in a sedan headed for the West Coast to the headquarters of the Pacific Fleet in Long Beach, California. He could have gone by train or bus. But, since he and three buddies—fellow ensigns at the academy—had the same orders, they decided to pool their cash and buy a car for a transcontinental drive. At the invitation of his older brother, Fluckey and his pals stayed overnight with Jim at his home in Ohio while heading west. Ensigns Fluckey, Frank Gambacorta, William Germershausen, and Robert Prickett made quite an impression on Jim, who greeted his brother with, "Congratulations, Commodore!" He was impressed with the uniforms, noting in the vernacular of the times, "naval officers look simply ducky when wearing their gigs."

By the time of Gene's visit, Jim had changed his last name. All the Fluckey children had endured some degree of hazing growing up. "Fluckey is a difficult name to live with. I know from personal experience," said one female relative, who explained that at a family reunion several teenagers and young adults agreed that their last name was a "trial." Gene had contemplated a name change, wondering about the consequences in the Navy for an officer called "Fluckey." But he decided he'd rather defend it, given the long and proud history of the family's service to the country. But Jim and Ken, his Ivy League brothers, made the change just as soon as they were able. Ken assumed the original Alsatian spelling to become Kenneth Newton Flocke. Jim simply switched around his birth name to become James Fluckey Snowden, after his mother.

Leaving Ohio, the four ensigns roared away in mid-June, taking Route 40 to Route 66 that led them through Missouri, Kansas, Oklahoma, New Mexico, Arizona, Nevada, and finally California. The journey was a panoply of extremes for the young officers. The contrast between abject poverty and wealth was undeniable. The Great Depression had coincided with years of drought through the midsection of the country, causing prodigious dust storms and suffocating black blizzards, one of which chased the ensigns through Oklahoma before a rainstorm settled it. What came to be known as the "Dust Bowl" had wiped out whole farming communities. Refugees with all their belongings took flight, many en route to a West Coast that by most standards seemed quite the paradise—especially California, where a burgeoning oil industry, thriving Hollywood film studios, agricultural abundance, and trade opportunities with Pacific Rim countries ensured a relatively stable economy. A buildup of Navy bases at San Francisco, San Diego, and Los Angeles further bolstered the economy. Among them, the anchorage serving the Fleet at Los Angeles—Long Beach—was one of the Pacific Coast's most unlikely ports.

In its brief history, the city had virtually willed itself into prominence at the mouth of the Los Angeles River. In 1911 investors had conceived draining eight hundred acres of mud flats between the river and the ocean, dredging them, building a stone breakwater at sea, and thereby creating a seaport that eventually would become the largest man-made harbor in the world. Discovery of oil fields offshore in 1921 drew new investors, who plowed an estimated $1 million per month into creating a downtown. Even when a major earthquake devastated the city in 1933, it was quickly rebuilt in an Art Deco style. By the time of Fluckey's arrival in the summer of 1935, another offshore oil gusher continued the fuel expansion of the port, which had become home base for the Pacific Fleet because of its temperate weather most of the year. With more than a dozen battleships, several carriers, and numerous cruisers, destroyers, submarines, and auxiliary vessels berthed there plus a naval shipbuilding yard in nearby San Pedro, the Navy projected awesome military clout across the Pacific to support bases in Hawaii and the Philippines and the atolls of Midway, Wake, and Guam between them.

As the four ensigns arrived in Long Beach, a letter from "Snowden" awaited Gene. "Can't Navy discipline teach you to take your junk with you?" Jim joked, noting Gene had left behind a pair of dress white pants. "You're one of the world's worst travelers in leaving everything behind, so naturally you'll spend your whole life traveling. Fancy losing half of your cruiser division during a war, Admiral, damned embarrassing, don't you think?" He closed by wishing his brother good luck.

Fluckey's orders were to join the battleship *Nevada,* one of about a dozen dreadnaughts forming the core of the Pacific Fleet. The 27,500-ton warship was home to more than a thousand officers, sailors, and Marines. It was one of two sister ships built in Massachusetts and commissioned in 1916 in time for World War I. The ship had seen duty with the Atlantic Fleet in the British Isles during the war but saw little action.

In 1922 the Atlantic Fleet was disassembled and sent to the newly formed Pacific Fleet command in California. The decision was the outgrowth of a burglary of the Japanese consulate in New York City that same year by the Federal Bureau of Investigation (FBI) and the Office of Naval Intelligence (ONI). The prize was the theft of Japan's naval code that allowed American code-breakers to decipher Japanese diplomatic and naval dispatches. They revealed that Japan had a larger peacetime fleet than the United States, that it was fully activated, and that Japan had well-fortified island bases stretching south into the Central Pacific. The Navy worried about its bases in the Pacific should war break out and redeployed its warships from the Atlantic to the Pacific Coast as a warning to Japan. Under the Navy's worst-case scenario envisioned by its so-called Orange War Plan, the United States would temporarily concede the Philippines to Japan, would rush the Pacific Fleet from California to Hawaii, then island-hop south to the Philippines to retake them.

With this in mind, the Navy began modernizing its coal-burning battle-ships like the *Nevada*. By 1930 the battlewagon had completed a three-year modernization that gave it a new superstructure and significant improve-ment to its armament and firepower, plus conversion from coal to oil power. Still, the battleship was one of the older behemoths in the Fleet. Newer dreadnaughts such as the 33,400-ton *Idaho, New Mexico*, and *Mississippi* were bigger, faster, stronger, and more heavily armed.

An invasion of China by Japan in 1931 exacerbated tensions in the Pacific. Japan's ever-more powerful navy and army needed resources, espe-cially oil, to sustain its war and fuel the heavily industrialized Japanese home-land. The fear in Washington was that Japan would move south against European colonies in Indochina. Mineral- and oil-rich Malaysia made a tempting target, and the Pacific Fleet was the only real hurdle standing in the way.

Indeed, Fluckey and his fellow ensigns had arrived in Long Beach at a precipitous time. The year 1935 foreshadowed in many ways what was to come. Fascist troops from Italy had invaded and occupied Ethiopia. The Japanese army had marched into Beijing in China. Nazi Germany had cre-ated a new Luftwaffe (air force), instituted a compulsory draft, and began rebuilding its navy. Japan began accelerating shipbuilding, having abro-gated the London Naval Treaty of 1930 that had fixed the size and type of warships that the major navies of the world could build with an aim to pre-venting the kind of arms race that led to World War I. Meanwhile, Tokyo fiercely objected to a plan by the U.S. Navy to conduct its annual Fleet exer-cise in the area of Wake Island, the American possession nearest to Japan. Adm. Joseph M. Reeves, commander in chief of the Pacific Fleet, wanted to test his theory that it was possible for Japan to spring a surprise attack on the big Navy base at Pearl Harbor by using aircraft flying off carriers. Reeves wanted to see if his carriers could take Wake Island by surprise in a mock attack. Tokyo demanded that unless the war games were called off, it would cancel a trade agreement with the United States that had made Japan its second largest market. President Franklin Roosevelt, unwilling to risk a disruption in trade, ordered Reeves not to venture close to Wake.

The ensigns aboard the battleships at Long Beach were not privy to any of this. Rather, their purpose was to learn how to be officers. The tradition was to rotate duty stations every few months so that over a two-year probationary period they would have a good understanding of all the various commands and responsibilities aboard. Engineering, communications, and deck management were primary objectives, as well as completion of the so-called ensigns notebook. "The notebook had a separate chapter for each department of the ship," explained Capt. Max Duncan, who was to serve under Fluckey in World War II.

> You were required to become familiar with each system (piping, circuits, pumps, motors, etc.) within the department and make drawings of many of the systems from inspections. You were required to qualify to stand the watch or duty in the department if one was established. The division officers signed off that you had satisfactorily completed his division's requirements and the department head had to sign off for his department. There was a schedule established and if you fell behind, you were not granted shore leave until you were back on schedule. The major check off was "officer of the deck-underway" so one could go flying or to sub school [with their inducement of extra pay]. To qualify, one had to successfully anchor the ship, conduct a successful man overboard, change station in a formation underway, and so forth. The notebook work was in addition to your assigned billet work. Overall, duty on a major ship was a busy time for ensigns.

Ensigns found a very formal setup on battleships and carriers. There was a junior officers mess with a separate wardroom, and the mess president was the senior lieutenant j.g. The junior officer mess was informal and was frequently the scene of dinners with dates on weekends. Many times the dinners were quite formal—and cheap. Cost was important. "Ensigns pay was $125 a month plus $18 a month subsistence," explained Duncan. "Only if you lived on the ship did you have enough money to go ashore and have a good time."

Maneuvers off Long Beach and spring voyages to Panama and Hawaii kept the Fleet battle ready.

Fluckey, at age twenty-two, preferred life aboard the battleship, focusing on all his tasks. He was not much for dating, a pattern he established during his academy years. But in December 1935, fellow Ensign Germershausen met a young woman in Long Beach by the name of Marjorie Gould. She was pretty with long blonde hair, high cheekbones, aquiline features, and a light build on a tallish frame. Her girlish mannerisms were irresistible. Socially she was outgoing and was a chanteuse for a local band and had joined a group of young ladies, including the wives of senior officers, who provided companionship to naval officers at formal teas and dinner dances. Ensign Germershausen thought Marjorie would be an ideal match for his good friend Fluckey and arranged a blind date between them. Afterward Gene was so smitten that he rushed back to the *Nevada* to report, "I've met the girl I'm going to marry." He wrote a letter to his father announcing the same news. The next day he proposed. But Marjorie demurred. It took her more than a month to reveal what wasn't outwardly apparent. In late January, she got up the courage to write a letter to Gene at sea, unveiling a story of tragedy, hardship, and perseverance.

Marjorie was the older of two daughters born to an affluent English immigrant couple. She grew up in privileged circumstances in Flatbush, then an upscale section of New York City in the 1920s. Her father was a department store buyer. Marjorie, well educated early in life at private schools, seemed destined for a comfortable life. But at age eleven she was on vacation with her family and was playing with other children on a second-story balcony at their hotel when she slipped and plunged to the ground. She wasn't seriously injured. However, perhaps by coincidence, her pancreas stopped functioning, bringing on profound and irreversible diabetes at a time when treatment was very limited.

The Goulds took her to the Joslin Diabetes Clinic in Boston, where doctors decided to start their youngest patient on insulin, an experimental drug first manufactured by the Eli Lily Company in 1922. Traditionally, diabetes patients practiced what was known as a "starvation diet"—fasting and consuming large quantities of fat and very few carbohydrates. Insulin made it possible to eat normal foods. But it could also be unpredictable; too much insulin could bring on serious reactions. The clinic's renowned "wandering nurses" visited the Goulds at home, sometimes staying with them, to teach Mrs. Gould how to inject the medicine and how to calculate the calories needed to balance her daughter's diet with her insulin. Large needles were needed, needles that had to be sharpened on a pumice stone. The syringes were made of glass and had to be boiled so they could be reused. If the calculations were inaccurate, if too much insulin was injected, sudden dips in blood sugar could bring on frightening mood swings and, in the extreme, diabetic coma. Marjorie had enrolled at public school in Flatbush after being diagnosed with diabetes, but the school couldn't handle her diabetic reactions. A Catholic school accepted her, but after two years it too let her go.

The Goulds separated when Marjorie was fourteen. She, her mother, and a younger sister moved to California at the invitation of an uncle in Long Beach. Again she was unable to enroll in any school. Meanwhile, her father fell upon hard times and sent less and less money to support his family, causing great distress. Out of economic necessity, Marjorie learned to sew, becoming an excellent seamstress who made all of her own clothes. She also became a voracious reader, becoming self-educated. As a diabetic, it was clear she could never have children. The doctors had told her as much. The risk to fetus and mother was too great. And it was because of this that she wrote to Gene that marriage to the ensign wouldn't be a good thing.

Marjorie mailed her letter in care of the *Nevada*, then had second thoughts and wrote a second letter. "Last night I stayed awake from eleven when I went to bed till 3:45 AM thinking of you and wondering what you were going to think of me when you get the letter I wrote on Saturday. I nearly sent a telegram asking you not to open it. I practically bared my soul to you and hon, it's almost like standing naked before someone. You don't think me awful, truthfully, do you?"

Quite the contrary—the revelations only deepened Ensign Fluckey's feelings for her. He wrote of his undying devotion, that having children didn't matter to him, that it was his love of her that mattered. On leave a few weeks later, Fluckey went to Marjorie's house and the couple announced their engagement.

Marriage under normal circumstances would have been possible within a short time. But in the mid-1930s the Navy frowned mightily on any of its ensigns getting married. War was coming and the Navy was determined to hang onto them for as long as possible. Rules were adopted to prohibit them from marrying until a full two years after graduation from the academy. Anyone who violated the directive was subject to immediate dismissal from the service.

Gene and Marjorie contemplated getting hitched secretly, perhaps in Mexico. But in the end they decided not to flaunt the regulation, though it meant no marriage until at least June 1937—a year-and-a-half away. They both were young and willing to wait. They could still see each other whenever the Fleet was in port, and when away steady correspondence—each letter numbered in a countdown to 6 June 1937—kept the flame burning. So absorbed was Ensign Fluckey in writing letters to Marjorie in his off-duty hours one day that while giving his messboy orders, he called him "honey." "That damn message has been laughing about that ever since," he wrote Marjorie.

Every week at sea Fluckey arranged for forget-me-not flowers to be delivered to his fiancée. Through daily correspondence, the couple exchanged poetry, thoughts about popular tunes, sometimes lapsed into French, and professed deep love for one another that at times was tested. In March 1936, for instance, the *Nevada* embarked for the Bremerton, Washington, Navy Yard for a month-long refit. On leave at the time, Fluckey took the train from Long Beach to rejoin the battleship at the shipyard. There he received a letter from Marjorie describing an encounter with a married aide to Fleet Admiral Reeves at a dinner party she was requested to attend as the aide's escort. "He was old enough to be my father," she wrote. "Franny [the hostess] warned me not to get cornered alone anywhere with him as he's very amorous. He has a '36 Buick sedan that's a honey but even that couldn't intrigue me. We all went to the Biltmore after dinner and had a very enjoyable time but when we arrived home he wouldn't let me out of the car. Gave me quite a fight until I told him I'm very much in love with someone and that I detested people who had no regard for other's feelings. After that speech he let me go. He said he'd like to call again but I told mother that I'm out if he does."

Fluckey started counting down the hours in his letters until the *Nevada* was back in Long Beach. There Marjorie noticed in a city newspaper that Gene was being transferred to the destroyer USS *McCormick* (DD-223), based in San Diego. "Your letter gave me the worst fright of my life," he replied. "I spent the whole afternoon running around the communication offices of the *Nevada, Maryland* and *New York* reading over all orders sent out in the last two weeks—my name didn't appear. I even went to the newspaper offices in town, checking the back file of orders sent to the news—still no orders for me. Darling, I'm so in love with you that the thought alone of being in San Diego this next year with only weekends to be with you, is enough to drive me nuts. Surely fate couldn't be that mean."

But mean it was. Six days later he sent another letter to Marjorie on USS *Nevada* stationery with the *Nevada* crossed out and replaced with a handwritten *McCormick*.

"Marjorie, darling," he began, "I'm aboard."

The change from the spacious battleship to the *McCormick* was incredible. "Hon, this is the first time I've ever written a letter to you on the overhead— one leg is out the port, the other over the side of the bunk to keep the steady rolling from affecting my writing. Gosh, I'm glad I'm a fairly good sailor, otherwise I'd have to install a one-way valve in my throat. It's such a change from a battlewagon. As a Junior Officer, one is wet-nursed perpetually [on a battleship]. The moment I stepped aboard the *McCormick* the executive officer informed me that I was Gunnery Officer, Assistant Engineer, Commissary Officer, Assistant Communications Officer, Ships Service Officer and Wardroom Mess Treasurer. I was flabbergasted."

On the way down to Panama, the destroyer was involved in wartime maneuvers with the battleships. "Yesterday was one I'll never forget," Fluckey wrote. "From two in the morning till a forlorn supper at ten last night, we ran around like a dog with a tin can tied to its tail. Making smoke to protect our dear, dear battleships till we all looked like coal miners."

So often did Fluckey begin his letters with "Marjorie, darling" that he mused he would name his flagship "Marjorie, darling" when he became admiral. "Then I'll never get mixed up. Anyhow it sounds good to me and the British call theirs 'invincible,' 'indefatigable,' and 'impregnable.' Naturally in time the U.S. will probably have a 'delightful,' 'delicious,' and 'delovely.'"

Ensign Fluckey adjusted well to life aboard the destroyer. Both he and his fiancée eventually viewed his reassignment as fortuitous. As she put it, "It could be lots worse, for it might have been one of the new destroyers on the East Coast." He agreed. "The final ensign to get orders from the *Nevada* is being sent to an oiler which travels any place and every place. Perhaps I could have done worse."

The *McCormick* was in and out of San Diego, often at sea with the Fleet off the West Coast, visiting Central and South America and Hawaii. When the ship was in San Diego and the officers got shore leave, Fluckey took the bus to Long Beach. He made the trip so often that he later joked he had put enough mileage in to circumnavigate the world.

On a return cruise to the Canal Zone, the *McCormick* docked in Panama City, where everyone got to go ashore. Fluckey was appalled by the city's squalor just beyond the shopping district. "Later I dropped into a small restaurant and received a shock. The most peculiar individual I have ever seen in my life dropped himself at a nearby table. One might call him a male—I wouldn't. He was blonde with a weak attempt to make his hair quite pink. His face was powdered, lipsticked, eyebrow penciled, with mascara. The climax was silver nail polish. Passing sailors laughed when he beckoned to them. I waited for someone to pop him, but he went unmolested. Pitiful sight."

At sea in the tropics, Fluckey suffered badly from sunburn due to his light complexion. As officer of the deck, he complained that his face was "one big blister . . . I'm so red I'm purple." During the cruise, the *McCormick* passed below the equator, bringing on an ancient naval tradition whereby crewmen who have sailed the Southern Hemisphere "baptize" those who haven't. In this case it was Ensign Fluckey and a few other "pollywogs" brought before a mock King Neptune's court convened on the destroyer. "Last night Davy Jones [a designated crewman] crawled aboard in proper fashion with his subpoenas for the 'pollywogs' to the court of Father Neptune," as Fluckey described it in a letter to his fiancée. Fluckey's three "offenses" were "overexposing his face to the sun," "flouting his blistered hide before his betters," and "being lubberly enough to attempt to bring a trunk aboard a destroyer." The next morning a sailor dressed up as Rex Neptune in a homemade crown and scepter presided with a school of "mermaid" sailors. The ensign was found guilty on all counts followed by an appropriate sentence, met with laughter all around: "First they stuffed me full of quinine, then, alas, clipped my golden locks (by far the worst of the ignominies). Off to a good start they proceeded to beat me to a frazzle, souse me from head to foot with fuel oil, and then dumped me into the tank. Naturally I'm a full-fledged shellback [satisfactory initiation into the Southern Hemisphere club], though slightly peculiar looking, being bald in spots with dark rimmed eyes where the fuel oil refused to come off. We passed the remainder of the day massaging ourselves with kerosene, hot water and rags alternately," he said of himself and fellow pollywogs. "Hon, when, oh, when will I ever be presentable again."

For the next year, as the destroyer tagged along with the Fleet up and down the Pacific Coast, Fluckey earned a reputation as being affable, well liked, capable of lightning-like calculations, and unflappable in emergencies. "I don't know anyone he doesn't like, nor do I know of anyone who doesn't like him," Marjorie would tell a reporter a few years later. "He fits into all crowds and doesn't know what it is to have a temper. In fact, he flatly tells me, 'There's no use trying to get into a fight with me—I just won't fight.'"

By May 1937—with just a month left until Fluckey was to get twenty-five days' leave to marry his fiancée—the ensign witnessed a tragedy involving a Navy pilot and radioman. "Our ship was port plane guard for the *Saratoga* and I was officer-of-the-deck when a plane whizzed past us attempting to take a short cut to make the landing on the *Saratoga*," he wrote Marjorie.

He crashed about 500 yards astern of us and we went emergency full ahead, trying to reach him as fast as possible. The plane sank immediately for when we reached the spot in less than six minutes it had disappeared leaving no trace. As I am in charge of the crash boat, I hopped in and searched back and forth in a very heavy sea for a half-hour in vain. The only articles I found were a cigarette butt, a couple of pencils and a radio notebook. Gasoline bubbles kept breaking on the surface, but as the water was miles deep, there will never be a chance of finding them. They were snuffed out like a pair of candles.

You know, hon, it gives you an awful funny feeling to see a couple of men die that quickly and know you can't do a damn thing to save them. Tomorrow I have to appear at the inquest aboard the *Saratoga* to give all the gory details and my part in it. It's so sad to think that they might be alive now if they had just taken their time instead of trying to save a couple of minutes.

As the *McCormick* headed back to San Diego, Fluckey scribbled "658 dragging hours" at the beginning of a new letter, noting the time remaining until the couple would be reunited and could wed. "Did you know I've grown a moustache? I was going to surprise you with it, but the captain thinks I'd better get rid of it before I see the high and mighty tomorrow. Truly I'm quite distinguished looking if one is not over five feet away. Still, as you can realize, at ten feet it fades out entirely just like my eyebrows. And I did so want to be married with a moustache."

With "2,030,400 seconds" left before leave, Fluckey wrote again of preparing for marriage and how the division doctor summoned the three husbands-to-be aboard the *McCormick* to a private conference to "top off" their knowledge of marital relations.

Gene Fluckey and Marjorie Gould were married right on schedule, 6 June 1937, in Long Beach in a simple ceremony that fulfilled the Navy's marital waiting period. The couple was desperately poor on an ensign's salary. Given the cost of insulin and other medicines, they eked by, barely. When the commanding officer of the *McCormick* came to call, the couple drew the blinds and didn't answer the door as they didn't have a single soft drink or anything to offer.

With trepidation Marjorie's mother turned over the duty of monitoring her daughter's insulin treatments to her son-in-law. Not only did he do so very successfully, but he had studied up on every available source of information on diabetes. "He frankly knew more than the doctors did," said a relative. Fluckey decided, based on his readings, that megadoses of vitamin B would help keep his wife healthy, contrary to medical advice of the time. But the vitamins were expensive and the Navy was unwilling to pay for them. Fortunately, a new, longer-lasting insulin was on the market, which helped medically. But as Fluckey put it in a letter after the *McCormick* cast off, "I am scared stiff and heart broken at the thought of leaving you in anyone's hands but my own. I've never detested going away so much in my life as I did that last night. I tried to feel perky. Still the minute the car drove off gloom and despair settled all over me."

The couple had no intention of having children; the risk to both child and mother from diabetes was just too great. Yet it wasn't long before Marjorie learned she was pregnant and due in March 1938—a scary situation. Mothers with diabetes at that time often died during childbirth.

In his desire to be home more during this time, Fluckey considered transferring to submarine duty; submariners seemed to have much more free time. "I have figured out that in destroyers, normally operating, I can be with you less than one-third of each year. Loving you as I do, there is no job at any salary worth that sacrifice. Submarines should do better," Fluckey noted in a letter home. But even with submersibles, as he put it, "If they don't bring the average free time up to 50 percent, the Navy and I will part."

Over the next nine months, the *McCormick* was in and out of San Diego and for a time was transferred to the Navy base in Vallejo on San Francisco Bay, where Marjorie relocated briefly. Most of the time, Ensign Fluckey was at sea, rekindling a romance of letters in which he regretted deeply the long absences.

Occasionally something out of the ordinary broke the monotony on the *McCormick*. On 20 March 1938, while at sea, a sailor fell overboard when a guard rail on the flying bridge gave way. He plunged onto the roof of the bridge, knocked off one of the radio antennas, then fell into the Pacific. He struggled to get his clothes off so they wouldn't drag him under. Though life preservers were thrown in his direction, he couldn't reach them. Fluckey ordered a boat lowered, jumped in, and raced toward the sailor. "We got to him in time to save him though he was cut up a bit and utterly exhausted," he wrote Marjorie. "When we brought him aboard, I mixed a shot of coffee and alcohol to bring him around. As the coffee was hot and the alcohol strong, I had to keep sipping it to be sure it was OK for him. We both recovered."

Three days later Marjorie Fluckey gave birth to a nine-pound, seven-and-three-quarters-ounce baby girl at Mercy Hospital in San Diego. Fortunately, there were no complications; both mother and daughter—Barbara Ann—were doing fine. The announcement was radioed to the *McCormick*. "When the news arrived I was just turning in after the evening 8–12 watch, so I really feel like I stood watch over you," he wrote back from the destroyer. "After a few joyous jumps I broke out a box of cigars and woke up everybody from the Commodore on down to tell them of the joyous event and to offer them a cigar. . . . Darling, I'm so very, very happy sitting here puffing a cigar and writing dribbles from the whirlpool of thoughts of you that encompass my being. The whole ship is congratulating me and my chest measurement has increased to a 52."

March led into April, April into May, with the *McCormick* still out in the Pacific and Fluckey longing to be home. He decided to put in for submarine duty. The benefits seemed to far outweigh the negatives. If he got a transfer, he and his family would first go to New London, Connecticut, for intensive submarine training over several months—time that he could be with Marjorie and his daughter. Submarine duty also offered hazardous duty pay—an extra 50 percent at sea—and a quicker route to promotions. In addition, active duty and former submarine officers that Fluckey had met seemed a cut above in intellect. And there was another reason—Fluckey's complexion. He suffered greatly from sunburn; he figured undersea duty would be more conducive to his physical well-being.

Of course, there was the risk of a sinking. During his lifetime, more than a few submarine disasters had grabbed the headlines. Between 1927 and 1935 ten submarines had been lost from the United States, Russia, France, Italy, and England, with the deaths of 408 officers and men. Despite the public perception of subs being "iron coffins," the disasters were few compared to the large number of submersibles in the American fleet. Lately the safety record had improved. New, larger submarines capable of enough speed to accompany the Fleet also were being built for transpacific operations.

Fluckey's orders to sub school arrived while the *McCormick* was in Pearl Harbor. He shared the good news in an effusive letter written in the wee hours of dawn. He calculated it would be 28,831 minutes until the destroyer finally returned to San Diego.

Sweetheart, it's sunrise. Would you like me to describe a sunrise over Hawaii? I'll have a try at it anyhow. First, close your eyes—imagine a low verdant land rising to the westward forming a long mountain ridge—to the eastward the land becomes hilly, then breaks into a very rickety range of mountains going down towards the sea. At the seaward end there is an old crater, as Diamond Head appears in the greying morn. The sea is a cobalt blue, smoothed and molded into place by a giant hand. The birds have stopped singing—there is a breathless hush—everything but time has stopped and it's so quiet you can hear a pin drop—even the sugar cane is standing straight and motionless—not a leaf whispers—not a foot walks—the sky has set itself—I am holding my breath in silent expectancy. Such a lovely dawn—it's hard to believe that I'm alive and seeing all this with my very own eyes.

In successive days the ensign composed poetry for his wife and wrote dreamily of his daughter. Marjorie wrote back, "You should see our blessed darling. She gets prettier every day and more adorable. Hon, you're just going to love her to death. . . . Darling, the poems you wrote were really very sweet, though I must admit that the second one rather made me blush, in fact Mrs. Germeinder said I had the rosiest look while reading one of your letters. If she but knew! However hon, I can quite believe and understand what you mean for they tell me that you realize how very much I love you."

As June arrived the *McCormick* dropped anchor in San Diego to an emotional reunion between Fluckey and his bride. For the first time, he got to hold his six-week-old daughter. On 6 June, the third anniversary of Fluckey's graduation from the academy and the first anniversary of his wedding, the couple christened Barbara Ann. That same day, all three left California for Connecticut, where the young ensign would find a home in the Silent Service.

Submersibles

Along with his orders to sub school, Eugene Fluckey had been promoted to lieutenant (j.g.) with a much needed pay raise. As he moved up the chain of command, he also had been moving down—figuratively. In three years he had transferred from a 27,500-ton battleship with a crew of more than 1,000 to a 1,550-ton destroyer with a crew of 270 to imminent duty in a 903-ton submarine with a crew of 38. Rather than wait forever to become captain of the battleship, he now envisioned himself as lieutenant commander of an undersea warship in just a few years.

The incredibly complex and expensive vessels were, in their time, akin to today's orbiting spacecraft. Diving and surfacing—like liftoffs and landings—required precision teamwork that was unforgiving if not carried out in split-second unison. The service was perceived as so dangerous it was an all-volunteer arm of the Navy that operated in complete secrecy, giving rise to its reputation as the "Silent Service." It was also an elite corps; not just anyone could join. Those who served had to meet exceedingly tough criteria for mechanical aptitude and psychological well-being. The wrong kind of man aboard a sub, on a long cruise and under attack, could be devastating for the rest of the crew. Adm. Charles A. Lockwood, a World War I submarine pioneer who would go on to command the Pacific submarine fleet in World War II, summed up the type of individual the Navy was looking for: "In no other branch of military service are men required to remain away from normal human contacts as long as submariners at depths far below the least glimmer of sunlight and far away from the feel and smell of natural air. Moreover, these conditions must be endured with good cheer in overcrowded, sometimes ill-smelling, dew-dripping, steel compartments. Those whose tempers or temperaments cannot stand the strain are soon eliminated."

On arrival in Connecticut, the Fluckeys rented a cottage in New London, a historic seaport on the south bank of the Thames River and five miles inland from Long Island Sound. In its colonial heyday, the city was an international port-of-call for tall-masted merchant ships that once lined its waterfront. As Marjorie and daughter Barbara settled in to their new quarters, Gene took a Navy launch to the opposite side of the half-mile-wide river to the village of Groton, where the submarine school sat overlooking the Thames. The base, originally a ship coaling station, was converted into a submarine operating and training facility in 1917, the year the Navy launched its first government-built submarine, the L-8. By the time of Fluckey's arrival, the school appeared much like a quintessential New England college campus, with tidy lawns and stately red-brick classrooms and dormitories. But it differed in a couple of aspects. For one, a 150-foot-high cylindrical tank loomed over it. The tower, appearing much like a midwestern grain silo, was filled with 240,000 gallons of purified, steam-heated water in which students practiced escape techniques from a mock submarine compartment at the bottom of the tank. Another distinguishing feature was a small fleet of stubby World War I–era O- and R-class submarines used for training and docked at slips along the river below the school.

Lieutenant Fluckey and 29 other junior officers drawn from the Fleet joined about 170 enlisted men at the school in a program that turned over every six months. A series of physical tests weaned the enlistees. First was night-vision certification. Since submarines primarily patrolled on the surface at night to increase speed while avoiding detection, the men had to be able to see the silhouettes of enemy surface vessels in a darkened room built to resemble the bridge of a submarine. The men also gathered in a twenty-foot-long steel chamber, where they were subjected to high atmospheric pressure and hundred-degree temperatures, the type of conditions they might face in a submarine. Anyone who could not endure the tests faced elimination and return to the surface fleet.

Classroom instruction included diesel mechanics, electrical systems, submarine tactics, torpedo weaponry, and communications. Exhausting hours were spent understanding the complex web of internal mechanisms of a submarine, one of the most complicated military weapons ever devised. Diesel engines used to propel the vessels on the surface were dismantled and rebuilt. Motors and generators for undersea propulsion were rewound. The men diagrammed all the electrical, pneumatic, and hydraulic systems and practiced using all the controls. They witnessed what would happen if lead-acid batteries in the keel of a submarine were doused in seawater. Deadly chlorine gas roiled up, a vivid reminder of a perennial danger of submarine operations. The men also learned how to use Momsen lungs, self-contained breathing devices that would allow them to escape from a stranded sub. Each lung consisted of a spring-loaded nose clip, mouthpiece, and air-inflated bag from which to breathe. To qualify for submarine duty, each officer and enlisted man had to swim to the surface from the bottom of the escape training tank while breathing through his Momsen lung. They made ascents of a hundred feet straight up the middle of the tank, guided by a line knotted every fifteen to twenty feet. To simulate actual conditions, the bottom end of the line was attached to a platform modeled to resemble a sub's deck and the top end was attached to a buoy deployed at the surface. The men methodically ascended, one knot at a time, pausing at each to blow and decompress the air in their lungs. As they ascended from the hundred-foot depth the air in their lungs expanded under the reduced pressure and would have ruptured a lung if not exhaled. As a safety measure, experienced divers worked in pairs from air-filled vestibules at various depths in the tank to assist anyone who had problems.

Twice a week the students boarded the school's submarines in small groups for hands-on lessons in diving, surfacing, and maneuvering the vessels in the river and Long Island Sound. Under the careful scrutiny of a veteran crew, they experienced for the first time the complexity of submergence, beginning with the explosive "ah-oo-gah" of the Klaxon diving alarm. In unison, crewmen cranked open huge Kingston valves to flood ballast tanks to begin a typical ten-minute dive. Simultaneously the deafening clatter of diesel engines shut down as electrical motors took over, drawing power from the batteries, each the size of a human and lining the keel, making up nearly a third of the submarine's weight. Simultaneously crewmen sealed all hatches and valves throughout the vessel to keep interior compartments from flooding. Planesmen manned two large, hydraulically powered hand wheels at amidships that controlled stern and bow diving planes, mechanical wings deployed from the craft to maneuver it up and down in the sea. Everything was timed; everyone aboard had to carry out his duty unerringly to perfect the dive. Practice emphasized the critical nature of teamwork: one mistake could cost the lives of every man aboard. Slade

Cutter, who graduated from sub school just ahead of Fluckey, described the unity of purpose that was needed in a Fleet boat:

> The engineman has to shut off the engines at the diving alarm. The man on the hydraulic manifold in the control room closes the outboard induction valve by hydraulic power. When the engine room personnel hear the outboard valve close, they close the inboard inductions. The guys in the maneuvering room have to shift to the batteries for propulsion. The fellow in the control room opens the vents, and then he closes the vents after the submarine is submerged. All these things have to happen independently. Nobody is supervising them; nobody can be there. The officers have their own responsibilities. All these things have to be done and you have to count on the people doing them in the proper sequence.

Rigorous oral and written exams each week continued to narrow down the number of enlisted men who could qualify for submarine duty. As for the officers, Fluckey seemed a perfect fit. Throughout his life, he had been fascinated with how things worked and nothing was more complex than a submarine. He also was a people person, and no crew worked more closely together in tight quarters than submariners. Officers and men viewed themselves much like a family.

The submarine classes of 1938 were important to the Navy because they would form the command nucleus for the service's new Fleet submarines, the long-sought answer to how to deal with the growing might of the Japanese military. Admiral Hart, superintendent of the Naval Academy during Fluckey's years there, proved in 1921 that the Navy's existing subs were incapable of doing that. He took a flotilla of the latest S-class boats accompanied by a tender, a floating hotel/machine shop that serviced the undersea fleet, on a voyage from New London to Hawaii, then southwest to Manila in the Philippines. The entire journey was beset by breakdowns, forcing overhauls in Hawaii and overtaxing the tender. The flotilla's ineffectiveness convinced the Navy of the need for a long-range, much larger submarine that would not be tied to a tender and would be capable of patrols that might last three months at a time and span the Pacific.

The new fleet-type subs were critical to the success of another revision of the Orange War Plan. Instead of the Fleet steaming directly to Manila from its base in Hawaii at the outbreak of war, it would move in stages, first to bases in the Marshall Islands, then to the more westerly Caroline Islands, before moving into Philippine seas. The new tactic required American and Philippine troops to stand their ground longer, to retreat if necessary to the rocky fortress of Corregidor at the mouth of Manila Bay until the Fleet arrived. In tandem with this strategy Fleet submarines would interdict troops and supplies sent south from Japan.

Plans for these amazing submarines had been finalized and the first generation was launched from shipyards in New England and California in the mid-1930s. The contrast to the S-boats was astonishing. The older vessels were 211 feet long; the fleets, 310. The S-boats contained 4 torpedo firing tubes; the fleets, 10. The S-boats could dive to a test depth of 200 feet; the fleets, at least 300. The S-boats had a maximum surface speed of 14 knots; the fleets, 21. The S-boats carried a maximum crew of 42; the fleets, 80. The S-boats had a range without refueling of 5,000 miles; the fleets, 12,000. And enough food and water could be stored aboard a fleet-type sub to facilitate patrols lasting more than two months without resupply or refueling.

Technically both the S-class and fleet subs weren't true submarines but rather submersibles capable of diving and staying submerged for periods of time measured in hours. In wartime, survivability was questionable. The discovery and development of sonar as a means of locating and destroying submarines posed a significant threat. During the latter stages of World War I, an Allied group known as the Anti-Submarine Detection Investigation Committee discovered an electronic method of locating German submarines. The resulting echo-ranging system, known as ASDIC (from the committee's initials), or sonar, came into being. With it, a sound pulse, or "ping," was transmitted from a surface vessel. When the pulse hit a submerged metallic object, it bounced back as an echo. At the sub school instructors believed that a properly equipped destroyer operating in tandem with other equally equipped vessels could determine the precise location of a sub with sonar and deliver a coup de grace. Still, the young sub officers-in-training shrugged off potential hazards. "That's the beauty of being young," said Cutter.

As graduation neared in the late fall, competition for class rank was intense because of the consequence of finishing last: assignment to the S-boat squadron patrolling the Chinese coast. It was the one place where you couldn't take your family and most in Fluckey's class were married. By sheer determination Fluckey avoided China duty. As a member of the 57th Submarine Basic Officer's Class, he graduated seventh out of thirty officers and received orders to report for duty to the S-42 based in Panama.

For the United States Navy in the 1920s, the S-class subs represented the highest evolution of a stealthy coastal defense weapon. After Admiral Hart's ill-fated voyage to Manila proved that the boats were ill equipped to travel with the Fleet, the Navy relegated them to guarding bases on the

West and East Coasts of the United States, the U.S.-owned Canal Zone in Panama, Hawaii, and the Philippines. The S-42, built in 1923 in the Bethlehem shipbuilding yard in Quincy, Massachusetts, was one of six S-boats stationed at the big Navy base in Coco Solo, Panama. The former company town constructed to house workers who built the American-owned canal was now a bustling naval bastion guarding the Caribbean entrance to the waterway.

It was because of the ambition of the United States to build the canal that Panama earned independence after a long struggle. The tiny country was among the first Spanish-owned colonies in the Americas to assert independence from Spain in 1821 by aligning itself with breakaway Colombia, which decided to absorb Panama rather than let it go. For eighty-two years Panamanians tried to reassert independence through forty administrations, fifty riots, and five attempted secessions. They were finally successful after the United States approached Colombia for permission to build the canal linking the Atlantic with the Pacific over the narrow isthmus of Panama. When Colombia rejected the overture in 1902, Panama again proclaimed independence, this time succeeding with American backing. In exchange for the ten-mile-wide, coast-to-coast canal zone in perpetuity, the United States agreed to pay Panama $10 million immediately and a $250,000 annuity, nearly doubling that amount by 1933.

Realizing the strategic importance of the waterway to commerce and military security after World War I, the Navy stationed a significant number of submarines and destroyers in Panama to guard the canal. The relatively new S-boats, including S-42 of Submarine Division 11, had been based in Coco Solo since May 1936.

Fluckey was the junior officer and would remain with the boat for two and a half years. He gained invaluable undersea experience as the boat patrolled the Caribbean as far north as Cuba and Haiti and as far east as the Virgin Islands. The sub played tag with destroyers (which Fluckey termed "greyhounds of the sea") and often dived and surfaced to avoid detection by planes. The S-boats were prone to breakdowns on extended duty, requiring the USS *Holland* (AS-1) sub tender to accompany them.

Lieutenant Fluckey quickly learned that sub duty had built-in hazards not found on surface ships. They were noisy, crowded, hot while submerged, and a plumber's delight of hand wheels, flapper valves, pressure gauges, pumps, levers, and switches. Occasionally, men were injured unwittingly, including Fluckey. "We had been down for an hour or more, so had started to pump the control room bilges, unbeknownst to me," he wrote Marjorie. "In doing this, they have to take up the central section of the deck—about two feet behind the place I was standing. With the noise in the boat, I didn't hear them lift up the deck, and being warm, I took off my shirt, then stepped back to hang it up on a valve wheel—but there just wasn't any deck to step back on and I went tumbling down into the bilges. Nevertheless, I didn't even break a leg, nor nary a bone. I luckily got off with a hunk out of my skin and a sliced thigh."

Among the reasons the lieutenant chose undersea duty was to escape the sun, which had left him terribly burned on the destroyer. Alas, even sub duty had its moments. In a letter to his family, now relocated to Coco Solo, he sighed, "So far this cruise, sunburn just comes and goes—first I get burnt, then we dive and I sweat it out. . . . I'm as red as a spanked fanny. A few more freckles will probably be the ultimate outcome. How I wish I'd tan for once."

Fluckey was away from his family far more than he had anticipated. His first mission lasted more than three months. At times, he wrote of Division 11 being forgotten by the Navy. "All the other ships are making some of the big ports around here 'cept good old subdiv eleven. We're just like a bunch of old drag horses plodding around working for everybody and nobody realizes we're here when it comes to a decent liberty port or going home." There were times far out at sea when Fluckey was mesmerized by submarine duty, however, like when the S-42 arrived on station 1,100 miles east of Coco Solo. "It was so darn calm we passed our day of leisure swimming over the side, a real treat to splash around in water crystal clean and so deep it would take a person over an hour to reach the bottom at a fast trot."

The sub docked periodically at the U.S. naval base of Guantanamo, Cuba, and in Puerto Rico, the Virgin Islands, and Haiti, where Fluckey couldn't believe conditions. "I thought I had seen the low in poverty but this takes the cake," he wrote Marjorie. "The people have nothing, have never had anything and the land seems to produce only dried up peanuts with an orange or so now and then." In the Virgin Islands, officers and sailors of the Fleet went ashore in St. Thomas. It was there that Fluckey became an accidental ambassador for the Navy at the governor's house.

He had been relaxing on the veranda of the city hotel when a fellow officer arrived, dressed in white service and under the impression that the officers had to attend a reception at the governor's mansion. "I told him I would gladly hop up to the governor's with him save for the sad fact that the two suits of white I had were dirty," Fluckey wrote to his wife. "The situation was cleared up by my returning to the ship, squeezing into one of the [officer's] suits and returning ashore to kill the fatted calf." Arriving outside the mansion, he noticed officers milling about in the road and in the gardens, not wanting to be first to enter the home. When Cdr. W. T. Waldschmidt entered the home, Fluckey strolled inside, signed the guest registry, and started up the stairway, expecting others to follow. He hadn't realized that the officers were to first go to a room on the first floor. The governor and his wife were on the second floor and dashed forward to greet the young lieutenant, who looked around with a jolt.

> A great big empty room, and I the first arrival with lots of officers down below but only the governor, his wife, her grandmother and I above to start things off. However, they were very amiable and we had a few minutes chat to ourselves before the thundering horde arrived. Honestly, hon, I'm going to be the first to arrive at anything like that from now on, for it's much nicer getting to know people like that before everything becomes a hurried formality. Between the rum punch and the Scotch, I passed the hour talking with the old lady who really was one of the most unbelievable characters I've ever met. To portray her, imagine a lively old lady about ninety in a wheelchair with an endless sparkle in her eyes, a joy in living, and a scotch and soda in her hand.

After the reception, Fluckey and his fellow officers adjourned to the hotel, where the orchestra off the *New York* and *Wyoming* battleships performed at a dance held at the hotel.

By the fall of 1939, with the S-boats continuing to troll the Caribbean, Germany's invasion of Poland had triggered war in Europe. Japan, meanwhile, was consolidating its conquest of China while threatening to overrun Burma, Thailand, Indonesia, Indochina, and the Philippines, the territorial possessions of Britain, France, the Netherlands, Portugal, and the United States. Tokyo also began a massive buildup of its navy and its bases in the Mariana, Caroline, and the Marshall islands inherited from Germany by the peace terms of World War I. President Roosevelt and the Navy looked with alarm on these developments since the bases were like a strand of pearls strung along vital U.S. sea lanes linking Hawaii with the Philippines. The president retaliated by ordering the Fleet to shift its headquarters from West Coast ports to Pearl Harbor in order to bring the warships closer to the Philippines and hopefully dissuade Japan from further expansion. The administration also stiffened defenses in the Canal Zone, believing Japan might stage a surprise attack to put the canal out of commission.

The S-42 maintained its vigilance in the Caribbean through 1940 and the first half of 1941, with brief periods of liberty for the crew in Coco Solo. The boat was away for holidays, including Christmas and birthdays, the passage of which were marked in letters between Lieutenant Fluckey and his wife. By June 1941 Mrs. Fluckey and her daughter returned to New London to await Gene's transfer back to the States, where he expected to assume command of his own submarine. Gene, along with his beloved Irish setter Penny, temporarily moved into a base dormitory and soon followed his family to New London—but not for long. Orders arrived for him to report as diving and engineering officer to the *Bonita,* one of the largest and most troublesome submarines in the undersea fleet.

War Fish

Beginning with its V-class, the U.S. Navy began a tradition of giving many subs the names of fighting fish. Thus, the first three became the *Barracuda* (V-1), *Bass* (V-2), and *Bonita* (V-3). The Navy thought it was naming the *Bonita* after a fish with a streamlined, silvery blue body that must swim continuously because it lacks an air bladder and is migratory, often traveling amazingly long distances—an ideal name for the original promise of the V-3 as a transoceanic submarine. But that fish is spelled "bonito." As it turned out, "bonita" is a Spanish adjective meaning "beautiful." That, too, seemed an apt description for the startlingly large vessel as seen on the surface with its bulbous nose sweeping upward from the bow, its smooth white skin, and its tapered teakwood deck. In actuality the boat—like the rest of the V-class—was a miserable failure. Even later "improved" versions—the V-8 (*Cachalot*) and V-9 (*Cuttlefish*)—were beset by so many problems that they were known to some as "Breakdown Division One." The Navy had pinned its hopes on the V-class with its range of 10,000 miles without refueling and a design speed of 21 knots, fast enough to keep up with the Fleet anywhere it went. But the Vs never measured up. They were unable to go faster than 18.7 knots. They couldn't meet the design goal of 9 knots submerged. And there were other problems. The fuel tanks often leaked, disclosing the sub's location when diving. The main diesel engines and electric motors failed frequently. And the vessels were heavy forward, making navigation on the surface and maneuverability submerged difficult. With its new fleet-type boats coming along, the Navy decided to decommission the V-class in 1937. But when a national state of emergency was declared by President Roosevelt in the spring of 1941 as conditions deteriorated in both Europe and the Far East, every sub was needed. Thus, the V-boats were recommissioned.

Originally the Navy intended, by terms of a secret agreement with England, to send the *Bonita, Bass,* and *Barracuda* plus twenty-two S-boats to Europe to operate under British command against German U-boats.

Navy Capt. Ralph Christie was selected to command the squadron. In order to train the crews, he began sending the boats on patrols to Navy bases in Bermuda, the Virgin Islands, and Guantanamo Bay. The performance of the Vs appalled Christie, who changed his mind and sent them back to Panama to help guard the canal.

In the summer of 1941 there was good reason for the Navy to worry about security in the Canal Zone. The Japanese had developed enormous *Jensen*-class cruiser submarines that could easily cross the Pacific. These I-subs were 373 feet long, could make 23 knots on the surface, carried 114 officers and crew, and had a range of more than 16,000 miles without refueling. Each carried a sealed hangar aft or forward of the bridge that housed as many as four catapult-launched planes or a midget submarine. It seemed to the Navy that the I-subs had been built with one purpose in mind—to attack American naval bases and especially to bomb the Panama Canal and stop the flow of war materiel once hostilities broke out. Another concern was the presence of German U-boats in the Caribbean. An alliance between Germany and Japan could imperil both ends of the canal.

Initially Fluckey was surprised to learn of his *Bonita* assignment. After serving so much time in S-42 in Panama, he had hoped for command of one of the old O- or R-boats operating out of New London. Instead, his orders were to become engineering and diving officer in the *Bonita*, which he joined in Bermuda on 11 June 1941 as a (j.g.) lieutenant.

Captain Christie considered the sub the worst of the V-boats. Even Fluckey had to concede he was right after reporting aboard. "I was shocked," he recalled on reading the old ship's orders: "This submarine goes totally out of control if she has over a 2 degree down angle. Diving time is five minutes 45 seconds." In sub school, instructors drilled into the young officers the necessity of getting submerged in about sixty seconds. Any boat on the surface longer than 60 seconds risked being spotted by a plane and being sunk. To Fluckey, the risk was unacceptable. "As we prepared for my first dive aboard *Bonita*," he recalled sardonically, "I told the skipper that when war comes, we will be sunk by a plane whose pilot is still in the ready room when we start to dive."

Just as startling as the diving characteristics was the average age of submariners aboard. Fluckey, twenty-six, looked at his chief petty officers and saw men in their sixties. Because of all the problems in the *Bonita*, the Navy had recruited volunteers from the original crew that put the sub into commission in 1925. "The average age of my chiefs was sixty-two," said a chagrined Fluckey, who would in the coming months retire his chief electrician at age sixty-five.

Fluckey approached the *Bonita* like he did everything in life—with boundless curiosity as to how things worked and innovativeness in devising ways to solve problems. He didn't take "no" for an answer. Just as he had conquered his eyesight problem at the academy when doctors said it was impossible, he applied himself to solving the ills of the boat. He knew how important it was for the big submarine to dive quickly. So he soon came up with a unique solution: steepen the descent to twenty degrees while pumping water aft into ballast tanks to counterbalance the force on the bow going under. It would save time and bring the boat to level once fully submerged. It took precise calibrations, but the technique worked; the *Bonita* made the benchmark of achieving submergence in less than a minute.

With enthusiasm and goodwill, Fluckey was relentless, constantly pressing crewmen, the executive officer, and even the skipper for new ways to do what had become routine. In some ways this was annoying for those plodding along in the comfort of normal operations. Fluckey's modus operandi was well known to fellow officers in Coco Solo. In a poll among his squadron skippers, he was voted the officer least likely to succeed because he "rocked the boat" with too many new ideas. Nevertheless, the lieutenant pushed ahead, unfazed, realizing improvements could mean the difference between life and death, success or failure, in a coming war.

Until October 1941 the *Bonita* operated along the Pacific coast of Panama in search of Japanese submarines. Sometimes that would take the sub seven hundred miles offshore to check out Japanese tuna fleets. Unfortunately, as was the case with other V-boats, the sub left a telltale stream of oil from leaky tanks, making its presence known wherever it went. That was one problem Fluckey couldn't overcome; there was no way to get to the tanks without returning to a shipyard for a major overhaul.

The hunt for the enemy turned up nothing. Days at sea led to spells of boredom. Fluckey sat in on poker games in the wardroom, studying the skills of the skipper and the executive officer, making mental notes on how to beat them. As the boat's censor, he also read all the enlisted men's mail to remove anything that might disclose the submarine's location, tactics, and mission. His longing to be reunited with his family intensified with each and every letter.

By the fall Marjorie and daughter Barbara were preparing to return to Panama from New London now that Gene had secured housing at Coco Solo. Finding family quarters on the base had always been difficult, as housing was parceled out according to seniority. Arrangements had been made for a Navy transport to bring Fluckey's family, though Marjorie worried about being sunk en route because of war in Europe. Gene had urged her not to worry. "Keep your chin up and stop letting things upset you. Sailing in the Atlantic is still very safe and I pray your transportation won't be canceled. However, if it does become dangerous, the Navy Department undoubtedly will cancel all transportation."

On 25 November 1941 Fluckey wrote of his excitement that the family would be together for the holidays. "Tomorrow morning I'll order the Christmas tree. I could kick myself for not bringing the ornaments with me. As usual my heart is ticking off the seconds until you get here. Sweetheart, 'till you arrive I'll be singing 'Deck the Halls with Boughs of Holly.' It cheers me knowing we'll be together for Christmas, then 'Joy to the World.'"

In New London Marjorie had all the family's belongings crated and stored for shipment, then learned the date for embarkation was to be 31 December, dashing any hopes of spending Christmas and New Year's with her husband. In a stroke of good luck, however, Fluckey's brother, Snowden, was able to secure passage for the family on an American Presidents luxury liner, due to cast off on 14 December.

Unaware of any of this on 6 December, Fluckey again wrote from Coco Solo: "Right now the best Christmas present I could possibly get would be to have you with me. For all I know, and if perchance the Gods have heard my prayers, you may be on your way down already. Please, God, make it so."

The next day—7 December 1941—the whole world changed as the *Bonita* docked at Coco Solo. Japanese dive bombers and fighter planes dealt a devastating surprise attack on the Navy base at Pearl Harbor as well as a crippling bombardment of Manila and the big Navy base at Cavite in Manila Bay. At 1900 on 7 December the *Bonita* received an encoded message that a state of war existed between Japan and the United States. Lieutenant Fluckey and those on the sub hurriedly prepared for their first war patrol in the Pacific.

The big sub cast off at 1345 on 10 December, bound for Balboa at the Pacific egress from the Panama Canal. A three-week patrol of shipping lanes leading to the canal was planned. Lt. Cdr. Stanley G. Nichols orders were to interdict Japanese submarines and warships and report any enemy aircraft. Arriving on station on 13 December, the sub assumed a routine of sailing to the west from daybreak until noon, then east from noon to darkness. The boat lay to at night to save fuel. There were no sightings of any ships or submarines. Aircraft contacts all turned out to be Navy.

On 31 December the *Bonita* headed in through the canal en route to Coco Solo to end the patrol. The pilot of a patrol boat who came aboard announced that all transportation from the States had been canceled and that dependents in Coco Solo were being evacuated. Fluckey could only won-

der if his family had arrived, only to be shipped back home. Letters from
Marjorie awaiting him, however, disclosed the shock of the Japanese attack
back home, the fact that her departure had been canceled, and how worried she was about her husband. "Most of the boys from the old Coco Solo
S-boats have written the girls telling them to go home," she noted. "Sweet, I
don't know how I'm going to stand this being away from you and specially not
knowing how long it is going to be. Why, oh why did we have to get Coco Solo
at this time? . . . Are you alright and is there any great danger in your vicinity?
I'm so terrified at the merest chance of anything happening to you."

Fluckey was crestfallen. "I tried to sit down and write you a letter calmly
accepting the situation, yet my eyes would fill and a lump rose up in my
throat at every thought of you," he wrote back. "Sweetheart, our present situation is one which we can't avoid and lack the power to do anything about
it. As much as I passionately desire you, as much as I long for the sight of
you, I feel that your being in New London is for the best—it's so much safer
there and you're free from the cause of jitters the families down here seem
to have had lately since being sandbagged and blacked out."

Fluckey urged his wife to approach the future as a series of stepping
stones. "You know, as well as I, that [the war] will be over on Barbara's birthday [March 19]—that's our first date to look forward to—let's keep that
date in mind." But that date came and passed with no end in sight to World
War II. After three consecutive war patrols in the Pacific zone, Fluckey was
discouraged, assigned as he was to one of the worst boats in the fleet and
stuck in Panama, where there was no action, no sign of the enemy. The
only thing to preoccupy him were the perennial breakdowns. On the second patrol, the bow planes became unreliable, followed by the stern planes
jamming when the boat dove at a seventeen-and-a-half-degree down angle.
That was solved only by going to hand operation. The upside for Fluckey
was his promotion to full lieutenant just before the *Bonita* cast off on 9 January. April and May passed with two more war patrols—the boat's fourth and
fifth. Still no sightings of any enemy aircraft, warships, or submarines. On
the fifth patrol, more mechanical problems afflicted the boat, this time a
failure of the starboard generator engine.

Fluckey was frustrated as others got promoted to new boats back in the
States despite his ability to keep the *Bonita* functioning. With no promotion
in sight, he applied for postgraduate studies in design engineering, a three-
year regimen beginning with one year at the academy and the final two at
the Massachusetts Institute of Technology. "I've stayed awake so many nights
lately arguing the pros and cons over and over again and wondering what was
the right thing to do," the lieutenant wrote his wife. "I must be hypersensitive

about any thing that would even look like I was trying to avoid the war. I looked up all the submarine people who had taken [the course] and almost all of them now command submarines. All that and the thought of being with you for three years finally brought about my decision."

Still, Fluckey clung to the hope of commanding one of the new fleet submarines. "I'm going to do my damnedest to get in a new boat," he vowed to his wife at the end of his fifth patrol. "At least then I'll get a chance to be with you for awhile and afterward I'll be heading someplace with a purpose and an opportunity to polish or rather help polish off this whole mess [the war]."

In June good news arrived. The Navy granted Fluckey's wish for graduate school. On 21 June 1942 he left Coco Solo for New London for a well-deserved thirty-day leave, after which he and his family would move to Annapolis, where he would begin his studies. But he would return to the war sooner than he envisioned on a boat that seemed to be jinxed.

The Boat from Scotland

Gene Fluckey's arrival in Annapolis in midsummer of 1942 coincided with a low point in the submarine war against Japan. After the debacle at Pearl Harbor, the Navy had hoped to strike back convincingly with its growing and vastly improved undersea fleet. Many naval experts considered the faster, more durable, deep-running fleet-style boats the best in the world. Intended for operations in the tropics, they were air-conditioned to cut down on electrical short circuits caused by humidity. They could dive quickly to three hundred feet or more, safely below typical blasts from enemy depth charges. They were equipped with targeting computers, the first use of such devices that made attacks more effective. They had ten torpedo firing tubes, six forward and four aft, and could carry as many as twenty-four advanced Mark 14 torpedoes. Most persuasive of all, the weapons were tipped with Mark 6 magnetic exploders. The existence of the exploders was a highly classified secret that very few in the Navy knew about. No longer did a torpedo have to depend on impact with a ship's hull before detonating. Naval engineers had come up with a triggering mechanism that detonated the explosive when the torpedo entered the target's magnetic field. Since all iron ships generate such a field, the new weapon seemed foolproof in laboratory tests, though they had not been tested at sea for cost-cutting reasons. Nevertheless, the Navy was convinced the exploders would be decisive in combat. In fact, Capt. John Wilkes, commander of U.S. submarines in Manila on the eve of war, had predicted "amazing results." Then just about everything that could go wrong did.

It became apparent early on that too many subs were commanded by older skippers who were less than aggressive. They were steeped in a 1930s naval tradition of very cautious tactics. In those prewar years, the fleet subs were intended as scouts for the battleships, cruisers, and aircraft carriers. The plan was for the boats to speed ahead of the battle line, then submerge when in the area of possible targets and await opportunity. Submerged attacks were time-consuming and often ineffective compared to surfacing and attacking slow-moving transport ships. Many older skippers also were convinced that Japanese sonar was so sophisticated that once it detected a submerged submarine, there would be little chance of escape. Division commanders reinforced that sense of caution after hostilities began, exemplified by Manila Cdr. Stuart "Sunshine" Murray, who, at a muster of skippers after news arrived of the attack on Pearl Harbor, impressed on them the need for caution. "Don't try to go out there and win the Congressional Medal of Honor in one day," he told them. "The submarines are all we have left. Your crews are more valuable than anything else. Bring them back."

Even when the boats did attack, they were hampered by torpedo shortages and, worse, scandalously defective weapons. The new torpedoes either ran too deep or the magnetic feature exploded prematurely for mysterious reasons. There were numerous additional reports that conventional contact exploders didn't detonate, but rather hit with a thud and sank. While laughable to the enemy, it was demoralizing for sub skippers who did get in close enough, only to be counterattacked by Japanese warships with devastating, sometimes fatal, consequences. Within the first months of the war, the fleet submarines *Shark* (SS 174), *Perch* (SS 176), and *Grunion* (SS 216) met their demise, with the loss of nearly two hundred highly trained officers and men. Indeed, the vaunted undersea fleet had proven mostly ineffective, save for one lucky hit by the *Grenadier* (SS 210) on 8 May 1942 on the converted passenger liner *Taiyo Maru* off the Japanese home island of Honshu. The 14,500-ton ship went down with nine hundred technicians and skilled workers employed by the Mitsubishi Company. They were en route to Java and Sumatra to restore oil fields captured from the Dutch. The loss was a major setback.

As the Navy wrestled with its torpedo and skipper problems, Fluckey tackled the books in postgraduate studies at the academy. He was very happy to be reunited with his family and anticipated that within a year he would be in position to get back into the war as commander of a Pacific submarine. Indeed, as many as three new submarines in need of officers and crew were being launched every month at shipyards spanning the nation.

Initially the Fluckeys moved into an apartment on Perry Circle within view of the academy, planted a "victory" vegetable garden, and enrolled Barbara in preschool nearby. Marjorie's mother, who was a registered nurse, remained by her daughter's side for years, ensuring that she followed a strict regimen to keep her diabetes under control whenever her husband was away. Typically, fresh orange juice was squeezed every morning and kept in the refrigerator. Whenever Marjorie showed symptoms of diabetic reaction due to a drop in blood sugar, a glass of juice was at the ready. Barbara grew up understanding how important that was.

> I had always lived with it—and saw what Mom did, and what Dad did, and what my grandmother did. Dad often had me get the juice. But I had never prepared it with white Karo corn syrup—he or Nana did that when Mom was really shaky. She would say 'I'm shaky' or 'I'm feeling shaky.' Although she was unaware of it, Mom's voice would change slightly and the cadence of her speech might also. I got to the point where I sensed when her sugar was getting low. That's something that could annoy her when I was older. I might start to hound her about taking orange juice and present her with some and if she was still feeling well, she might blow up, although that, too, was a sign that her sugar was falling. I had seen enough insulin reactions by the time I was five or six to last a lifetime.

The thing that worried Gene most whenever he was away was how the insulin was administered. The medicine was still in its infancy and even doctors had difficulty. "Dad handled Mom's insulin when he was home and she had very few problems. When she did have a problem and had to have medical help, she got totally messed up," recalled her daughter.

Fluckey's calculation that naval postgraduate school was the route out of Panama and into the Pacific War proved to be correct in the fall of 1943. With his promotion to lieutenant commander, he received orders to Prospective Commanding Officers' (PCO) School at the submarine base in New London in November of that year. He and Marjorie decided it was best for her, her mother, and Barbara to remain in Annapolis to wait out the war.

In the early spring of 1944, with his schooling behind him, he reported to the commander Submarine Force, Pacific Fleet, with expectations of immediately sailing into combat. But Capt. Karl Hensel had no intention of sending him outbound on the next submarine. Rather, the division commander assigned him to two months' duty repairing new fleet subs coming in off patrol. Hensel's intention was to go easy with Fluckey because his service had been only on an old S-boat and the *Bonita,* neither of which had engaged in battle. The captain wanted him to learn the modern boats and read the war patrol reports before going out as an understudy to an experienced skipper.

The young officer did his best to hide his disappointment. He checked into his cabin aboard a submarine tender in Pearl Harbor with its brood of toothpick-like fleet boats nested tight to the mother ship to await repairs and re-provisioning. Fluckey, now one of the more senior PCOs in the fleet, looked at the boats with longing, itching to make his mark in the war. Then, just two nights into Fluckey's assignment, around 0200, an old acquaintance showed up. It was Lt. Cdr. John R. Waterman, a graduate of the Annapolis class of 1927. The strain of war patrols in the Atlantic and Pacific as the skipper of the fleet sub USS *Barb* (SS-220) was etched into his face. He was exhausted—and worried. The *Barb* had been Waterman's boat from its launch. It had come down the ways at the Electric Boat Company shipyard in Groton, Connecticut, in 1942 with high hopes as the latest *Gato*-class vessel, the final version of the fleet submarine derived from the mistakes of the V-class. The *Barb* and five sister submarines making up Submarine Squadron Fifty initially were deployed to the British sub base at Roseneath, Scotland. In late October 1942 the squadron sailed for Morocco to make a photo reconnaissance of the coast in preparation for Operation Torch, the Allied invasion of North Africa. The *Barb* patrolled off Safi, where it radioed in weather reports and enemy fleet activities, then sneaked in under cover of darkness to put two Army scouts ashore, equipped with blinkers and a radio to guide two destroyers in close to the landing zone in advance of the invasion force. On the night of 8 November 1942, amid occasional flashes of lightning that illuminated an armada of 105 approaching transports, the *Barb* and the other boats took position with twinkling infrared aircraft landing lights mounted on their bridges to guide Task Force 34 to the beach heads. Waterman was apprehensive throughout the operation. His boat was unmarked and could easily be mistaken for a German U-boat by Allied warships and aircraft. A constant barrage of radio communications and recognition signals had to be sustained, the difference between life and death during the ten-day operation.

The squadron returned to Scotland and for the next six months sought out German U-boats and enemy transports off the coast of western France and northern Spain in a notch of the Atlantic known as the Bay of Biscay. The missions were perilous to the extreme. Allied aircraft buzzed overhead with orders to sink any submarine they came across. Scores of enemy submarines also prowled the surface at night. Many were outbound from Nazi sub bases on the French coast to wreak havoc on Allied convoys in the North Atlantic. The *Barb*'s orders were to attack the subs and to interdict Axis ships carrying supplies to Nazi bases in occupied France. However, Waterman was restricted from attacking any vessel flying the Spanish flag; Spain had declared neutrality and had agreed to post lists of its vessels, sailing times, and their destinations. It was soon obvious to the *Barb* crew that many more ships were being encountered than what was posted. Waterman, like other skippers, concluded that German ships were sailing under the ruse of being Spanish.

In early December, on the boat's second war patrol, the sub moved in on a ship that Waterman was convinced was a Nazi oil tanker. The skipper fired four torpedoes, sinking the tanker *Campomanes*. Spain, however, lodged a protest, claiming it was a neutral ship. Rather than create an incident, the Allies apologized and blotted out any references to the sinking, to Waterman's chagrin. During the rest of the month-long patrol, observers on the *Barb* watched in frustration as a parade of 225 ships went by with suspicious cargoes. Suspect targets were tracked, approaches made, and firing tubes readied, only to be foiled by discovery of a Spanish flag.

On the *Barb*'s third war patrol, the sound of frequent explosions from Allied aircraft attacking U-boats in the Bay of Biscay kept the crew on edge throughout the run. Waterman sighted even more ships—upwards of 600, with 127 large transports singled out for possible attack. The *Barb* had to snake between smaller surface craft in order to close in on each ship, only to be foiled each time because they turned out to be "Spanish." "The feeling of futility engendered by such numerous contacts which failed to develop into attacks was hard to overcome," the skipper reported on his return to Scotland. "The tendency was to become lax and the effect on morale was noticeable."

Waterman was temporarily relieved for the *Barb*'s fourth war patrol. The results were the same for Lt. Cdr. Nick Lucker: lots of targets, no attacks.

Reassuming command for the boat's fifth war patrol, Waterman asked the British to conduct a sound test on his boat. For some reason, the sub had not encountered a single U-boat in its first four patrols. Something didn't seem right. "We took the *Barb* up into one of the lochs where the British had an underwater sound measuring range," noted Lt. Robert W. McNitt, who was the boat's gunnery officer. Captain Waterman was ashore with a telephone connection between the sub and the British sound station. Explained McNitt, "We got a call back from the Brits saying, 'You are so noisy you're off the meter. We can't measure you. You've got a trim pump that's bloody noisy. We can hear floor plates in the engine room as your crew are walking around because they're not screwed down. Your cook is washing dishes in the sink, we can hear the silverware.' That got our attention . . . all kinds of things were wrong that hadn't been thought out ahead of time. It was a real eye-opener." Worst of all, the *Barb*'s sail area—the conning tower rising above the deck at amidships—was twice the size of a typical U-boat. The reason for the large size was the Navy's insistence that its subs carry a standby compass. The only ones available were those built for battleships and standing six feet high with a big brass nonmagnetic structure built around them that required the massive sail structure.

It was now apparent to Waterman why the *Barb* had been so unsuccessful in its patrols in the Bay of Biscay and a foray up the Norwegian coast in a futile hunt for the German battleship *Tirpitz:* the boat was too noisy when submerged and its conning tower was too large when surfaced. U-boats could see the *Barb* long before it could detect them, allowing the Germans to skirt around the Americans or dive under them. Furthermore, the *Barb* made so much noise that a good soundman on an enemy ship would hear the sub coming long before it arrived.

The *Barb*'s fifth patrol was into the North Atlantic in a futile search of German "milch cows," large submarines deployed to refuel and rearm U-boats at sea. The sub ended its Atlantic adventure on 1 July 1943 in New London, where the boat's sail was cut down and the compass was replaced by a small armored-vehicle unit no larger than a man's hand. Other measures were taken to silence the clatter detected by the British and to correct engine problems. Also, two 20mm guns were added to the bridge and a 3-inch gun on the after deck was moved forward at Waterman's direction.

It was during this time that a *Barb* enlisted man accused a warrant officer of molesting him in his bunk when the officer was on watch. The following morning, the skipper and McNitt, who had moved up to executive officer, interviewed the officer, a family man with children. As Waterman went to consult the squadron commander about what to do, McNitt relieved the warrant officer of his duties. As the exec went into the log room to write up a report on the incident, the warrant officer went down to the pump room below the control room, where he buckled on a 45-caliber pistol and shot himself in the chest. McNitt, like the rest of the crew, was shaken by the tragedy. He considered the warrant officer a good man, "but something overcame him."

After the refit, the *Barb* embarked for Pearl Harbor via the Panama Canal, arriving in September 1943 and going right back out on its sixth war patrol to the coast of Taiwan. Despite numerous chances to go after enemy targets, however, few attacks were made. Many aboard were very frustrated at a perceived lack of aggressiveness on the part of the captain. "I thought we were much too cautious," said McNitt, the boat's executive officer. "We'd come up, and if there was an aircraft that passed by we'd dive immediately and stay down. Or if there was any risk of attack, why, we'd be very, very cautious, and I think that was the main problem we had with that patrol." Perhaps some close calls had unnerved the captain. An enemy plane dropped a bomb that just missed. "Only his poor marksmanship saved us," noted Waterman in his official war patrol report.

McNitt didn't question Waterman about his tactics. "I was new to this," he said of his early promotion to executive office while the boat was in the Atlantic. "I was not critical of Captain Waterman because I didn't know how this could be done and what the proper way of handling it was."

The *Barb* came in off patrol in late November in hopes of a major overhaul. The failure of the main hydraulic plant came close to "causing the loss of the boat," the skipper noted in his official report. There were numerous other problems: grinding in the rudder mechanism, a fuel leak, sound equipment leaking badly, the bow plane magnetic brake failing, the auxiliary engine needing overhaul, and outboard exhaust valves leaking excessively. The condition of the crew was another concern. "This is the sixth war patrol of this vessel and many of those aboard have made them all," concluded the captain. "The cumulative effect is becoming apparent in some cases in the form of slacking interest or increased nervousness."

The boat returned to Pearl Harbor and then continued on to San Francisco for its overhaul. But on the approach to the city, the vexed *Barb* was attacked by a freighter coming out of San Francisco Bay. "We were on the surface, and we'd thought we were back home now," explained McNitt. "All of a sudden this ship opened fire on us with a deck gun. The first round was about a mile astern. The next one was about half a mile astern. They were getting closer, and we thought we'd better dive. So we pulled the plug, and we went down like a rock. We had to blow main ballast before we got to test depth and came up like a cork, burst out of the water, and broached. He opened fire again at us and we got [the *Barb*] under again and finally got control of the ship. It was a close call."

Captain Waterman was all but certain he would be relieved and move up to division commander. But it wasn't to be after the *Barb* returned from its overhaul to Pearl Harbor. Now in Gene Fluckey's cabin on the sub tender, the skipper disclosed his orders to make one last run before being detached. He confided he'd bow out as captain right then and there if it wouldn't be disastrous for his career. He was worn out—and fearful the *Barb* would be sunk on its next patrol. The story was going around that subs disappeared on either their first or fifth patrols—the first because the captain was inexperienced and the fifth because the same skipper was fatigued and complacent, letting down his guard. In the first nine months of 1943, eleven submarines had been lost. Waterman was beyond fatigue and worried that the string had run out for him and the *Barb*.

He offered Fluckey a deal.

The skipper had long been aware of Gene's high efficiency ratings for both engineering and torpedoes while attached to the S-42 and *Bonita* in Panama. That sort of technical know-how was exactly what the *Barb* needed. Waterman also believed Fluckey's youthful vigor would help reenergize the *Barb*. He suggested Fluckey come aboard as prospective commanding officer, that the two alternate every other night as skipper so that Waterman could get sufficient rest and Fluckey the experience he needed as captain. Sensing reluctance, Waterman assured Gene that if they returned alive and the *Barb* was intact, he would relinquish command to Fluckey and make it stand with higher-ups.

That was the deal-maker.

The next day Fluckey approached the division commander about making the next run with Waterman. Hensel, having ordered the would-be skipper to hang around a few months to learn the fleet boats, was taken aback by such a precocious request just two days after Fluckey's arrival. Without flinching, the lieutenant commander did some fast talking, unleashing an encyclopedic knowledge of every job of every single member of the *Barb* crew.

Hensel gave in.

"Gene, if you've got that many ants in your pants, get going," he replied curtly. "You'll get your orders."

PART TWO

They have attacked me.
The counterattack will be terrible. Go below!

—CAPTAIN NEMO,
Twenty Thousand Leagues Under the Sea

Rift (Seventh Patrol)

Thirty minutes after convincing his division commander that he was ready to become a boat captain, Lt. Cdr. Eugene Fluckey was aboard a submarine that he believed could do much to win the war against Japan. The *Barb*, after its overhaul, was back in fighting condition and ready for remarkable events with eager shipmates rejuvenated by new blood.

Captain Waterman had worried after the boat's most recent sixth war patrol that the crew had been together too long and that changes were warranted. The Navy agreed. But the skipper was surprised at the "unusually large turnover" at Mare Island—about a third of the crew. Out of sixty-nine veterans, thirty new rates, including three first-class petty officers, had come aboard. To make room for them, twenty-six crewmen, including five petty officers, had been transferred to other boats. That was consistent with a growing practice of transferring about a third of each crew after three or four war patrols. It provided a veteran core for new boats and improved morale on the older boats by melding new rates with experienced hands who took personal interest in training them. What concerned Waterman was the fact that eighteen of the new men had never been to sea. Training began at once to school the men in air and surface craft recognition, night lookout techniques, torpedo mechanics, gunnery practice, gas welding, and optical, gyroscope, and sound equipment repairs. Cross-training and critical split-second timing in diving and surfacing routines were practiced. The skipper was impressed. "The newcomers turned to with remarkable enthusiasm which was soon reflected in the efforts of the old timers to help them along," he noted in the deck log. Still, with so many inexperienced sailors, it was comforting to have Lieutenant Commander Fluckey aboard with his wealth of technical experience in keeping the old *Bonita* running. The best news for the entire crew was that problems with the Navy's infamous Mark 14 torpedoes had finally been resolved, thanks to the tenacity of Vice Adm. Charles Lockwood.

"Uncle Charlie," as he was known in the undersea Navy, was a submariner's submariner, a sparkplug of a man who was a legend in the force going all the way back to the early days of the Silent Service. After the outset of World War II, he had taken command of U.S. submarines in the southwest Pacific and vigorously defended his boat captains who insisted the Mark 14s were defective. The Navy's Bureau of Ordnance bristled at criticism of the secret weapon, blamed submariners for fouling up, and wouldn't field-test the weapons. Lockwood, refusing to buckle under, took a submarine into the harbor off Albany, Australia, and fired Mark 14s into a net, proving they ran too deep, deep enough to miss a ship's hull. Henceforth sub captains adjusted depth controls accordingly, ignoring bureau directives. Still, magnetic triggers tended to explode prematurely during attacks. No one could figure out why. Lockwood, by then promoted to commander of all Pacific Fleet submarines, and Adm. Chester Nimitz, commander of the Pacific Fleet, ordered the exploders deactivated permanently.

Sub captains continued to experience many duds. In July 1943 the *Tinosa* (SS-283) fired fifteen Mark 14s with conventional contact exploders at a Japanese whaling ship; eleven were direct hits but failed to explode. In August the *Sculpin* (SS-191) attacked targets on three occasions off the coast of Formosa (Taiwan). The torpedoes hit with a metallic "clunk" but didn't explode.

Lockwood was fed up with the Bureau of Ordnance's inability to explain what was happening. He ordered tests in which live Mark 14s were fired at various angles into a submerged Hawaiian cliff. Navy divers recovered one dud with its warhead split open. Big chunks of TNT littered the seabed. Upon examination of the firing mechanism, it was determined that the steel firing pin never reached the detonation cap. The motion of the pin was guided by a sleeve and the fit was so close that the shock of hitting the target crimped the sleeve enough to prevent the movement of the pin. Those torpedoes that hit the target at an oblique angle were not so affected. It was decided that a lighter material be used for the firing pin and a stronger spring be used to propel it. Lockwood had a lighter, tougher prototype tooled at Pearl Harbor from the propeller of a wrecked Japanese Zero fighter plane. It solved the problem. New firing pins and stronger springs were thereafter installed in all torpedoes. In what seemed an odd directive, captains at sea with unmodified torpedoes were ordered to fire obliquely at targets to give them a better chance of sinking ships. After twenty months of war, the Mark 14 was at last combat worthy and boat captains soon reported success.

As 1943 slipped into 1944 the undersea war finally was showing major results. American subs had sunk more than three hundred enemy ships in 1943, twice the success rate of 1942. Imports of raw materials to sustain Japan's factories dropped sharply, and Japanese shipyards for the first time were unable to keep up with losses. But just as the offensive began to bite hard, so did Japanese antisubmarine warfare. The Navy lost fifteen submarines in 1943—more than twice the 1942 rate. In the first two months of 1944, three more subs joined them—*Scorpion* (SS-278), *Grayback* (SS-208), and *Trout* (SS-202).

On the afternoon of 2 March 1944 Lieutenant Commander Fluckey sidled up alongside Lieutenant Commander Waterman on the bridge of the *Barb* with every expectation of a superior war patrol as the submarine's four powerful diesel engines roared to life. In a major surprise, another officer jumped aboard at the last minute. It was Admiral Lockwood, hitching a ride to the Navy base at Midway, the first leg of the *Barb*'s seventh war patrol.

Lockwood was a chatty people-person, much like Fluckey, who wasted no time engaging him in conversation. Waterman and others, though, were a bit taken aback by the admiral's presence. "Everybody was polite, subdued, and listened more than they talked with Lockwood. However, Gene was quite chatty, and two or three times he told the admiral he hoped he would get a chance to get a command," recalled Lt. Everett "Tuck" Weaver, one of four junior officers aboard.

Lockwood was unlike other admirals. His tradition, established in Australia, was to personally greet every sub coming in off war patrol by jumping aboard as the boat tied up and climbing to the bridge or going to the wardroom to congratulate and interview the captain. Fluckey, like many in the undersea fleet, knew of Lockwood's disdain for skippers who did not press their attacks. The admiral had relieved a number of them, replacing them with younger, more daring captains. Fluckey—quick-thinking, imaginative, and bursting with ambition—was the kind of individual Lockwood could keen to in his search for top guns. Gene used every occasion to discuss tactics and experiences with Lockwood. His knowledge of submarines soon showed itself.

On the fourth day out from Pearl Harbor, the *Barb* encountered heavy seas. While the sub was submerged, a fire erupted on an auxiliary generator terminal board in the engine room and was quickly put out. The cause was traced to an electrical short circuit caused by seawater leaking into the sub from the main induction pipe, the largest external opening of the boat situated high up on the conning tower. A mushroom-shaped, hydraulically controlled valve normally sealed the external opening of the induction pipe, which snaked down aft of the conning tower and into the boat's engine rooms, where it stretched along the overhead above the vessel's four diesel engines. The tube, twenty-two inches in diameter, provided the tremendous air flow to the engines needed during surface propulsion. It was imperative to find the cause of the leak because the valve might fail during night surface patrol, making it virtually impossible to dive. To find out what was wrong required someone to enter the ribbed pipe in the engine room and wiggle up through the wet, tortuously narrow opening, follow the conduit to the topside valve, and tighten a nut on the valve stem seal as the boat remained submerged. It was too risky to sit like a cork on the surface with the engines shut down, unable to dive because of a man in the induction pipe.

"I didn't like having somebody go up in there submerged under the conditions, so I did that myself," recalled Executive Officer Robert McNitt. The fact that he was tall and slender helped. "I took a wrench and crawled in. You have to crawl like a snake through it. It was too small to get on your knees. I got all the way up there and found that I had an oversized wrench. Crawled back out again. If I'd had any sense, I'd have taken a rope with me."

McNitt slithered up the pipe a second time, tightened the lock nut, then backed out again. Still there was water leakage. The exec was stumped.

Fluckey, studying the situation, posed a solution. "Have we looked at the zerk fitting?" he asked McNitt. The zerk, external to the main induction valve, was a small plug to which a grease gun could be attached in order to force grease into the valve. Replacing the zerk fitting stopped the leak.

At Midway Lockwood disembarked and the *Barb* resumed its patrol. Now alone and unmarked, the boat headed west on the surface at seventeen knots toward enemy shipping lanes off the east coast of Formosa, a round-trip voyage of more than six thousand miles. The bridge atop the conning tower bristled with lookouts, each intently scanning the horizon for ships, submarines, or approaching aircraft, friend or foe. Down below radar operators searched for contacts beyond visual range.

Less than a day into the voyage, mountainous seas and high winds slowed the sub's progress, making for a roller coaster ride for the nine officers and seventy-one enlisted men aboard. For three days seventy-foot breakers and seventy-knot winds made it impossible to gain forward momentum. The wild surf crested and broke above the sub, crashing down in a gray blur on the conning tower where the lookouts and the captain—Waterman and Fluckey alternating duty—were lashed into the bridge superstructure. Repeatedly so much seawater was taken down the conning tower hatch that it grounded out a periscope-hoisting control panel, temporarily disabling the scope.

Finally, on 12 March, the storm abated enough for the *Barb* to attain thirteen knots. But one of the boat's propeller shafts began emitting a loud squeal, easily heard through the hull and a threat to future silent running when under enemy attack—a sobering thought to Waterman. For a week the submarine pushed west into the Philippine Sea but made no contact with the enemy.

Opportunity finally arrived on 24 March.

ComSubPac had radioed an ULTRA directive for the *Barb* to intercept an enemy convoy at a specific location. ULTRAs were command dispatches to submarines on patrol, giving precise details of Japanese ship movements. Very few in the Navy knew where the information came from but it was very accurate. In fact, U.S. cryptanalysts had cracked the Japanese naval code. As the "ultra secret," it gave the American Navy an unparalleled advantage in the Pacific that would remain throughout the war. The intelligence was so precise that the Navy knew the names of vessels leaving port, when they were embarking, what course they were taking, their final destinations, and their arrival times. Unfortunately the Navy had been unable early in the war to capitalize on the information due to torpedo problems and old-school tactics by senior captains.

Until now.

The *Barb* made haste on all four engines on an intercept course that took all morning and afternoon. As the sub neared its target, an enemy patrol plane spotted the *Barb* and jettisoned two bombs as the boat dove to 175 feet. Explosions rocked the boat but caused no damage. The captain kept the *Barb* submerged for an hour. When another bomb exploded at great distance, he ordered the sub to remain deep. Fluckey was beside himself. Fifteen minutes of submergence was enough in his book. Precious time was being lost. Matters boiled over in an animated debate in the wardroom. Lieutenant Weaver and others could hear every word. Fluckey was firm. The *Barb* should surface and head for the convoy. Waterman was just as firm. It was too risky because of aircraft; the *Barb* would stay down.

The crew was on Waterman's side for the most part. "Gene and Captain Waterman were polar opposites on tactics," explained Weaver. "Though Gene and the captain had radically different ideas of how to operate a boat in wartime, these differences were never discussed between them in our presence. Captain wasn't there when we heard Gene's ideas, and vice versa.

Gene's ideas seemed a little radical, and in view of the fact *Bonita* never had a Japanese contact, we took them with a grain of salt." Fluckey's ideas were "far out," as Weaver put it.

But the lieutenant commander viewed a submarine as a kind of torpedo boat that ought to operate on the surface, where it could use its fast speed to outmaneuver ships in hit-and-run attacks and could dive quickly when planes approached, only to pop back up minutes later. He had other ideas too. When the *Barb* approached the east coast of Formosa and lookouts sighted a railroad bridge, Fluckey was inspired. "Gene wanted to take the rubber boat and a scuttling charge ashore to blow it up," said Weaver. "He talked a lot about using rockets from the deck too."

Waterman, on the other hand, couldn't shake the cautious regimen of his earlier training and politely overruled Fluckey at every turn. Executive Officer McNitt, though viewing the captain as too cautious, did not try to dissuade him. The captain had taught McNitt much about seamanship and was responsible for his rapid ascendancy to exec. Thus the exec was in no position now to question the skipper's judgment.

Junior officers like Weaver who hadn't had much experience in fleet-type boats were confused. "We didn't know who or what to believe," he said.

Despite tactical disagreements, Fluckey and Waterman were respectful of one another. "It would be very difficult to dislike either man and they got along very well on a personal basis, even though their philosophy on wartime operations was 180 degrees apart," explained Weaver. "Captain told us Gene was a nice young man who would mature if he got a command, or if he didn't, he should be flying a one-person airplane and not having eighty people depending on his judgment for their survival."

Ultimately, the *Barb* stayed down for nearly three hours following the attack by the plane. By the time the boat surfaced, all hope of overtaking the convoy was lost. Fluckey was supremely disappointed. The degree of his frustration was imparted later to Weaver and Lt. Paul Monroe in a private moment. "If I ever get command and stay down more than fifteen minutes for a Japanese plane, you are to kick me in the rear end and that's an order!" he told the two officers.

Discontinuing the search, the *Barb* turned back toward the Mariannas. Given the importance of a phosphate mining plant on Rasa Island that produced more than a hundred thousand tons of the explosive annually, Captain Waterman decided to reconnoiter the facility. The skipper thought it possible to bombard it with the sub's 4-inch deck gun. If the gunnery crew were lucky, it might catch an ore ship being loaded and blast it as well.

In the predawn darkness of 28 March, the sub moved in toward the coast, where it made radar contact with a ship. The *Barb* dived. At periscope depth, the captain identified it as the freighter *Syona Maru* and began closing for attack. The ship, however, acted erratically. Rather than preparing to dock, it moved off, circled the tiny island, stopped and started, and continually changed course abruptly. Waterman suspected a Q-ship—a vessel disguised as a transport but actually armed to the teeth, a decoy to lure submarines in close so they could be destroyed. Such ships had a very shallow draft so that torpedoes fired at them usually missed because so little of the hull was below the waterline. Waterman decided not to attack, turning his attention to the phosphate operations instead.

The periscope view of the factory indicated operations had been expanded greatly from what was reported by another submarine the previous November. There were new barracks and homes for workers, a large roasting and processing plant, huge warehouses, conveyor assemblies, and steel hoists lining the dock. As the skipper began filming the target through the periscope, the *Barb* broached in plain view of the town, necessitating an emergency dive. The film, developed onboard, turned out to be blank; no prints could be made. After sunset the *Barb* surfaced and angled back toward the port. But the sea was too rough for an accurate bombardment.

Captain Waterman turned back toward the mystery ship, still circling the island. The *Barb* got within 4,500 yards while the target continued to stop and start at irregular intervals. The skipper was convinced the ship was a listening post and had in fact picked up the *Barb*. "We felt he could hear us but not see us, and that he was cunningly drawing us closer to the beach, possibly for searchlights and shore batteries [to light up the sub]," noted the skipper in the ship's log.

Waterman began to lose confidence, according to Weaver.

Captain was on the bridge. I could hear Gene talking to the crew down below in the control room since my station was in the conning tower on the phone. I heard the darndest commotion. It was Gene acting like a high school cheerleader, giving a pep talk to those around him— "The *Barb* was going to strike tonight. It would no longer be a virgin." I thought it was a bit strange as it was a time of tension. Gene then came through the conning tower on his way to the bridge, where I could hear the conversation with Captain Waterman. They concluded the target was a Q-ship and Captain didn't want to mess with him. But Gene said, "Johnny, you were the best torpedo shooter in Panama. Set the fish for three feet depth. We can't miss. Let's get him."

I felt Gene coerced Captain into firing.

A few minutes before midnight the target stopped, giving the *Barb* an opening from 2,200 yards. Waterman fired three torpedoes from the bow tubes with very shallow depth-control settings. Within a minute the first hit aft. The second passed astern. The third hit under the smokestack with a loud explosion, breaking the ship in two. The stern sank in twenty seconds. The bow followed thirty seconds later. There was no doubt it was a Q-ship. Fluckey was ecstatic, as was Waterman and the rest of the crew. After more than two years patrolling both the Pacific and Atlantic, there was now no doubt that the *Barb* could claim officially it had sunk an enemy ship.

The sub resumed patrols of shipping lanes linking Manila and the east coast of Formosa. False radar contacts provoked searches for bogus targets for days to come. When a distant plane was sighted on 13 April, the *Barb* dived. Waterman kept the sub down for more than two hours, to Fluckey's great irritation. The skipper reasoned that the plane was an advance scout for an approaching convoy and that staying submerged put the sub in position to sink passing warships. When none appeared, the *Barb* surfaced just as a dozen planes turned toward the boat. Waterman ordered an emergency dive to 150 feet and stayed down for another hour though the planes did not attack and went on their way. For the next week the submarine encountered no targets, just a single plane, necessitating another lengthy dive. This time the captain stayed down for more than three hours, using the time for torpedo maintenance.

By 19 April the boat returned to Rasa. After dark the *Barb* exchanged recognition signals with the USS *Steelhead* (SS-280), which had just reconnoitered the phosphate operations. Both boats in a column a thousand yards apart simultaneously bombarded the docks and factory the following night. "The night was dark but clear and cloudless. Although the island and installations were clearly visible from the bridge, only a vague outline could be seen through gun telescopes," Captain Waterman noted in the patrol log. "Closed to 3400 yards and commenced fire with the 4-inch gun. The first shot was a hit in the congested area of the island. *Steelhead* opened up with her 3-inch gun immediately and did some nice shooting. Continued closing to 2800 yards and opened up with our four 20 MM and two .50 Caliber guns. *Steelhead* joined with automatic guns and a respectable barrage resulted."

Small fires erupted everywhere. Direct hits from deck guns toppled a large steel conveyor loading hoist. Another shell hit a chemical storage facility in the center of the island, throwing up a hundred-foot blue-white flare, followed by a tremendous explosion. Other shells fell on the warehouses, shattering them. The subs made another pass. Again the big deck guns shelled the plant, igniting volatile phosphorus that burned with blue-white intensity.

The *Barb*'s 4-inch gun misfired during the attack. A shell casing with a live explosive was jammed in the barrel. "Captain Waterman wanted to conclude the exercise with the faulty round still in the gun. But Gene volunteered to go down on deck, get it ejected, and throw it over the side," explained Weaver. Fluckey, as was his nature, was relentless in getting his way. The skipper gave in.

All except the gun captain cleared the deck and reentered the submarine as Fluckey dropped down from the bridge. He ordered the gun captain to eject the shell through the breech of the gun, where Fluckey caught it before it could hit the deck and pitched it overboard. Simultaneously for unknown reasons, Lieutenant Commander Waterman ordered the boat to accelerate. "For some reason he went ahead full, made a sharp turn while Gene was down there," said Weaver. "Water came over the deck, Gene got soaked, and it was lucky he wasn't washed off the boat."

The young lieutenant commander shrugged off the incident, very satisfied at the aggressiveness that the *Barb* had shown off Rasa. The crew was electric, certain the bombardment had put the plant out of operation for months to come.

Low on fuel, the *Barb* headed for Midway, where Fluckey had every expectation of finally getting his own boat. Hopefully it would be Waterman's boat, or, as Gene put it, "I looked forward to the captain's promise being fulfilled."

But plans had changed.

Kito (Eighth Patrol)

The *Barb* arrived at Midway to a rousing welcome from high-ranking officers who came aboard to extend congratulations for action that only they and those in the undersea Navy fully understood. Though the submarine offensive was beginning to isolate Japan, little was known publicly about the submarine offensive.

Waterman had returned triumphant due to the successful sinking of the Q-ship and the bombardment of the phosphate factory. His reward was orders to take command of a submarine division. For the skipper, the risk of war patrols finally had ended. Still, there was the matter of living up to the promise made to Eugene Fluckey at Pearl Harbor. When Waterman presented a letter recommending him as the next skipper of the *Barb*, however, the officers looked perplexed. They had no idea that he was aboard as prospective commanding officer. In fact, another man—Lt. Cmdr. Jake

Fyfe—was waiting to take over. It was an awkward situation, to say the least. "My heart plummeted," Fluckey later said.

Waterman coaxed the squadron commander to send a radio dispatch to Admiral Lockwood in Hawaii to see if the orders could be switched. The following day, a change order arrived, giving Fyfe command of the USS *Batfish* (SS-310). The *Barb* now passed to Lt. Cdr. Eugene Fluckey. It was made official on 28 April, when Waterman quickly arranged for a formal transfer of command. The new captain had finally achieved his dream and was eager to test his theories of submarine combat with a crew that he hoped would share his passion for dynamic action. He wanted to make a good impression right away at a muster of crewmen on deck. In his hand, he held up the captain's mast book. Carefully maintained by Captain Waterman on previous patrols according to Navy protocol, the book noted infractions by enlisted men and what the punishments were. With a heave, Fluckey threw it into Midway Harbor. There would be no captain's mast on his boat, he announced. Rather, he expected all hands to perform to the utmost of their ability. He would trust them, demand all their skills, be creative in finding new and better ways to do their jobs, and press the attack on the enemy and sink ships.

Preparations began at once for the *Barb*'s upcoming mission. Twenty-four torpedoes were packed aboard, fourteen forward and ten aft. Provisions to feed nine officers and seventy-five enlisted men for two months were stored. All systems were checked out. Test dives and practice attacks got under way.

During the refit, crewmen on liberty took rides aloft, courtesy of Marine pilots. In return, the submariners invited the aviators to take a ride in the *Barb*. Fluckey decided to give them something memorable below three hundred feet, where immense water pressure squeezed the hull, causing it to groan threateningly. One of the pilots was in the conning tower when a packing gland broke loose. Seawater exploded overhead, thoroughly soaking Lt. John Glenn, who thought he was a goner before a crewman quickly stemmed the leak. Glenn would never again ride a submarine. However, he would one day become the first American to orbit the earth.

By mid-May, as the *Barb* prepared to cast off, Admiral Lockwood radioed Midway that he would fly to the island. He wanted to talk to the thirty-year-old skipper. Had Lockwood reconsidered his elevation to command? Fluckey was worried.

The admiral arrived on 19 May. With a stern expression, he headed for the dock, where the skipper was standing on the sub's deck. Both exchanged salutes. "Good morning, Admiral," smiled the captain with boyish good nature. Lockwood was terse. He wanted to know how confident the captain was on the eve of a very dangerous mission to the little known Okhotsk Sea, a frigid, 18,000-foot-deep ocean shaped like a teacup north of Japan. The sea spanned four hundred miles between Japan's Kurile Islands to the east and Sakhalin Island hugging the coast of Siberia to the west. Fluckey said he was eager to get going. "How many ships do you want me to sink, Admiral?" Lockwood, his countenance lifting, wondered how many this young upstart thought he could sink.

"Will five be enough?" replied the skipper. Did Lockwood want tankers, freighters, cruisers, destroyers, submarines, or maybe a battleship, an aircraft carrier? With a smile, the admiral said five of any type would be sufficient. Indeed, five would match the most sinkings of any submarine in the war.

The admiral came to the point of his visit.

The *Barb* would be sailing with the USS *Herring* (SS-233) and the USS *Golet* (SS-361). ComSubPac wanted all three to serve as a de facto wolf pack on arrival in the Okhotsk, coordinating attacks on any convoys encountered. The tactic, pioneered by Germany's U-boats, had been highly successful in the North Atlantic. The arrival of so many new American subs in the Pacific allowed Lockwood to employ similar tactics against Japan. The admiral's concern was that Lt. Cmdr. David Zabriskie Jr. in the *Herring* and Lt. Cmdr. James S. Clark in the *Golet* were, like Fluckey, making their first war patrols as a wolf pack. One of the skippers had to lead. Was Fluckey, the senior captain, ready for that? As wolf pack commander, he would call the boats together and plan strategy when a convoy was sighted. He would decide who would attack and in what sequence. If difficult decisions had to be made, he would make them.

Fluckey was more than ready to assume the role, adding, "You will have your ships."

Satisfied with the response, Lockwood gave him a firm handshake and a slap on the back, wishing him well. The skipper was delighted with the vote of confidence. Yet he hardly could have predicted the outcome of the mission. Only one boat would return.

On 20 May 1944 the *Barb* cast off from its mooring pier to begin its eighth war patrol. Destination: the Kurile Islands. The next day, the *Herring* also embarked for the volcanic island chain stretching a thousand miles like a beaded necklace between northern Japan and the Soviet Union's Kamchatka Peninsula and separating the Pacific Ocean from the Okhotsk Sea.

A week later, the *Golet* followed, setting a course for the northeast coast of Japan's main island of Hokkaido, where the Kuriles begin.

Outbound, there were high expectations in the *Barb*. Fluckey began molding the crew into a cohesive force. He listened to them, got to know each on a personal level, and tutored them in all aspects of submarining. "He had a wonderful willingness to try new ideas," recalled McNitt, the executive officer making his third patrol in the *Barb*. One of those nuances was shortening up the watch cycle for officers on the bridge. Fluckey had long noticed how exhausted the officers were. He wanted his men as rested and alert as possible. He coached all the lookouts on what to do when aircraft were spotted, as explained by "Tuck" Weaver, the officer of the deck.

> His training on how to deal with airplanes was as follows. It is important to spot the plane while he is six or seven miles away. If he is closer, dive. When he is at a distance, observe him as he may not have seen us, and if he hasn't and doesn't approach, do not dive. If he turns toward us, dive, go to three hundred feet with left rudder. But always know the depth of the water under us since when near land or in a shallow sea, depth of the water is frequently less than three hundred feet and we do not want to strike bottom on a dive. Lastly, U.S. or Allied planes are at least as dangerous as Japanese planes, so if you encounter them, do not stay up and try to exchange recognition signals with them.

The captain popularized a special saying when the watch changed, said Weaver. "The officer being relieved would say 'SLIPKEEP' and the one going on watch would repeat it. This was short for 'one slip and it's for keeps.' It was a constant reminder to stay alert."

Those aboard the *Barb* melded well with their new captain. "Gene Fluckey was a no-pain, no-strain, easy-on-the-nerves individual whose good-humored, upbeat personality was infectious," said Weaver. "He had a unique and wonderful ability to make all of those around him feel good about life. He made them better than they really were."

It took an uneventful seven days for the *Barb* to make the 1,800-mile transit between Midway and the lower Kuriles, where the sub passed into the Okhotsk through the wide Etorofu Strait. The sea, which freezes over in winter, was heavy with patchy fogs and ice floes in the spring of 1944. It was the beginning of the shipping season and numerous Japanese and Russian ships crisscrossed the sea. Enemy warships and aircraft from bases all around the lower edge of the sea patrolled relentlessly. Hidden mines guarded ports and waterways. The risk of being sunk was extremely high. Any man left adrift by a shipwreck would freeze quickly.

Passing into the Okhotsk, the *Barb* encountered an ice floe five miles wide with peaks a hundred feet high. Soon the sub made contact with a freighter but let it pass. It was Russian, an ally, though Fluckey didn't trust the Soviets. The next day, just past midnight, radar contact was made with another large vessel in dense fog. Fluckey closed to within two thousand yards on a perfect setup. One more attempt to see the target through the fog and then fire. At the last minute, a tanker loomed into view. It was Russian. The *Barb* sat there, unseen, as the ship lumbered by. "Frankly I was tempted to order the lookouts to do an about face and let go anyhow. However, we sat and watched her quickly pass into the fog," Captain Fluckey noted in the ship's log.

Overnight, the *Barb* received an ULTRA revealing that a four-ship Japanese troop convoy was about to leave the northern Kurile island of Matsuwa on a route that would take it into the vicinity of Fluckey's wolf pack. The skipper issued a call for the *Herring* and *Golet* to rendezvous as planned. Only the *Herring* responded. The two boats danced around each other like scorpions ready to strike until prearranged radar signatures confirmed their identities. The two then planed up alongside each other just before midnight on 31 May.

From their respective bridges, the two captains communicated with megaphones. Fluckey reasoned that the convoy would make for La Perouse Strait and pass into the Sea of Japan on the opposite side of the Okhotsk. A plan of attack was agreed to. The *Herring* would patrol a ten-mile square north and east of an imaginary line drawn between Matsuwa and the strait, while the *Barb* would search south and west of the line. The first boat to make radar contact would alert the other before attacking. The subs quickly separated.

Fluckey went below to gauge the readiness of his crew. In the stern torpedo room they had a favor to ask. Could the captain attack with the stern torpedoes? Through its many war patrols, the *Barb* had yet to fire a stern shot. Fluckey promised not to forget this time. In the engine rooms, with the clatter of diesels drowning out conversation as the sub streamed along, the so-called "black gang" gave a thumbs up and a "V" for victory as the captain passed forward into the crew's mess, where the men burst into applause as the skipper entered. "Sink 'em all, Captain! Give them back more than they gave us at Pearl Harbor!" In the control room, men were so busy exchanging information that Fluckey simply gave a clenched fist in acknowledgment. In the wardroom, as meals were being served, Executive Officer McNitt reported that all was in readiness.

The *Barb* was the first to make contact. Fluckey ordered the bridge watch to head for the target while sounding the battle stations alarm and getting off a contact report to the *Herring*. Gongs blared as men scrambled to their stations. The captain, slipping into a rubberized parka and grabbing a pair of gloves and binoculars, climbed the control room ladder through the conning tower and onto the bridge, a pedestal forty feet above the surf. Though it was early afternoon, Fluckey couldn't see a thing because of low-hanging fog. However, trailing clouds of smoke from coal-burning engines could be seen through thinning upper layers of the fog. As the captain directed the boat at high speed to get around and ahead of the vessels, the fog disappeared, leaving the sub exposed. The captain and the lookouts dropped down into the conning tower, Weaver following close behind and dogging the water-tight hatch amid the loud "A-ooga!" of the Klaxon diving alarm.

A bomb blast could be heard, then the sound of depth charges. They were a long ways off. The *Herring* obviously had engaged the enemy. In fact, Skipper Zabriskie had attacked the convoy's lone destroyer escort. A single torpedo put the *Ishigaki* under, scattering the convoy's three transports. The *Madras Maru* headed south, the *Koto Maru* west, and the *Hokuyo Maru* turned east back toward Matsuwa.

Fluckey, from the periscope in the conning tower, made a 360-degree circle. No airplanes were in sight. One ship with large guns forward and aft was heading directly at the *Barb*. The sub would attack with three of its six bow torpedo tubes, then prepare for a stern shot if the ship eluded the first shots. In quick succession, he ordered the periscope up and down, exposed for no more than four seconds at a time to avoid detection. Each time trajectories to the target were checked and rechecked. When the ship was within 1,400 yards, the captain gave the order.

"Fire 4!"

The boat shuddered as a blast of compressed air launched a twenty-foot-long torpedo.

"Fire 5!"

"Fire 6!" yelled the captain.

Seconds passed. Then a tremendous explosion amid cheers throughout the boat.

Fluckey ordered the periscope raised and held there. He watched as a waterspout from the first explosion fell on the target. Then another fireball. "Directly under the stacks!" he shouted, followed by the sound of another direct hit. A secondary explosion from munitions aboard the ship shattered the vessel.

Fluckey gave those in the conning tower a quick look at the sinking *Madras Maru*. Landing barges loaded with soldiers floated off the deck. Motorized lifeboats and row boats pulled away. One got caught in the whirlpool of the ship going under and disappeared.

After ten minutes, with the forward torpedo tubes reloaded, the submarine surfaced among the lifeboats and landing barges, one only fifty yards off the port beam. Weaver and Fluckey were the first to emerge on the bridge, the captain intent on offering medical assistance to survivors. He heard a Japanese officer's scream, then the sound of a machine gun sending a spray of bullets whizzing overhead. Fluckey and Weaver hit the deck, crawling back to the conning tower hatch and diving below while ordering the sub to roar ahead, leaving the survivors behind.

"One ship down, four to go!" shouted the captain.

For Tuck Weaver the near brush with disaster on the bridge reminded him of his days aboard the S-30 (SS-135) when it was stationed in the Aleutian Islands in 1943.

The boat was on patrol on the Pacific side of the Kuriles when Skipper Bill Stevenson attempted a daring down-the-throat attack on a charging Japanese patrol boat that was firing 5-inch shells at the sub. The captain was preparing to fire four bow torpedoes when his periscope dipped below the waves, foiling the setup. Yelling to bring the boat up, the planesmen overcompensated and broached the sub right under the nose of the *Chidori*. Stevenson ordered a crash dive with no time to close the outer doors of the torpedo tubes where the weapons were exposed. The S-30 was only a hundred feet deep when the patrol boat crossed over and dropped depth charges.

Weaver described the scene for Fluckey. "Standing in the control room, I saw the hands fly off both depth gauges before the lights and everything electrical went dead. Having no propulsion and being nearly twenty tons heavy we just sank until with a thud we hit the bottom."

Fortunately the boat landed on an ocean shelf three hundred feet down, sparing it from crush depth. But the first round of depth charges smashed all four torpedoes, one so badly it couldn't be removed. As electrician mates toiled to repair damage throughout the boat, patrol craft overhead used grappling hooks in attempts to hook the submarine. It was nerve-wracking to hear them rattling across the hull. But none took hold. After dark the boat surfaced and escaped using radar to thread its way through the circling patrol boats.

Back on the *Barb*, Fluckey resumed the hunt for targets and soon spotted the fleeing *Koto Maru*. It took three hours for the sub to get ahead of the transport and settle into a submerged position. Under a clear sky with no sign of overhead aircraft, the *Barb* let loose with three torpedoes from its stern tubes. A minute ticked by. Raising the periscope, Fluckey watched as all three hit the ship, breaking its bow and turning it on its end. Lifeboats, dangling from their lines, began spilling survivors into the frigid sea. Within three minutes the ship disappeared.

The skipper, making a periscope sweep before surfacing, was taken by surprise when a plane came roaring in undetected and dropped two bombs. Concussions slammed against the hull, shaking the boat wildly and causing seawater to rush past as if it had been holed. "Down scope! Rig ship for depth charge!" Fluckey shouted. "Take her deep—three hundred feet! Left full rudder!" Two more explosions were more distant as the *Barb* made its narrow escape with only minor damage.

The boat stayed submerged for an hour, then surfaced to return to the wreckage in hopes of taking a prisoner who might provide valuable intelligence. The resulting spectacle was gruesome and eerie in daylight on a flat sea with ice shards everywhere. "This was the first time that I'd ever returned to the scene of a sinking and it was a rather unholy sight," the skipper later noted. "The atmosphere was much like one you'd expect from *Frankenstein*. The people were screaming and groaning in the water. There were several survivors on rafts. The water at that time was very cold, about twenty-seven degrees. These people were gradually freezing and dying."

When one of the gunners aboard the *Barb* took a shot at one of the survivors, Fluckey angrily rebuked him, demanding why he had done so. The enlisted man stammered, then replied, "He pulled a knife on me."

McNitt, the exec, was alongside Fluckey on the bridge as the submarine trolled through the flotsam and doomed soldiers. "We could only take one prisoner. I remember coming up close to this man who was sitting on a hatch cover or a piece of wood. There was ice in the water. He was wearing nothing but a singlet and a pair of pants. We invited him aboard, came up to him, and he turned his back to us. One of the crew pointed a submachine gun at him, at which point he seemed happy to come aboard. I've often thought this was a matter of saving face for a moment. His alternative was not good."

Three seamen hauled the prisoner on deck, where a pharmacist's mate bundled him in a blanket after unwinding a twenty-foot-long spool of wool that he had wrapped around his abdomen, which had saved his life. The rescuers passed him through an access door to the bridge and lowered him through a hatchway, where others took him under guard, removing him to the after torpedo room where he could be watched. Fluckey ordered everyone aboard to treat him kindly and asked to be informed when he was sufficiently revived to begin interrogation.

Two hours later, guards led the prisoner into the officers' quarters, where McNitt had laid out a chart of the Okhotsk on the wardroom table. No one knew any Japanese. Luckily the skipper had pirated a single page of Japanese phonetic vocabulary from a Navy bulletin two years earlier and had kept it with him. He greeted the prisoner with "Konban wa" (Welcome). The sailor, short with a slender build, bowed and returned the greeting. The skipper had him sit next to him on a bench and proceeded with a line of questioning. Asked his name, he declined, putting his finger to his lips and moving it back and forth as if to say he could not divulge anything. Fluckey produced a .45 revolver and placed it on the table out of reach of the prisoner. Again he asked for the seaman's name.

"Kitojima Sanji!"

Fluckey indicated that he and the crew would call him "Kito." The prisoner nodded. With a combination of broken Japanese, sign language, and facial expressions, the officers were able to extract some information: Kito was a second-class gunner's mate. He once went AWOL after being ordered to execute a Chinese captive. He became a schoolteacher. Then he got drafted. He had been a lookout on the *Koto Maru* and had seen the torpedoes coming. The convoy had embarked from Matsuwa. There were four ships. He named them all. He confirmed that the *Herring* sank the escort.

The skipper reasoned that the *Herring* was chasing the *Hakuyo Maru,* the convoy's sole survivor, back toward Matsuwa. He ordered McNitt, the boat's gifted navigator, to set a course for La Perouse Strait in case the ship had evaded the *Herring* and was making a desperate run for the Sea of Japan.

Warming up to the interrogation, the prisoner used a pencil to draw a line on the map where mines were located in or near the strait. Fluckey wanted to know if there were more, motioning that the sub would be headed through the passage and could strike a mine, killing everyone—including Kito. He understood. He drew more lines and revealed that each of the explosives was about fifty feet below the surface. The captain was satisfied.

Guards led Kito back to the torpedo room while Fluckey convened a strategy session. The captain appointed torpedo and gunnery officer Lt. Jay Alan Easton to teach the prisoner English, have the enlisted men watch over him at all times, assign him various tasks, get to know him, and treat him gently. Based on the interrogation, Fluckey decided the boat would not venture through La Perouse Strait—too risky. He ordered everyone to rest overnight while posting a minimal watch. The next day he would have the ship's cook bake a cake to celebrate the dual sinking and pass around rations from the sub's whiskey allotment, known as "Black Death" because it was so poorly manufactured.

On the evening of 2 June, as the sub continued its westward trek across the Okhotsk, there was still no word from the *Herring*. Later reports would confirm what Fluckey suspected: Skipper Zabriski had set a course for Matsuwa in hopes of intercepting the fleeing *Hakuyo Maru*. There was no sign of the transport when the submarine arrived off the port. However, Zabriski noticed two other ships docked at the island and moved into the harbor at night to attack them. The boat fired several torpedoes that destroyed the *Hiburi Maru* and *Iwaki Maru*. Soldiers manning a shore battery, however, saw the tracks of the torpedoes and counterattacked. Two direct hits shattered the *Herring*'s conning tower and the boat plunged to the bottom with the loss of its entire eighty-three-man crew.

Just past midnight on 2 June, the day after *Herring*'s loss, the *Barb* made radar contact with a fast-moving Japanese *Chidori*-class frigate paralleling the submarine as both neared La Perouse Strait. Sounding the battle stations alarm, Fluckey prepared to attack. The destroyer continued its course without deviating, oblivious to the submarine. Fluckey hoped to get in closer but minefields loomed just ahead. He had no choice but to launch three torpedoes from long range. Lookouts on the warship saw them coming by their luminous tracks. The warship dodged the torpedoes, dropped a dozen depth charges, and fled through the strait.

Two hours later the diving alarm sounded again as the *Barb* made radar contact with a plane at dawn. The sub made an emergency dive to 260 feet as a bomb exploded overhead but not close. Resurfacing, the sub headed up the east coast of Sakhalin Island north of La Perouse. In the journey northbound, crewmen were mesmerized by a fantasy of floating ice. Windchiseled icebergs rose over the sea. Men crowded the bridge for a glimpse. Most had never seen such a proliferation of fifty-foot columns and pinnacles sculpted by the wind into exotic shapes. Around them, white seals basked in the sun on ice floes—"a lost world smothered in diamonds," as the captain later put it. The boat steered around the bergs and approached a thirty-foot ice cliff reflecting a dazzling kaleidoscope of color. The sub paralleled the ice pack for twenty minutes until lookouts reported masts and funnels of four trawlers, apparently ice bound. The battle stations alarm sent sailors scrambling to man the 4-inch gun on the afterdeck plus the boat's 40mm cannon and twin 20mm guns on the bridge. The gun captain reported the ships were in sight. Fluckey was just about ready to order a bombardment when the ice shelf began moving. And it picked up speed. With a shocked expression, Tuck Weaver asked Fluckey if the *Barb* should speed up too. "All ahead standard!" the skipper replied. Yet as the sub accelerated, so did the ice shelf—and it disappeared!

"All stop!" the captain ordered.

Those on deck were dumbfounded. Before them appeared an open, flat sea with nothing in sight. The whole engagement had been a mirage.

Weaver announced that maybe he'd been on patrol too long and needed some rest, that all the men were apparently "a bit touched." Moments later, he sighted another ice floe. Reporting it to the captain, Fluckey took a look and concluded it, too, was a mirage. Weaver said it was the real thing. Fluckey bet him a quart of whiskey that it wasn't. It was.

The captain went below to the wardroom to take stock of himself. There he mulled over childhood memories, recalling the literary adventures of Gen. Adolphus W. Greely, whose arctic explorations in the 1880s were once compared to those of Lewis and Clark in opening up the Old West to the United States. Fluckey recalled Greely's descriptions of phenomenal mirages produced by ice and sun in the arctic. As the skipper was lost in thought, a message arrived from Weaver: "It's twelve o'clock and all chronometers are round." Weaver had replaced the *w* in *wound* with an *r* to humor the skipper.

After a fruitless search for targets, including a near attack on a poorly marked Russian freighter, the skipper turned south toward the northern coast of Hokkaido, where he contemplated an attack on the port of Abashiri. Kito warned him that the city was home to seven major air bases that could easily swarm the sub. Fluckey changed his mind.

The prisoner, who was learning English rapidly, had proven to be extremely likeable. "He was as accommodating as could be," said McNitt. "When we'd tell him where we wanted to go, he would show us that there are minefields here, or there were airplanes located here, or guns emplaced here. The places he showed us that we knew about were accurate, and he showed us a lot that we didn't know about."

On 9 June the *Barb* headed for the lower Kuriles, hoping to destroy a cable relay station on Etorofu Island. To get within range of the station, the sub would have to navigate its way into a U-shaped cove. Low-hanging, patchy fog kept frustrating the captain as he edged in and out of the cove. The lookouts were surprised to hear him utter an expletive for the first time—"Damn charts!"—when the depth measured under the sub was much shallower than shown, putting the boat at risk of grounding. Fluckey made several more approaches from different angles. Each time fog or the shallows stymied the boat. Occasionally, the gritty fog lifted to reveal the cable station and an exotic landscape of smoking volcanoes. Still, the sub could not get close enough.

The skipper finally gave up and resumed a northward patrol of the Kuriles, where the boat encountered tremendous currents and eddies caused by tidal differences at the boundary between the Pacific and Okhotsk. The sub skirted numerous whirlpools, some several hundred feet wide. The ever-curious Fluckey directed the *Barb* through one of them "to see what happened." The boat heeled over ten degrees but righted itself as it passed through.

The boat made radar contact on 10 June with another swift-moving *Chidori* and gave chase for five hours before the destroyer outran the sub. The following day, as the sub navigated past icebergs, the port lookout spotted a fishing trawler hiding behind one of them. The *Barb*'s orders, like those issued to all other American submarines, were to clear the sea of enemy vessels until Japan surrendered. Fluckey wasn't crazy about sinking fishing trawlers, many of which were unarmed. But he and his men rationalized that most had radios and could be sentries on the lookout for submarines. Also, starving the enemy by denying its food supply seemed a good way to speed up an end to the war.

Fluckey ordered the gunnery crew to man the 4-inch gun, sufficient to sink the trawler. But the fishing boat kept out of sight behind the ice. McNitt suggested lobbing a shell over the iceberg into the ocean behind the ship. That could alarm the captain, causing him to speed forward into view. As predicted, the trawler took off at full speed, the submarine in pursuit. The two vessels zipped in and out among the icebergs, the sub firing thirty rounds that made Swiss cheese of passing ice columns. The thirty-first shell tore through a larger iceberg, toppling ice boulders that fell onto the deck of the ship, sinking it.

The sub encountered a second trawler, this one armed. An exchange of gunfire ensued but the fishing boat was no match for the sub's 4-inch gun.

Three hours later lookouts reported columns of smoke over the horizon. Radar plots showed two ships following a zigzag route. The sub caught up, submerged, and prepared to attack. Fluckey raised the periscope and noticed the ships' silhouettes jump into the clouds. Another mirage. He called off the attack. "I don't want to waste torpedoes on phantom ships," he told the crew. Rather than chase the mirage from submergence, Fluckey decided to wait for dark, surface, and then use a burst of speed to go after the ships, which were actually ten miles distant.

The *Barb* overtook the convoy off the coast of Sakhalin Island. The ships had embarked three days earlier from a naval base on the opposite side of the Okhotsk at Paramushiru, the northernmost island in the Kuriles. The 2,738-ton *Chihaya Maru* was carrying 260 tons of military cargo and 173 soldiers. It was accompanied by the *Toten Maru,* a 3,823-ton crab factory ship carrying another 200 troops. Both were armed with deck canons and steaming west toward La Perouse Strait.

Fluckey, on the bridge with Weaver, issued a whirlwind of directives. "All engines ahead one-third. Make ready all tubes fore and aft. Phosphorescence is very heavy, but I believe we can mosey in another 1,000 yards without being seen. Use tubes 1, 2, and 3 on the lead ship and 4, 5, and 6 on the trailer. Tuck will mark amidships bearings. Spread the torpedoes from aft forward with 50 yards between torpedoes. All hands on your toes. We're heading in!"

Just before midnight Fluckey gave the order to fire. One torpedo wrecked the stern of the *Chihaya Maru.* Two others holed the factory ship. The mournful sound of its whistle emanated continually from the *Toten Maru* amid automatic gunfire blinking wildly in the dark from its deck. Those in the *Barb* watched from afar as the *Chihaya* turned to flee. Fluckey had no intention of letting it go and proceeded after it. The ship reversed course, as if to ram the sub, its deck gun lobbing shells at the boat's luminous wake. Fluckey and Weaver instinctively ducked behind thin metal sheathing that wrapped around the bridge as each shell whistled past. Suddenly the captain stood up, laughing. Weaver wondered what was so funny. "Tuck," he replied, "it's so idiotic to cower behind this thin sheeting. Any shell would pierce it." So both men stood, ignoring the shelling as the speeding *Barb* roared past the crippled ship. One canon blast was so loud at two hundred yards that it left ears ringing on the bridge.

The *Chihaya* turned and crossed the sub's wake. Fluckey was ready. He fired three stern torpedoes. Seconds later the transport disintegrated in one massive explosion.

Tracking east back across the Okhotsk to the Kuriles, the submarine arrived in the vicinity of the big Paramushiru naval base just as the destroyer *Hatsuharu* left port, escorting the 5,633-ton army icebreaker *Takashima Maru* with a cargo of six hundred troops and equipment headed for the Philippines.

Fluckey worried that the boat's vertical periscope shears might be seen during the chase. He had four enlisted men climb up and drape white sheets over the shears, then lash them down. With so much ice floating in the sea, the captain reasoned, this would help disguise the boat as it closed on the convoy. It worked. The *Barb* moved in undetected. Radar imaging on the sub revealed the ships often stopped, sometimes reversed course, than went ahead full, making it very difficult for any submarine to position itself for a methodical submerged attack.

Fluckey decided to go after the icebreaker in a risky night surface attack using the boat's speed to mimic every turn of the target. To the captain, it was the only feasible way of sinking the transport. However, the boat's phosphorescent wake and engine exhaust risked giving away the sub's position. Fluckey ordered a full stop ahead of the convoy and abruptly changed tactics. He would depend on radar to direct an attack, crossing his fingers that the stationary submarine was in the right position at the *Takashima*'s predicted zig away from the sub as it plowed forward toward the *Barb*. Fluckey positioned the sub with its stern torpedo doors opened, torpedoes armed and pointed at the oncoming ship. The massive bow of the icebreaker approached, looming higher on a collision course. "We are holding our breaths for the expected zig away," noted Fluckey in the sub's log. "The bow wave of the target looks tremendous bearing down on us." The captain, on the bridge, held steady. At the last moment the ship zigged away as anticipated and into the sub's cross-hairs. Fluckey fired two torpedoes. Forty-five seconds later they exploded, ripping away the ship's fantail. The target came to a halt and began sinking, its whistle blaring.

In the confusion, the destroyer *Hatsuharu* got a visual on the luminous wake of the *Barb* speeding away. The warship turned and gave chase, lobbing depth charges. The sub pushed nineteen knots. The destroyer was faster and gaining but finally turned back to the *Takashima* to rescue survivors.

Fluckey ordered all stop.

The *Barb* idled in the distance, looking for an opening to attack the destroyer. The escort, noting the sub's presence, broke from the sinking ship, spilling soldiers into the sea, and raced anew after the submarine, driving it away while lobbing depth charges, then turned back again. The scene repeated itself through the night, keeping the sub crew on edge. Rumbling explosions from thirty-eight depth charges repeatedly rocked the boat. The sub remained on the surface in Fluckey's attempt to outwit the destroyer and ensure the sinking of the transport by putting another torpedo into it. There was no need. Just before dawn, the *Takashima Maru*'s bow rose high and disappeared into the Okhotsk.

The destroyer, with a cargo of rescued soldiers, began a more intense search for the *Barb*. Fluckey, still watching from the distance, asked for a five-gallon milk tin filled with oil and the top punctured. The captain directed an enlisted man to climb down to the deck and cast the tin into the sea. Fluckey reasoned an oil slick would spread and in the early light would be mistaken for a sunken submarine, allowing the Americans to escape. It worked.

The *Barb* set off at flank speed back across the Okhotsk to the Kamchatka Peninsula at the top of the Kuriles.

Fluckey had achieved his quota of five major ships sunk. With four torpedoes left, he went after more as the *Barb* patrolled southward along the Kuriles over the next few weeks.

From a distance of thirty miles off Paramushiru, the *Barb* observed airplanes practicing dogfights in the crisp arctic air against a backdrop of three-thousand-foot volcanoes belching smoke and fire. Numerous Russian ships passed. The sub dived under scores of sampans, too small to attack. At one point it got caught in a fishing net and had to surface to free itself. Nearer to the Japanese main island, the *Barb* dodged many aircraft by diving and quickly popping back to the surface.

Attempts to contact the overdue *Golet* continued to fail. Fluckey feared that it, like the *Herring*, had been lost. Later reports indicated Lieutenant Commander Clark's boat had arrived in the lower Kuriles on 14 April, when an antisubmarine patrol discovered it, delivering a death blow off the east coast of Hokaido. All eighty-two men aboard perished.

The *Barb* exited the Okhotsk Sea on 29 June and set a course for Midway. All those aboard celebrated the Independence Day holiday—4 July— twice, on both sides of the international dateline. In a single war patrol, they had coalesced to make the *Barb* one of the war's most formidable submarines. The captain's lightning-like ability to analyze any situation and execute a determined plan of action, while methodically plotting an escape route, had impressed the crew. Said McNitt, "During attacks, he had an uncanny ability to keep the tactical picture clearly in his head, focus on the battle plan, and change it at the last minute as the situation changed."

The *Barb* arrived at Midway on the boat's second 4 July. The submarine's 51-day patrol included 33 days spent crisscrossing 8,700 miles of the Okhotsk Sea. The men had bonded with Kito during the time and hated to see him go. They filled a seabag with cigarettes, extra clothes, and comic books for him to take along. He, in turn, told them he hoped one day to become an American citizen, that going back to Japan would be a death sentence for revealing so much to the submariners. When Marines came aboard to take charge of the prisoner, they began roughing him up. "These were Marines that had not been to war yet and they thought they'd be tough with this Jap, you know, and knock him around," explained McNitt. "The crew got between the Marines and Kito and shook his hand. Every one of them shook his hand when he left, and these Marines couldn't understand this.

Aftermath of bombing of IBERLANT headquarters in Portugal in 1971. *Courtesy Fluckey family*

Exterior of IBERLANT headquarters showing how windows had been blown out by bombs planted by terrorists. *Courtesy Fluckey family*

Isaac Newtown Fluckey and wife Louella with their children (*clockwise from lower left*) Eugene, Jim, Lucille, and Ken in 1918. *Courtesy Fluckey family*

Eugene B. Fluckey after graduation from the Naval Academy as an ensign assigned to the battleship *Nevada*. *Courtesy Fluckey family*

Portrait of Marjorie Fluckey following marriage to Ensign Fluckey on 6 June 1937. *Courtesy Fluckey family*

Lieutenant Fluckey served in S-42 operating out of the Canal Zone in Panama in 1938–40. *Naval Historical Center, NH42155*

The *Bonita* (*from the right*) and *Bass* of the V-class submarines moored in San Francisco in the early 1930s. Lieutenant Fluckey honed his seamanship and engineering expertise in the *Bonita* leading up to World War II. *U.S. Naval Institute Photo Archive*

Portrait of Marjorie Fluckey and daughter Barbara during World War II. *Courtesy Fluckey family*

SS-220 coming in off patrol to Midway during World War II. *Courtesy Fluckey family*

Japanese prisoner "Kito" with (*from left*) Lt. Everett "Tuck" Weaver, Lt. Cdr. Gene Fluckey, and Lt. John R. Post at end of the *Barb*'s eighth war patrol in the Okhotsk Sea. *Courtesy Fluckey family*

The submarine roars along at flank speed in the Pacific as lookouts keep a steady watch for targets and danger. *Courtesy Don Miller*

USS *Barb* Executive Officer Bob McNitt (*left*) and Skipper Gene Fluckey flank Kitojima "Kito" Sanji, a Japanese prisoner of war rescued from a sinking enemy ship. Sanji later provided crucial intelligence to the success of the submarine's eighth war patrol north of Japan. *Courtesy Bob McNitt*

Barb crewmen line up for rescue duty on storm-tossed South China Sea in 1944. *Courtesy Fluckey family*

Lt. Cdr. Eugene Fluckey (*center, front*) and *Barb* crewmen celebrate rescue of Australian and British prisoners on arrival in Saipan. William E. Donnelly, the *Barb*'s chief pharmacist's mate, has his arms wrapped around the shoulders of two of the Aussies rescued adrift for six days on the South China Sea. *Courtesy Fluckey family*

Sea bird that kept foiling attack on enemy target during *Barb*'s ninth war patrol sits atop periscope. *Courtesy Fluckey family*

Vice Adm. Charles A. Lockwood Jr. presents Navy Cross to a proud Cdr. Eugene B. Fluckey aboard the *Barb* on 6 December 1944. *U.S. Navy photo*

The entire crew of the *Barb* poses with the sub's battle flag after completion of the boat's twelfth war patrol at Midway. Commander Fluckey is in the middle at top of the flag. The submarine sank more enemy tonnage than any other submarine under a single skipper in the Pacific war. *Courtesy Fluckey family*

This guy was an enemy. The Marines hustled him off the ship, and away he went. But he'd been very helpful to us."

Added McNitt, "I think he may have saved the ship."

Fluckey, meanwhile, was hopeful for a quick turnaround so the *Barb* could head back into action. That would have to wait for a refit at Pearl Harbor four days later. There Admiral Lockwood wanted to talk to Fluckey. So did the president of the United States.

Lost (Ninth Patrol)

The phone jangled insistently in Gene Fluckey's room at the Royal Hawaiian. It was 0900. The captain, his officers, and the *Barb*'s enlisted men had been ensconced at the four-story luxury hotel on Waikiki Beach for only the second day in two weeks of much deserved R&R, courtesy of the Navy. Now someone was on the line sounding awfully curt.

"Get down in front of the hotel in ten minutes," demanded the unidentified male caller. "President Roosevelt wants to meet you."

Fluckey wasn't falling for the prank. "You've been drinking!" he interjected.

"Captain, this is Admiral Lockwood. Be there!"

It was no joke. The president was on his way to meet the skipper. The *Barb*'s record of five ships and two trawlers sunk in the Okhotsk Sea had generated quite a buzz. More fantastic were details revealed in the *Barb*'s war patrol report being circulated among sub captains: whirlpools hundreds of yards wide that the ship dived through . . . volcanoes spewing ash and fire . . . icebergs and white seals drifting by . . . running battles amid ice floes . . . dense fog that appeared and disappeared in an instant . . . incredible mirages of enemy ships far over the horizon . . . Japanese pilots practicing dogfight maneuvers overhead . . . dramatic attacks . . . a near ramming . . . aerial bombardments . . . a prisoner taken . . .

It seemed the stuff of fiction. Yet every detail was vouched for by crew members. "Gene had a skill in writing patrol reports that gave a vivid picture of what had happened without exaggeration. He didn't need to exaggerate, as the events were always bigger than life," said McNitt, the *Barb*'s executive officer. Lockwood was so enthralled after reading the report that he sent the narrative to Admiral Nimitz, who passed it along to Franklin D. Roosevelt for overnight reading. The president had arrived in Honolulu for a strategy meeting with Nimitz and Army Gen. Douglas MacArthur. After reading the *Barb* report, Roosevelt insisted on meeting the skipper the next morning. So precisely at 0910 Fluckey joined Lockwood in front of the Royal Hawaiian as the president's limousine rolled to a stop. Lockwood went to the right back door and opened it, helping the polio-afflicted president put his legs out so he could face the skipper, who greeted the commander in chief warmly. Roosevelt introduced Fluckey to Admiral Nimitz, sitting in the middle, and General MacArthur on the far side. Nimitz shook Fluckey's hand while MacArthur gave him a wave. Looking into the face of the Army's Pacific commander, Fluckey flashed back to Washington in 1932, when he watched as a much younger MacArthur ordered "fix bayonets!" and drove World War I veterans out of the District of Columbia and across a bridge into Virginia. The protesters, 15,000 strong, had bivouacked in the so-called Bonus City to demand bonuses Congress had promised eight years earlier but never paid.

Roosevelt and Fluckey chatted briefly. The president was intrigued that the *Barb* had spent only a single day submerged during its fifty-two-day patrol. Fluckey explained his strategy. Waiting in ambush for something to float by in daylight while submerged with three feet of periscope exposed was too limiting. By his estimate, only thirteen square miles of ocean could be scanned. A surface search, on the other hand, allowed the boat to raise the periscope to fifty feet, enabling a view of 206 square miles. "You see more ships and sink more ships," said the captain with a grin.

"Battle reports like yours let me sleep, confident that peace is inevitable," the president replied. Turning to Admiral Nimitz, he added, "Chester, I want you to personally see that I am sent a copy of *Barb*'s patrol reports whenever Captain Fluckey returns from patrol." The five men then exchanged salutes before Roosevelt, MacArthur, and Nimitz drove off.

Roosevelt had been so impressed by Fluckey's enthusiasm and the results of his first war patrol that the next day he asked Lockwood if he'd have the skipper rev up the *Barb*'s engines and cruise past a landing at Pearl Harbor. The president would be waiting to film the boat from his wheelchair; he loved making home movies and wanted to take back a memento of the *Barb*.

How do you turn down the president?

At Lockwood's direction, Fluckey assembled his crew and cast off. The *Barb* puttered by the landing as Roosevelt filmed the scene. He wasn't happy. The sub was going too slow. Its battle flag and pennants hung limply. Could Fluckey do it again, but this time faster?

The admiral ordered the skipper to take the *Barb* back out and come back in, this time with a head of steam. This angered the captain since there was a great risk of crashing into a ship moored at the landing. Any damage to the *Barb* certainly would put a crimp on the upcoming war patrol. Lockwood didn't want to hear it. "Don't worry about it. I'll be responsible."

Fluckey, furious, took the conn as the sub backed out into the channel for another run. As Roosevelt gave the signal by dropping his hand, the skipper bellowed, "All ahead full!" The *Barb* surged forward, its flags and pennants fluttering wildly to the president's satisfaction. But Lockwood feared the sub was coming in too fast. The admiral cringed. Just when it seemed a crash was inevitable, Fluckey shouted, "All back emergency! Left full rudder!" A whirl of foam erupted as the boat reversed thrust and shuddered violently to a stop, the bow ten yards short of the ship ahead. Roosevelt clapped approval as crewmen secured mooring lines from the *Barb*. Captain Fluckey crossed the bow to greet the president, pushing by Lockwood, who fumed, "Don't you ever do that to me again." Fluckey snipped back, "Admiral, then don't ask me to endanger my ship again."

Later, at Lockwood's office, the two shrugged off the incident. The admiral lavished praise on young Fluckey, noting that only five boat captains—Slade Cutter, Walter Griffith, Richard O'Kane, Charles Kirkpatrick, and Thomas Klakring—had equaled his record of five ships sunk on a single patrol. He asked if the skipper wanted to lead the *Barb* back to the Okhotsk. Fluckey demurred, preferring an assignment south of Japan on enemy convoy lanes. "Okay," replied the admiral. "Get ready for wolf packing in the South China Sea. It's hot as a firecracker."

"Great!" said the skipper. "Can't wait to get started."

It took another week for a relief crew to repair minor problems aboard the *Barb*. Meanwhile, Fluckey and his men relaxed in Waikiki. The order of the day was swimming and surfboarding, or hanging out at the Outrigger Canoe Club, the beachfront nightclub near the Royal Hawaiian. The hotel, leased by the Navy for aviators and submariners, was cordoned off by barbed wire and shore patrol guards. Inside, drinking, partying, and gambling were inevitable. "There was no night in my room I didn't hear dice banging on the floorboards up and down the hall there," said McNitt. "And every once in a while somebody would fall out a window and land in the bushes down below. So it was kind of a crazy place as it was. But it was necessary. You had to get your mind off the war." Indeed, the mortality rate among submariners had risen to the highest of any branch of the service. The *Barb* crew understood that all too well, having been the only sub in its wolf pack to return from the Okhotsk Sea.

The *Barb*'s crew was among the youngest in the undersea fleet. The captain was only thirty, McNitt was twenty-eight, and most of the crewmen were twenty-two or under. During liberty, the skipper did what he could to be one of the guys yet retain control. When crewmen decided to have an afternoon party in a field near the hotel, the skipper thought a few females would liven up things. He visited the Navy laundry and got the manager to invite women who worked there. So many came forward that Fluckey needed a bus but couldn't get one. What he did obtain was a flatbed truck. "As I remember," said McNitt, "this truck came up with all these girls shrieking and singing and everything and hanging over the edge of the truck and jumped out, and the party was on. My job was to make sure we got everybody back all right, and it turned out fine."

The captain was willing to bend the rules if it helped build morale. For instance, when one of his junior lieutenants insisted it was impossible to get a woman to the second floor of the hotel because of security, Fluckey bet it could be done. A nurse, engaged to an Army lieutenant stationed in the South Pacific, had gotten to know the submariners and agreed to participate. "So Gene and I engaged the shore patrol and the guy at the desk in conversation," said McNitt. "While we asked them for directions to town, the rest of them got Martha Hendrickson up the backstairs and into the room. But we hadn't been there more than a couple of minutes when there was a hammering on the door and the shore patrol was there."

The skipper was more successful in procuring twenty-four cases of beer from a supply officer for the upcoming war patrol. Few *Barb* veterans liked the regulation Schenley "Black Death" whiskey. What they did like, especially the younger ones, was beer. Despite a rule against having it aboard a Navy sub, Fluckey was determined to reward his crew for successful attacks. "We loaded the cases of beer in a jeep over at the officers' club [in Pearl Harbor], where we'd made arrangements to get them," said Fluckey's partner in crime, his exec. "We stowed them in the officers' shower; filled it right up to the overhead."

The *Barb* got under way for its ninth war patrol on 4 August 1944 in league with the USS *Queenfish* (SS-393) and the USS *Tunny* (SS-282). All three practiced coordinated mock attacks on an accompanying destroyer until the ship turned back two days out. Aboard the *Barb* was Capt. Edwin R. Swinburne, Lockwood's flag secretary, who would serve as wolf pack commander. Realizing the potential for strenuous action, the admiral reasoned it would be unfair for Fluckey to again coordinate the boats. Swinburne, ten years older than Fluckey, had never made a war patrol, though he was a veteran of the service. Lockwood and Cdr. Richard Voge, architect of the undersea offensive, coined the term "Ed's Eradicators" for the wolf pack. Lockwood posted Swinburne in the *Barb* because both of the other skippers—Charles Elliot Loughlin in the *Queenfish* and George Pierce in the *Tunny*—were new to their commands. Fluckey knew Swinburne was a stickler for rules and probably would put the kibosh on the beer stash. The skipper asked his officers to keep it a secret to give him time to think of something; it was too late to offload the beer.

En route to Midway cross-training continued. Every man had to know another man's job in case of an emergency. The value of that showed itself during a practice dive.

"We were trying to see if we could increase our diving speed, and we were diving with almost a thirty-degree down angle," explained McNitt, noting the normal dive is ten degrees. "With the bow planes on full dive, the relay burned out, leaving the bow planes on full dive and no way to bring them back other than shifting to manual and cranking them up. There wasn't time to do that." The diving officer ordered "Blow main ballast!" as the boat rushed downward. A petty officer on the main ballast blow manifold needed to open the main ballast blow valve to rapidly force seawater out of the ballast tanks with compressed air to get the buoyancy needed to surface. However, the petty officer slipped on the steep deck and tumbled to the lower end of the compartment. The ship's third-class baker reacted instinctively from his cross-training. "Russell Elliman jumped out of the galley, where he was watching this, realized what had happened, dove through the watertight door, grabbed the main ballast blow manifold handle as he went by, and blew main ballast," continued McNitt. "It caught the boat at about 350 feet."

It was a close call; the cook had saved the boat.

Fluckey and Swinburne meshed well. The commander was perfectly willing to leave operations of the *Barb* to the skipper. In fact, he studied Fluckey's leadership traits, impressed by how he listened to any and all suggestions that anybody on the boat anted up. Said McNitt, "He was quick to make up his mind but if he saw a better way of doing it, he'd jump on it. He was cheerful, fun loving. Serious when it came to serious things on the boat but always looking for a way of putting a little bit of amusement or fun into the day."

So far Swinburne hadn't discovered the beer in the officers' shower. The boat was crammed with food and provisions. It wasn't unusual for the shower to be stowing provisions early in the patrol. Normally no one took showers until four weeks or more had passed and the smell of diesel fuel and body odor became pronounced. Even when the men did shower, it was quick—about a minute—due to limited fresh water aboard.

During an overnight layover in Midway, Captain Swinburne called a meeting of the sub captains to go over details of the upcoming mission. The plan was to stearn due west 3,600 miles to the Luzon Strait. There

Ed's Eradicators would be joined by the *Growler* (SS-215), the *Pampanito* (SS-383), and the *Sealion II* (SS-315)—"Ben's Busters." Senior skipper Ben Oakley in the *Growler* was wolf pack commander. The objective was to harass and sink Japanese convoys plowing the ninety-mile-wide passage between the Philippine island of Luzon and Formosa (Taiwan) on the eastern edge of the South China Sea. The strait was known in the Navy as Convoy College for the great numbers of ships passing through and the difficult test posed to sub captains in sinking them.

Prior to departure for Midway Commo. "Shorty" Edwards hosted a luncheon for the wolf pack officers. Fluckey still was seeking some way of legitimizing his cargo of beer. He casually brought up the fact that younger crewmen in *Barb* did not like whiskey. Edmonds remarked that new regulations allowed ships to carry a half-case of beer per man. Fluckey quickly went to a phone within earshot of Swinburne and made an exaggerated request to officers in the *Barb* to order some beer and take it aboard. They could store it in the officers' shower.

The submarines embarked on the morning of 10 August. Fluckey was confident since the *Barb* was armed with twenty-four electric torpedoes. The new Mark 18s were powerful and left no wake. No longer would the boat's position be revealed by the bubbly trail of a steam-driven Mark 14.

The boats formed a scouting line at twenty-mile intervals and proceeded at twelve knots for two weeks in an uneventful Pacific crossing. Arriving in the area of the Philippines, the two wolf packs spread out across the strait to engage a very wary, sophisticated enemy. Convoys were well guarded by destroyers, torpedo boats, and mine-layers. Numerous midget submarines and radar-equipped bombers operated from many islands near the strait.

For seven days no targets were encountered. Finally on 30 August an ULTRA reported that a convoy of nine ships escorted by five destroyers had embarked from Formosa en route to Manila. All six subs rushed to intercept in the Bashi Channel fifty miles south of Formosa. In the predawn of 31 August the *Queenfish* was the first to make contact and torpedoed a 4,700-ton tanker that exploded in a fireball, illuminating the night sky. The *Barb,* diving to avoid aircraft, came to periscope depth. Fluckey couldn't believe his eyes. Three columns approached: a freighter and tanker in the starboard column; a large freighter, a tanker, and a smaller tanker in the center; and, on the port side, a much larger tanker, a smaller oiler, and another tanker or a freighter. Enemy destroyers prowled the peripheries while planes crisscrossed overhead. The captain called down on the intercom so all could hear. "Jackson, put four cases of beer in the cooler." It would become the skipper's signature affirmation in expressing confidence and easing tension.

Fluckey thought a single salvo might wipe out the entire center column and the lead tanker in the port column. The *Growler,* however, had taken aim at one of the destroyers and fired two torpedoes, one of which passed above the *Barb*. The convoy zigged radically to the east, foiling the *Barb's* opportunity. Still, the captain's primary target—the largest of the freighters in the center column—lumbered into range, overlapped by a medium-sized tanker. Fluckey prepared to attack, his mind racing and changing tactics in a flash amid a cacophony of telemetry and verbal feedback from the fire control party. He fired three stern torpedoes from a thousand yards. Two ripped apart the freighter. The third struck the tanker.

The *Barb* went deep to escape a flurry of depth charges and aerial bombs. Back at periscope depth, both Fluckey and Commander Swinburne took turns viewing the sinking freighter. Meanwhile the *Sealion* inflicted damage on a freighter and a tanker, forcing the convoy back to Formosa.

Throughout the day Japanese bombers sought the submarines, dropping numerous explosives. Several detonations were close but astern as the submerged *Barb* tried to keep pace with the retreating convoy. Losing position, the sub turned west to investigate a smoke plume seen from the periscope as the sun set. A small armed transport led by two patrol boats soon sailed into view. Fluckey closed, not realizing the ship was a decoy in a submarine-killer group. The danger to the *Barb* was pronounced because its day-long submergence had drained most of the power from its batteries. Still, the boat was in position to sink the ship. Fluckey wanted to try. As the *Barb* maneuvered astern of the target, a bird landed on the periscope, plopping its tail feathers over the view port. "This proved extremely confusing for the approach officer in the final stages," Fluckey noted in the ship's log. "He banged on the scope, shook it, hooted and hollered at the blasted bird, swung the scope around quickly and raised and lowered it desperately. The bird clung on tenaciously, hovering over the scope while it was ducked, then hopping back on when it was raised. As a last resort both scopes were raised for observations, one a few seconds ahead of the other as a feint, while the approach officer followed the other scope up. This completely baffled the bird and he was noted peering venomously down the other periscope."

Fluckey, laughing, had a camera brought up and took a photo of the "feathered fiend." Then, in a flash, the *Barb* launched four torpedoes from its bow tubes, breaking the decoy ship in half as the bird flew off. The two escorts turned and charged, dropping fifty-eight depth changes as the submarine descended to three hundred feet with a left full rudder and escaped.

The boat surfaced five miles away under an inky, moonless sky. The boat's diesels roared to life, powering a getaway at seventeen knots. *Barb* crewmen were glad to be out in the open seas. By Fluckey's count, the sub had endured two hundred bombs and depth charges over a twenty-four-hour period.

Around midnight Fluckey reestablished contact with the *Tunny* and the *Queenfish*. The subs assumed a new patrol area off the northwest coast of Luzon. Through the night and into the next day the *Barb* dived and popped back up as antisubmarine aircraft hounded it with surface radar. As dusk fell on 1 September Fluckey and Lt. Max Duncan, one of two new officers assigned to the *Barb*, were on the bridge studying the sea for any sign of periscopes or mines while lookouts higher up in the periscope shears watched for approaching planes and ships. Duncan was the first to notice a silver bomber roaring in low toward the sub. "Plane astern!" he shouted. "Clear the bridge! Dive! Dive!"

The plane roared past without dropping any bombs. Through the periscope, Fluckey saw it head straight for the *Tunny*. At the last minute the sub dove. But it was too late. A bomb exploded near the tail, lifting the stern as the *Tunny* was going under. The plane circled, dropping more explosives plus flares to illuminate the area. Swinburne directed Fluckey to send a sonar message to the *Tunny* telling Skipper Pierce to stay deep. There was no reply. Two hours later the *Barb* surfaced on a dark sea. Again Fluckey tried to contact the *Tunny*. No answer.

At midnight radar picked up another fast-approaching aircraft. Again the lookouts and officers dropped into the conning tower, riding the ladder rails down in a single motion. McNitt, who had been taking star sightings to establish the *Barb*'s location, had a jacket on and zipped it up as he went through the hatch. "My beard was caught in the zipper and it held my head forward so that it banged every rung on the way down," he explained later. "It went clunk clunk clunk. Played that thing like a xylophone all the way down."

The sound of the plane passing over was so loud it brought a sleep-deprived Fluckey running from his cabin in his underwear. "Three hundred feet! Left full rudder!" he shouted. The bomber circled back and dropped four bombs. One of them exploded above the forward deck, shaking the boat violently. Fuses jumped from their lodgings. Lightbulbs exploded. Emergency lights snapped on. Glass gauges shattered, sending shards tinkling down through deck plates into the keel. Flakes of insulating cork and paint fluttered down from the overhead. Crewmen were visibly shaken.

As quickly as the attack began, it was over. To break the tension, Fluckey directed that the four cases of beer being refrigerated in the below-decks meat locker be brought to the control room to celebrate the sinking of the sub-killer. McNitt, nursing a nasty welt on his forehead, further enlivened things by reciting an old prayer from his Scottish ancestry: "Good Lord, do deliver us—from all the ghosties and ghoulies, and long-leggity beasties, and things that go boomp in the night."

An examination of the deck on surfacing revealed just how close the *Barb* had come to destruction. "I went out on the foredeck and I found the tail fins of a bomb stuck in the deck and wrapped around the bitts," said McNitt. "And there were bits of shattered casing stuck in the wood all over. I think it hit the forward part of the submarine where the deck was level but the pressure hull sloped down to more of a point. And the pressure hull was farther from the deck that detonated the bomb. If it had been farther aft, where the pressure hull was right underneath the deck, it might have finished us. That close."

The exec's bumpy ride down the conning tower ladder got him to considering what could be done to give the crew a few more seconds to dive to avoid aircraft. Radar warnings had been useful but precious time was lost getting the warning to the captain or officer of the deck. McNitt came up with a novel idea. The scope for the air search radar located below decks in the radio shack in the bowels of the boat showed an electronic spike that rose as a plane was coming in. The exec put a piece of tape on the scope at the point it was necessary to dive. "When this spike got up to the level of that tape, the radioman would dive the boat from his radio shack—not the officer of the deck, not the captain," explained McNitt. The radioman would buzz the bridge electronically, alerting the officer of the deck to commence the dive. It saved a few seconds, critical time that could mean the difference between life and death. The *Barb* employed the method from then on.

For the next two days the sub continued to dodge night fliers. Miraculously the *Tunny* reported in with no casualties. However, its stern was severely caved in, disabling four torpedo tubes and damaging the rudder. Swinburne ordered the boat back to Midway. The *Barb* and *Queenfish* continued on. Days went by as both dodged aircraft and midget submarines. Fluckey was able to shell and sink a four-masted armed sampan. A few days later the *Queenfish* came upon a convoy at midnight and alerted the *Barb*. Loughlin made an end-around and submerged ahead of the ships, which passed over the submarine. The *Barb* was angling up the far side of the convoy on the surface when the *Queenfish* fired ten torpedoes at four separate targets, sinking two large freighters. In the resulting commotion, Fluckey spotted a destroyer lagging behind the convoy. He ordered three torpedoes calibrated to run at a shallow four feet. "Dislike shooting at this target, really against my better judgment—if we hit they'll keep us down and the convoy will get away, if we miss the same results," the captain noted in the patrol log. "However once in every submariner's life there comes the urge to let three fish go particularly after a convoy skids across his nose while his hands are tied. I dood it."

Two torpedoes missed the target and the third made a circular run over the *Barb*, which went deep to avoid it, losing the convoy.

The *Barb* continued to be harassed by Japanese bombers, day and night. "These boys are varsity," Fluckey said of the enemy pilots. So often did the boat dive and resurface that the quartermaster, closing the hatch, remarked, "Is there any use in closing it?" The *Barb* also was pinned down by a destroyer that dropped twenty well-placed depth charges, "enough to jar your fillings," noted Fluckey.

On 15 September 1944 the wolf pack received orders to rescue Australian and British prisoners of war from Japanese transports sunk by the *Growler* and *Pompanito* in the middle of the South China Sea. The *Pompanito* had returned to the area and found more than a thousand prisoners floating on improvised rafts among miles of debris and dead bodies. The *Pompanito* picked up seventy-three survivors, the *Sealion II* another fifty-four. They could take no more. The remaining castaways' only hope—the *Queenfish* and *Barb*—was still more than 450 miles away. The problem was where to find those adrift.

That responsibility fell to McNitt, the boat's brilliant navigator. In the previous patrol in the Okhotsk Sea, it was his ingenuity using radar mapping that enabled the *Barb* to dash through fog-shrouded inlets in the Kurile chain without fear of grounding. He prided himself in delivering the boat to precisely the destination the captain had in mind. Now, as the *Barb* and the *Queenfish* awaited coordinates for the rescue mission, McNitt drew on all available data. Tidal information. Estimated wind direction. Strength of current. "Fortunately, I had in my navigator's notebook a clipping I'd taken from the *Naval Institute Proceedings* written by a Coast Guardsman," he explained. "Never knowing when this would be handy, I'd cut it out and stuck it in my book. It gave a very good description in a few paragraphs of how to combine wave, current, coriolis effects [the effect of the earth's rotation on sea currents], and wind and calculate what the drift would be. We laid these vectors down on a chart, ran it out to where we thought they'd likely be, set a course for it, and took off on the surface at maximum four-engine speed."

After seventeen hours the subs were within 150 miles. Traveling on the surface at night the *Queenfish* reported contact with a large enemy convoy traveling north at twelve knots. Commander Swinburne decided it was too important to let pass. Radar imaging revealed four large ships in two columns, a destroyer leading, escorts on the flanks and quarter, and one large vessel in the middle between the two columns. The *Queenfish* initiated the attack on the far side of the convoy. Loughlin fired his last four torpedoes, two of which damaged a tanker. The *Barb*, with all ten of its torpedo tubes armed and ready, prepared to attack three heavily laden tankers led by a destroyer. When they suddenly veered away, Fluckey had no choice but to target the last tanker in the column. The destroyer saw the boat coming, turned, and charged.

On the bridge, Fluckey had his eyes glued to the closing escort when Tuck Weaver shouted, "Captain, there's a flattop in the middle overlapping the bow of the tanker. We'll have to change our firing setup." The quartermaster nudged the captain. "Destroyer, six hundred yards coming in to ram!"

"Tuck!" shouted Fluckey. "Shift your point of aim to the tanker's bow! Fire six torpedo spread! Dive! Rig ship for depth charge! All watertight doors locked!"

In a fifteen-second span the submarine fired all of its bow tubes as the boat was going down. Fluckey hoped to hit both targets. One was them was the twenty-thousand-ton aircraft carrier *Unyo*, which had long been hunted by American submarines.

In December 1943 the *Sailfish* (SS-192) had attacked the *Unyo*'s sister ship, the *Chuyo*, during a typhoon off Japan. Imprisoned on the *Chuyo* was half the surviving crew of the submarine *Sculpin* (SS-191), scuttled a few weeks earlier near the Japanese naval fortress of Truk in the Central Pacific. Sailing in tandem with the *Chuyo* was the *Unyo*, in which twenty other *Sculpin* prisoners were under guard. In a tenacious ten-hour attack, the *Sailfish* sank the *Chuyo* as the *Unyo* escaped in the storm. Only one *Sculpin* prisoner survived the sinking. He was picked up by a Japanese warship and later reunited with his shipmates off the *Unyo* in Japan. Now, nearly a year later, Fluckey had his chance to sink the carrier.

In less than two minutes three of the *Barb*'s six torpedoes struck the tanker. Its volatile cargo of aviation gasoline erupted in a five hundred-foot fireball, consuming the vessel. Two other torpedoes smashed into the carrier, rupturing it. Surfacing an hour after the attack, the *Barb* remained a safe distance away as enemy destroyers picked up survivors. The rest of the convoy had disappeared to the north. The *Unyo* limped along with them as crewmen attempted damage control. But seven hours after the attack, the carrier sank.

Fluckey had contemplated going after the *Unyo* with his three remaining torpedoes. But time was of the essence if the boat hoped to reach the Allied prisoners they had been dispatched to rescue. "The seas have been rising and if we don't reach the survivors today, their fifth day in the water, there will be none left alive," noted Fluckey in the boat's log. The *Barb* and the *Queenfish* raced ahead through the night against winds gusting above twenty knots with rough seas. Aboard the *Barb*, all torpedo skids were converted into three bunks each as Fluckey organized the ship to take up to a hundred survivors.

At dawn on 17 September the boats arrived at the position calculated by McNitt. The bridge watch was horrified. "There were bodies all over the place, grossly inflated," recalled the captain. "The crew came up on the bridge but it was such an awful sight that nobody wanted to stay there and watch. So we went through this mass of wreckage and bodies until we found three men on a raft that seemed to be alive."

The *Barb* pulled alongside.

"We tried to pass them a rope with a bowline in the end of it right close aboard and handed, almost threw it across the raft, and these men would just sit there and look at it," said McNitt, who was in charge of the rescue party.

> They were beyond comprehending what was happening to them. They were so far gone. You'd tell them to put it over their shoulders and they'd pick it up and look at it. They were just too weak and too uncomprehending then. So the only thing to do was to just get them. So three or four of us just took these lines, put them around our shoulders, took another line, swam out, and got them. Brought them back with the cross-chest carry and helped drag them up over the side of the submarine. In an open sea, with big swells and a rounded shape of a submarine, it was not easy to get them aboard. All of them fainted when they got on board. None of them could even stand up.

The men were stripped of their clothing, wiped down, bundled up, hoisted up onto the gun platform at the bridge level, then passed down the hatch by a chain gang to the crew's mess, where a table served as a receiving station. Chief Pharmacist Mate William Donnelly, aided by crewmen, wiped away the oil; treated enormous skin ulcers caused by sun, salt, and oil; and cleaned the survivors' eyes, which were in bad shape. Their tongues were seriously swollen as well, very red, dry, and sore.

The rescue operation was repeated throughout the afternoon. When one swimmer tired, another would take his place. In two and a half hours, the *Barb* found seven more improvised rafts, some with two, others with a sole survivor sitting on them. They were in pitiful condition, covered with sores, soaked in oil, emaciated, barely alive. They were all Australian or British. Once aboard, the survivors slowly came around. The stories they told were incredible, as was the account of Aussie army gunner Neville B. Thams of the 2nd/10th Field Regiment.

He and others had been in captivity for nearly three years after the fall of British-controlled Singapore in 1942. They were among 61,000 Australian, British, Dutch, and American prisoners put to work building a 265-mile railroad through the nearly impenetrable jungles of Malaysia. The men endured ghastly confinement in rat- and bug-infested "hell trains" after long work hours. They suffered terribly from dysentery, malaria, pellagra, beriberi, cholera, tropical ulcers, malnutrition, starvation, and beatings. More than a third succumbed. After the railroad was completed, the hardiest of the prisoners were transported back to Singapore for shipment to Japan in the holds of two unmarked transports. The intention was to put them to work in Japan's factories and mines.

The *Rakuyo Maru* took 1,350 prisoners aboard, most of them stacked on wooden platforms in the forward hull while others were confined to the forward deck. The *Kachidoko Maru* took an additional 900. Accompanied by five escorts, the ships cast off on 6 September. American code breakers intercepted news of the departure but were unaware of the prisoners aboard. Japan had not asked for safe passage, which would have been granted. At dawn on 12 September Ben's Busters—the *Growler, Pompanito,* and *Sealion II*—attacked. Both the *Rakuyo* and *Kachidoko* were torpedoed. Most prisoners were able to get off the ships before they went under.

"The sun rose at 7:00 a.m. It was dismal. One group of about nine hundred men had drifted far from the ship. I was one of these," Thams told his *Barb* rescuers.

The gunner, while sharing a floating hatch cover with four other survivors, watched as Japanese frigates came toward them, pulling men from the sea. "With the transport reasonably close our hopes of rescue soared. Unfortunately, it did not happen. When the English prisoners of war realized this, some started singing 'Rule Brittania.' Others joined in. Also the Australians. It rose to a great crescendo. Words cannot describe this act of defiance. Why they did not fire on us at close range I will never understand. The three ships turned away. We watched the freighter as long as it was visible, then we were all alone. All hope of rescue disappeared. Men began to die at once."

On the second day of their ordeal, 14 September, the men were in need of a miracle. "Oil covered us from head to feet, clogging our eyes and ears," continued Thams. "It coated the surfaces of the rafts and wreckage, making them very slippery and difficult to hang on to. We had no food or water and while we survived long periods of hunger on the railway, thirst was another matter. Many gave up. Scores succumbed and gulped seawater. Men who had already endured unspeakable hardship and grief now had to endure the unnerving sight of their own mates going crazy. There was nothing we could do for them."

On the third day the *Pampanito* passed through the wreckage and began taking as many aboard as it could. The *Sealion II* also arrived and helped. But there were far too many who had to be left behind.

On the fourth day only four men were left in Thams's group on two rafts. They found a fifth, a sailor who had survived the sinking of the Australian cruiser *Perth* in the Battle of the Java Sea, the building of the railroad, and the sinking of the *Rakuyo*. But overnight, the sailor disappeared, as did two others.

By the morning of the fifth day all that remained were Thams and an Englishman, sitting on a half-sunken hatch cover. They were semi-delirious and dozing a lot. "Almost alone in the sea, my English mate and I hang on we did, though chances of rescue were nil," Thams continued. "The sea was starting to toss our hatch cover about. Neither of us had much strength left and it was extremely difficult to climb back on the slippery raft. My eyes were covered in oil and I used a small piece of wood to scrape the oil from my eyelids. A shark circled us for about fifteen minutes, then it was gone. We were not unduly concerned. We were past the stage of worrying about death by shark attack or drowning."

The sea turned angry by the sixth day. Both men caught a few raindrops but not enough to quench their thirst. In the late afternoon the Englishman was the first to see a submarine heading toward them.

It was the *Barb*.

"I waved my shorts," said Thams. "I had removed them about the fourth day. They were chafing me. And they became our flag if ever we had the opportunity to wave at something. I can still see the submarine, like some gray ghost, as it came our way, blowing out spray as it plowed through the waves. There was a sailor in blue with a white cap. When a rope was thrown, I placed it under my armpits. Another two hours and I would have drowned."

Thams was the last man pulled aboard.

The weather worsened as the *Barb* and the *Queenfish* searched through the late afternoon of 17 September for more survivors. As darkness fell wind velocity exceeded sixty knots, tossing up waves more than thirty-five feet high. Lookouts and officers of the deck used lanyards to tie themselves to the bridge to keep from being washed overboard. In the chance that survivors were still alive, Fluckey was determined to try and find them. "It was a dangerous thing on a submarine," explained McNitt. "You can be pooped easily. We had to put the seas on the quarter, these huge seas running. We had to close the hatch almost every time when the sea flooded the conning tower, with the watch officer standing there with his foot on the hatch to close it. When the water subsided he'd let it open again, close it again. We were all drowned, soaked. We kept the searchlight on in the rain and the wind and the gale searching all night."

They saw nothing. A search all the next day yielded no other survivors. By nightfall the *Barb* gave up and submerged so those below could recover from the battering they had taken for more than twenty-four hours.

At dawn the *Barb*, with its fourteen survivors, and the *Queenfish*, with its eighteen, laid a course for recently captured Saipan. En route Donnelly, the pharmacist mate, hardly slept in order to attend to the survivors. They continually expressed their gratitude while recovering a sense of humor. "I take back all I said about you Yanks," laughed one. Another joked, "As soon as I can I'm going to write my wife [in Australia] to kick the Yankee out—I'm coming home."

The real hero of the patrol was McNitt. "The challenge [of locating the survivors] was like finding a needle in a haystack," Tuck Weaver recalled years later. "Bob's knowledge and skill not only saved thirty-one lives but also placed *Queenfish* and *Barb* in position to intercept the convoy."

On 24 September 1944 the two submarines arrived at Saipan. The *Barb* moored against the *Queenfish*, which had tied up alongside the sub tender USS *Fulton* (AS-11).

As the survivors prepared to disembark for treatment at a hospital, *Barb* crewmen and officers collected three hundred dollars—every cent that was aboard—to give them. Don Miller, second-class *Barb* torpedoman, saw the survivors off as hundreds of Navy men and Marines stood by and cheered. The men, wobbly and thin, were dressed in white navy hats and clean khaki dungarees. A dozen, including Thams, were able to walk. Two others were brought up on stretchers. Each insisted on clasping the hand of Captain Fluckey as they passed, tears of gratitude rolling down their cheeks. He choked up as well.

Said Miller, "A lot of tears were in the crews' and ex-POWs' eyes, very emotional for all of us."

Chaos (Tenth Patrol)

Saipan didn't mark the end of the war patrol. Rather, rest and relaxation would have to wait until both the *Barb* and the *Queenfish* made the week-long voyage southeast to the burgeoning Navy base on Majuro, the capital of the Marshall Islands in the Southwest Pacific. The *Barb* took on an extra torpedo for one of its forward tubes since wolf pack Commander Swinburne planned a little gun action against Japanese-controlled Wake Island en route. Three days into the mission, however, ComSubPac negated the bombardment, ordering the boats to Majuro without delay. There, the scene was far removed from the luxury the submariners had enjoyed at their preferred "barn"—Pearl Harbor and the hotel on Waikiki Beach. Majuro was quite the antithesis.

The atoll is just north of the equator, hot and humid, "a place much easier to forget than remember," explained Tuck Weaver. Conditions were miserable, agreed Fluckey in a letter to Marjorie. "Reserved this morning to answer a few of your letters, if the ants and gnats don't carry me off. Coco Solo and its sand flies were insignificant compared to these gnats. They're everywhere, unbearable at night. Crawling all over you, getting in every bit of hair on your body. Even when we mix a drink, the bugs have to be picked out before a sip."

To give the submariners a place to swim, explosives were used to blast out a section of reef. The coral was so sharp the men had to wear shoes to get to the water. "Majuro was a very austere place," recalled Max Duncan. "The quarters for officers and crew were Quonset huts. The skippers had a larger one. One thing I remember is that the thing to do at night, after the movies, was to throw beer cans on the metal hut roofs and yell 'depth charge!' Not funny very long."

The foremost thing on everyone's mind on arrival was the "the mail buoy," a metaphor for mail collected and waiting for the men at scattered island bases about the Pacific. Letters and packages—lots of them—were dispensed immediately. For Gene Fluckey, it was a chance to relax and finally catch up with his family in Annapolis—and get news of his safety back to them. "Between us'uns," he wrote, "let me know if you read anything published in the newspapers about Australian and British survivors being rescued by submarines. If so, I'll have some interesting dope for you. If not, don't mention it."

One of the letters to Gene was distressing. Marjorie had suffered three diabetic blackouts in the span of a few days. One had occurred when no one was home but seven-year-old Barbara, who saved her mother's life. Marjorie assured her husband the problem was under control and not to worry. Fluckey wrote back, unable as he was to phone home. "Hon, you can give me more scares than I'd have attacking Tokyo single-handed with a brick bat. Please be careful and take your tests as you promised me." The skipper was impressed by his daughter's ability to adapt in a moment of crisis. "She's got so much more on the ball than I had at her age," he wrote.

One of the facts of wartime was tight censorship to prevent operational details from getting back to the enemy. Fluckey, among the censors in his boat, described the process in a letter to Marjorie on the way to Majuro. "The wardroom is jammed with everyone including Commander Swinburne, dashing off a letter to respective wives. Most of the time they're jibber jabbering about what's confidential and what's not. Whether they can write this or that—and I bat them down. It's a shame, 'cause so many interesting things happen."

Captain Fluckey had a nickname for his daughter after his favorite bird, the bobolink. "Barbolink" had gotten into the custom of sending her father treasured Crayola drawings and the Sunday comics, which he took along on patrol. In a letter thanking her, he added, "Say, wasn't it nice of Uncle Sam to name our submarine after you?"

During the layover on Majuro, the skipper asked Max Duncan to take an early morning ride with him on a Catalina flying boat to watch a practice bombing by a carrier group on an island about an hour's flight away. "The strike force was from a carrier group that used the small Japanese-occupied island, not heavily defended, as a warm-up for major assaults," explained Duncan. "The strike was not on time so the Dumbo pilot flew in closer to get a good view of the island. The shore batteries opened up, the carrier plane strike was cancelled and the Dumbo beat a hasty retreat back to Majuro." On the way the "zoomies"—the pilots—offered Fluckey a chance to fly the plane in exchange for a sub ride. He compared the experience to "driving a truck."

Back on Majuro a ship's picnic was well under way when the captain and his officers arrived on the back of a loaded beer truck. With a band playing, crewmen lustily sang "For He's a Jolly Good Fellow." The skipper had just been promoted to full commander and the crew decided to christen him properly by bearing him off to the ocean. "I dunked six of them before they finally threw me in—shows you what jujitsu can accomplish," he smirked in a letter home. "Then with so many soaked down, they decided the other officers shouldn't be dry if the skipper was wet and all the officers were tossed in. And so the picnic went on, playing football with coconuts, drinking beer, grilling steaks, a few innings of softball."

Fluckey, whom Admiral Lockwood had recommended for a Navy Cross, the Navy's highest honor, for his first war patrol, thought it possible that his just completed second patrol would earn him a second Navy Cross. Sinking five ships was the standard for earning one. Another sterling run could put the crew in line for a Presidential Unit Citation, a much-coveted award extended by President Roosevelt. But this time, the *Barb* would have to do without its remarkable navigator. Bob McNitt had received orders to naval postgraduate school in Annapolis. For the exec, who was in *Barb* for five war patrols, the timing was perfect since the fall semester was about to begin.

Fluckey needed another executive so Lt. James G. Lanier, who had made the last two runs, moved up. The captain and the reserve officer "clicked together," as Gene put it. Lanier was a graduate of the University of Alabama, and his family came from a nautical tradition as owners of a big shipbuilding yard in Pascagoula, Mississippi. He also had been schooled by McNitt in his navigation techniques.

Making the *Barb*'s upcoming run was newcomer Lt. Cdr. Tex Lander, a prospective commanding officer assigned to gain experience under Fluckey before getting his own boat. The Navy also intended to infuse the *Barb* with many new enlisted men. "I told the squadron commander no one wanted to go and that I didn't intend to transfer anyone," Fluckey wrote Marjorie. "At this he gave me a long song and dance about their health being imperiled if they stayed aboard too long and ordered me to transfer a certain number of old hands. These practically cried on my shoulder at having to leave and swore that if they were still around Gooneyville [Midway] when we came through again, they'd be waiting on the dock with the sea bags and would expect to be taken aboard, having fully recovered."

One of those on the list was Buell Murphy, who had been aboard for nine patrols. "The great big gunners mate came around to me bawling like a baby, saying I could do anything to him, stick him in the bilges, disrate him, God knows what else—but please don't take him off the *Barb*—it would break his heart. That got me—I scratched his name off the list."

In the end, a bare minimum were transferred.

By the morning of 27 October 1944 the *Barb* was ready to go. Minor repairs had been made, twenty-four Mark 18 torpedoes had been hoisted aboard, and a requisite supply of beer was in storage. The sub's battle flag, with its angry "One-eyed Hoiman" caricature of a mackerel-like fish throwing firecrackers, fluttered from the conning tower as the sub's powerful diesels came alive in a haze of bluish smoke. Slipping the mooring lines, the boat fell in behind the *Queenfish* and just ahead of the *Picuda* (SS-382) in a single-file procession from the harbor. Destination: Japan. Loughlin in the *Queenfish* commanded the newly formed wolf pack, dubbed "Loughlin's Loopers" by ComSubPac. The mission was to sail from Majuro to the western coast of Kyushu, the southernmost of Japan's home islands. The wolf pack was to link up with another three-boat group known as "Underwood's Urchins"—the *Spadefish* (SS-411), *Sunfish* (SS-282), and *Peto* (SS-266). All six subs were to stifle convoy activity in and out of the industrial cities of Sasebo and Nagasaki on Kyushu. The sister cities were separated from the East China Sea by the Koshiki Strait running north and south between Kyushu and Goto Island to the west.

On 7 November the *Barb* arrived off the southern entrance to the strait. The five other boats patrolled farther west in the sea. The following afternoon, while the *Barb* trolled south below the strait along the Kyushu coast, Fluckey decided to stay in plain view as a ruse. His hope was that the presence of the sub would be reported and cause the Japanese to shift convoy departures and arrivals to the northern entrance to the strait. After dark the *Barb* sped up the coast, rounded Goto Island to the west, and took position at the northern end of the channel. The boat arrived undetected. On the night of 10 November a darkened lighthouse suddenly blinked to life. At the same time radar contact was made with a large ship approaching from the north without escorts. The 10,500-ton *Gokoku Maru* had been rerouted because of the earlier sightings of the *Barb* in the south. A destroyer sent to protect the ship was overdue. The *Gokoku*, which had been converted from a freighter into a light cruiser, slowed to twelve knots and began zig-zagging as it neared the strait. The *Barb*, rapidly closing, submerged and fired three forward torpedoes from 2,500 yards. Two hit, ravaging the target's amidships and bringing it to a complete halt with a thirty-degree list. As the *Barb* surfaced, the cruiser moved away at two knots in a desperate attempt to run aground. Antiaircraft guns blinked fire in all directions as seamen dived off the side and lifeboats dangled from the sinking ship. The *Barb* moved in. Fluckey sent the lookouts below, leaving only him and Tuck Weaver on the bridge. The captain realized the cruiser's big guns couldn't be lowered enough to bring the submarine within their sites. Just 970 yards from the target, the boat launched another torpedo from a forward tube. It broached, veered off course, and disappeared. Another, fired a minute later, also lurched off course, passing harmlessly down the side. Weaver jokingly suggested Fluckey try another tactic—put the nose of the sub up against the ship and roll it over.

Rethinking his options, the skipper decided on a submerged attack to steady the torpedo. As the diving alarm sounded, the skipper and Weaver went below. Neal Sever, a second-class signalman, lowered the hatch cover and prepared to set the watertight seal with a handwheel as the boat descended. Unbeknownst to anyone, however, Lt. (j.g.) Dave Teeters, the boat's electronics officer, was still up in the periscope shears. He had gone to the bridge earlier to watch the sinking. This was his third patrol in the *Barb* and he had never seen battle action before. With nothing else to do, he had slipped topside past the skipper and Tuck without notice. In the darkness and the commotion, he was enjoying the spectacle when the *Barb* began venting compressed air to dive. He looked down on an empty bridge with the deck hatch closing over the red glow from lights inside the conning tower. As the sea swirled up over the deck and rose against the conning tower, Teeters dropped down and hit the intercom button.

"Hey!" he yelled. "Let me in!"

Sever pushed the hatch back open and with a grin looked up at the officer. "Do you want to come in too, Mr. Teeters?" Water splashed down behind the lieutenant as he bounded down the ladder in a single motion while Sever closed and dogged the hatch.

The sub resumed its descent, and at periscope depth Lieutenant Commander Lander, the boat's PCO, fired a third torpedo at Fluckey's direction into the side of the ship from 1,400 yards. The *Gokoku* finally rolled over and sank.

The submarine surfaced and sped away as the belated destroyer arrived. At dawn Japanese aircraft and more destroyers swarmed the area, plastering the ocean with more than three hundred bombs and depth charges intended for the submarine—all for naught.

Throughout the next day the *Barb* remained submerged, the crew resting until orders arrived from Loughlin for the two wolf packs to join up for lifeguard duty during a B-29 bombing strike on Kyushu from a new base deep inside China. The six subs repositioned themselves before dawn on 11 November at forty-mile intervals along the flight path of the bombers over the East China Sea. Dozens of enemy aircraft crisscrossed the sky above the clouds on the lookout for American aircraft while oblivious to the submarines below. An hour before noon the silver bodies of the high-flying bombers appeared in the sky en route to Kyushu. The pilots exchanged recognition signals with the *Barb* as they thrummed past. For the submariners it was a particularly thrilling moment. Said watch officer Lt. Richard Gibson, "What a beautiful sight! It's good to see something American besides a submarine so close to Japan."

The raid was so intense that the thump of explosions was audible in the ocean beneath the boat. After a few hours the B-29s passed over on the return to China. One crashed, however, 170 miles to the southwest, close enough for the *Barb* to speed to the scene.

As Fluckey got under way, a coded message arrived from the *Queenfish*. Loughlin had attacked a large convoy, had damaged one ship, and had taken a terrific beating from depth charges from a pair of frigates working in tandem. Since the convoy was roughly in the same direction as the downed B-29, Fluckey set an intercept course. Two hours later an enemy plane dropped out of the clouds in an attack dive. The *Barb* got under in one minute, diving to two hundred feet—just thirty feet from the bottom—as a bomb exploded. The sub moved off unscathed, though the detonation sent a knife flying in the galley, slicing the forearm of the ship's baker while pots of boiling water toppled over, scalding his hand. When the boat surfaced in the later afternoon, wind velocity approached forty knots from the west, throwing up towering waves. Fluckey knew the impending action would be exceedingly difficult—and risky. Sea depth of only two hundred feet—two-thirds the length of the boat—would give the submarine little room for evasive maneuvers. Five hours later, in total darkness, radar revealed the approaching convoy. It took another hour for the boat to complete an end-around in force 6 seas. With no moon and a tumultuous ocean, the boat moved in unseen. Visual contact was established at midnight with a formation of ten ships in three columns with four destroyers patrolling the edges. With Captain Fluckey, PCO Lander, and the lookouts lashed to the bridge to keep from being washed overboard, the *Barb* skidded down mountainous seas in a path of foam two hundred yards wide to the head of the convoy. The plan of attack was to fire all six bow torpedo tubes and four stern tubes as the sub moved into the middle of the formation. Erratic ship movements in the heaving seas forced the fire control party in the conning tower to constantly readjust targeting data. With a destroyer edging up alongside the convoy on a collision course with the sub, Fluckey could wait no longer. In a three-minute span, six torpedoes exited the boat, two each for three ships. Multiple hits on the targets resulted in chaos, the destroyers wheeling about to find the yet unseen intruder. The *Barb* crossed ahead of one of the warships at a range of eight hundred yards to fire two stern torpedoes at a large freighter beyond. Another hit, this time sinking the 4,823-ton *Naruo Maru*.

Fluckey looked around for another target but couldn't find one as the ships fell out of formation and zigzagged in "utter confusion," as he described it. At Lander's suggestions, the *Barb* pulled away to reload the torpedo tubes, await the convoy reforming, and then go in for a second attack.

It was a difficult rearm. Corkscrew motions and severe battering by cresting fifteen-foot waves made footing very difficult for crewmen using hoists and their own strength to maneuver eight 3,154-pound torpedoes off their storage skids and into the firing tubes.

An hour later the *Barb* regained attack position and submerged ahead of the convoy. Spindrift reduced visibility through the periscope. Deep troughs between waves also made it difficult for the skipper to keep the targets in view until a freighter loomed only four hundred yards distant. As the *Barb* crossed its bow, Fluckey walked the periscope back and forth in order to view the entire ship, from bow to stern. Noticing a lagging second ship overlapping the target, the captain relayed targeting data in a continuing stream to the fire control party. The assistant approach officer called out bearings as fast as he could. The distance to the lead target narrowed. "She must be a lot closer," muttered the torpedo data computer (TDC) operator. "A whole lot closer," thought the skipper, who had overhead him. "But we control the situation. Gyros are racing toward zero. We can't miss."

Fluckey, still at the periscope, bellowed, "Fire 8!"

"Fire 7!"

"Fire 10!"

In the span of a few breaths, the first torpedo exploded against the hull of the freighter and "right in my face," noted the captain. In the after torpedo room, the crew thought it was a depth charge. Fluckey ordered silent running. The boat fell quiet as crewmen shut down all equipment that might reveal their location. Parts of the doomed 5,396-ton *Gyokuyo Maru* rattled off the *Barb*'s superstructure as the submarine slid past on low motor propulsion to escape. At 185 feet the sub was unable to maintain depth and was at a slight up angle. The worry was that its twin propellers might strike the ocean floor at two hundred feet, damaging them. The captain had two choices: rev up the motors to control the depth, or blow the ballast tanks to lift the sub slightly. Either way, the noise would be noticed by destroyers overhead.

Fluckey chose a quick blow, leveling the boat at 190 feet. On cue the warships charged for the kill. "Screws of one escort could be heard through the hull above us," Fluckey noted in the ship's log. "A hush descended on all hands. . . . Escort has shifted to short scale pinging. . . . Commenced evasive turns. . . . The escorts have us sandwiched. . . . Pings are ringing off our sides."

The splash of the first depth charge was audible. It exploded at 150 feet. Close. A minute later, another splash and another explosion—this time at the same level as the boat. Very close. Several more splashes. The sub hung near the bottom. Would this be the coup de grace? Everyone braced, staring at the overhead. This time the bombs landed in the mud on the ocean bottom without detonating. The fuses were set too deep.

The *Barb* floated motionless. So did the destroyers, pinging to relocate the sub. More splashes could be heard. Three bombs went off close.

Then all was quiet. An hour passed.

The destroyers had returned to the convoy. The *Barb* surfaced just before dawn. Fluckey briefly considered making another foray but decided to leave the follow-up attack to the Urchins.

When the search for the downed bomber crew proved to be futile, Fluckey set a course for Quelpart, a large island off the southern tip of Korea. Fluckey thought overcast conditions would be ideal for a little gun action.

Like most American submariners, those in the *Barb* were motivated by a desire for unconditional surrender and complete victory over the enemy. The sneak attack on Pearl Harbor and stories of atrocities against Allied prisoners inflamed them. In a letter earlier to his wife, Fluckey wrote of what the war had done to him. "So now I'm a veteran of the greatest game there is. And what a pleasure it is to eliminate Japs. Funny thing, I seem to be the most bloodthirsty one of the bunch and I never could steel my heart enough to kill a rabbit—but these slant eyes aren't man nor beast, so it's a different matter. Does make life out here seem kind of cheap though. So cheap I could stick a pistol in a Jap's ear and pull the trigger without a qualm."

The commander of the *Barb* would have no mercy as he came upon two Japanese schooners on the morning of 14 November. Sailors on the two vessels saw the sub coming. One schooner turned as if to ram, an action Fluckey termed "real courage." In doing so, the two vessels separated, giving the gunners on the sub the opportunity to fire port and starboard broadsides. "I knew the crew would enjoy this, so we easily slipped in between them," noted the captain, who observed dummy wooden guns mounted aft of the two schooners. Forty rounds of 40mm gunfire and 4-inch shelling dispatched both vessels. A half hour later the submarine encountered a third schooner and sank it as well. No regrets.

Later in the day, as the skipper relaxed in his cabin, Chief Pharmacist's Mate Donnelly interrupted. Lanier, the executive officer (XO), had suffered a heart attack. Fluckey couldn't believe it; the XO was only in his mid-twenties. As Donnelly explained it, Lanier had been taking star sights on the bridge when he felt tightness in his chest, shortness of breath, and pain in his neck and shoulder. Donnelly accurately diagnosed a case of angina pectoris and treated him with nitroglycerin tablets. Fluckey contemplated returning at once to Saipan. But Donnelly assured the captain that his XO was resting comfortably and if the symptoms lessened, there would be no need to return. There was plenty of nitroglycerin aboard to handle the situation. He recommended Lanier stay in his bunk for the time being and remain in the officers' quarters at all times. By all means, he must avoid climbing ladders and through hatches, and no battle stations.

Fluckey asked Max Duncan to assume Lanier's duties. Later the captain discussed the situation with his exec, who came to tears. Fluckey bucked him up, saying that he and the other officers would come to him for advice during the rest of the patrol. Besides, he said, the boat only had seven torpedoes left; any action would be limited.

The following afternoon the distant rumble of numerous explosions in the direction of the *Queenfish*'s patrol sector indicated a convoy had been encountered. At dusk a report radioed from Loughlin's boat revealed the *Queenfish* had put two torpedoes into one of two carriers, sinking it. The rest had fled in the *Barb*'s direction. Three hours later the sub made radar contact while racing forward on the surface and knifing through gigantic waves. Columns of spray lofted high into the air made Fluckey fearful the boat might be sighted. He slowed to standard speed, lowering the spray but causing it to drench the bridge watch instead.

Three, possibly four, destroyers guarding a carrier soon appeared. With the convoy's zig pattern mapped out, Fluckey decided to attack the carrier with five bow tubes. At thirty-seven minutes to midnight the skipper gave the order at a range of 2,580 yards. The first torpedo hit the stern but the others missed when the carrier *Jinyo* zigged to avoid. The ship slowed to twelve knots as the destroyers threw up a defensive screen of depth charges to keep the *Barb* away.

Fluckey got off a report to all other subs in the two wolf packs and began an end-around for another attack. But before he could get in position, the carrier suddenly accelerated to nineteen knots. The *Barb* attempted to close, notching up to more than twenty knots. The sub gained slowly but could not make up the distance before morning light. After a three-hour pursuit Captain Fluckey called off the chase.

As it turned out, the *Jinyo* was doomed anyway. Two days later—17 November—Lt. Cdr. Gordon Underwood in the *Spadefish* intercepted the wounded carrier and sank it.

With only two torpedoes left, both in the stern tubes, the *Barb* patrolled off Noma Misaki, the southern cape of Kyushu. About noon lookouts spotted two small ships skirting the coast. Fluckey moved in close to the beach for a stern shot, aiming one torpedo at each ship. Both missed.

Out of torpedoes, the submarine departed its patrol sector and set a course across the Pacific to Midway and the end of a nine thousand-mile, thirty-six-day war patrol in which the boat sank a light cruiser and two freighters and damaged an aircraft carrier. At Midway a refit and turn-around would send the *Barb* to the coast of China, where Eugene Fluckey and his submarine would make history.

Secret Harbor (Eleventh Patrol)

Midway Island was a welcome relief from the high tension of the *Barb*'s tenth war patrol. As usual officers and crew had lost weight despite a plenti-ful, rich diet. The skipper, who weighed 180 pounds leaving Majuro, arrived on Midway at 160. Losing weight was a manifestation of the ardor of the patrols. The Navy worried about that. Psychologists had long concluded that four war patrols was enough for any skipper. And though there was a period of rest and relaxation between patrols, the skippers needed a much longer break, preferably back home. Admiral Lockwood and the high com-mand in Hawaii had already decided that Fluckey could make just one more run, his fourth in command.

At dockside a Navy band, military brass, and a large entourage hailed the *Barb*'s arrival. It was a poignant moment for the captain, his officers, and his men, who believed that in the span of eight days they had sent five enemy freighters to the ocean bottom, damaged a large carrier, and crippled two cargo ships. The boat in three patrols had taken a toll on the enemy like no other Pacific submarine—fourteen ships sunk and four damaged. Fluckey's success was remarkable by any measure. Still, those who met him for the first time were taken aback that this smiling, six-foot redhead could be the Silent Service's ultimate warrior. As one put it, "He looks like the stub-toed boy of the magazine covers, the one with the homemade fishing pole and can of worms and the eighteen-inch trout." Some in the Navy speculated that the *Barb*'s ability to sink ships was simple luck, that "Lucky Fluckey" had been in the right place at the right time. The skipper, however, knew success had little to do with luck. What gave the *Barb* its edge was ingenuity, the quality of its personnel, careful planning, tenacity, and avoiding undue risks. Above all the boat did the unexpected. The captain followed the "Law of Contrar-ies," as he put it when grilled by sub captains. He said his daughter, Barbara, taught it to him in a letter. From Annapolis, she wrote that she prayed for rain when she wanted a sunny day for a picnic because "you see, Daddy, that's the law of contraries—pray for what you don't want and you'll get what you really want." The *Barb* employed the Law of Contraries by never doing what the Japanese expected, thereby retaining the element of surprise.

For the boat's upcoming patrol, Fluckey would have to do without two key officers. Lanier, his executive officer, had caught the first flight to Oahu for a complete physical and follow-up care at Aiea Hospital, where Donnelly's diagnosis of a heart attack was confirmed. Also shipping out was Tuck Weaver, the dependable battle stations officer of the deck. In every surface engagement, he and the captain had manned the bridge, directing the battle action. Weaver, a veteran of four war patrols in the *Barb* and five in the S-30, had received orders to new submarine construction in Manitowoc, Wisconsin.

One week into the *Barb*'s layover, Captain Fluckey boarded a cargo plane for Hawaii for a turnaround visit to ComSubPac. The only other passenger aboard was Weaver. Both men sat on a wooden bench reminiscing during the six-hour flight. Fluckey regretted losing Weaver, his "right arm" as he had put it in a toast at a farewell party on Midway. Tuck, he said, was a "rare gem," among the greatest officers he had known for his dry wit to relieve tension at dire moments and his fearlessness in combat. He was also, as Fluckey reminded everyone, the only shipmate that had experienced a sub sinking, a reference to those harrowing hours aboard S-30 when a deep ocean shelf in the Pacific saved the boat from sinking to crush depth after being depth-charged.

After the two men parted on Oahu, Fluckey went to the hospital to check on Lanier, then visited ComSubPac headquarters, where he learned that Laughlin's Loopers—the *Barb*, the *Queenfish*, and the *Picuda*—would be deployed to the Formosa Straits and South China Sea in December. The Navy expected the Japanese to rush reinforcements through the strait to the Philippines to blunt an American invasion of Luzon and Mindanao, now that Leyte had fallen. The mission of the Loopers was to bottle up the strait.

While at headquarters Fluckey met in private with Lockwood, who marveled at the *Barb*'s tenth war patrol. The admiral expected a solid eleventh, after which he wanted the commander to join his staff. He feared the *Barb* would be lost if Fluckey made a fifth run. The skipper begged him to change his mind, that he hoped to try all kinds of new tactics and deserved a follow-up "graduation" patrol unfettered by wolf pack duty. Lockwood agreed to consider it, but only after reviewing the results of the upcoming patrol and if Fluckey submitted to a complete physical.

Three years into the war Lockwood was directing an undersea offensive honed to deadly perfection. Despite the loss in the previous two months of the *Darter* (SS-227), *Shark II* (SS-314), *Seawolf* (SS-197), *Tang* (SS-306), *Escolar* (SS-294), *Albacore* (SS-218), *Growler* (SS-215), and *Scamp* (SS-277), there were still 140 boats on patrol—from north of Australia to the coast of Japan. The submarines were drawing an ever-tighter noose, denying Tokyo critically needed fuel and materiel to keep the war going. Furthermore, Japan was unable to build ships fast enough to replace those lost. It seemed Tokyo could not continue too much longer. Yet the Nippon government—especially the army—would not surrender. The war went on.

After his conference with the admiral, Fluckey flew back to Midway, where the relief crew worked to prepare the *Barb* for its eleventh war patrol. "A strange place," Fluckey noted of the two-and-a-half-square-mile Midway atoll in a letter home after he returned from Pearl Harbor. "Not a female in sight. White coral sand everyplace that forces you to wear sunglasses if you're outdoors long, ironwood trees and the birds. Thousands of them and darn near one for every square yard."

A presentation of medals to Fluckey and his crew on the deck of the *Barb* on 6 December broke the relative monotony. Admiral Lockwood flew in for the occasion and personally pinned the Navy Cross on the captain's shirt for the sub's extraordinary eighth patrol in the Okhotsk Sea. The admiral also parceled out additional awards to the officers and men. He confided to the skipper that more honors were in the pipeline for the eighth, ninth, and tenth patrols—Silver and Bronze Stars, dozens of letters of commendation, and a prestigious Presidential Unit Citation.

On the midafternoon of 19 December 1944 the *Barb* began its eleventh war patrol, bearing west toward China. Nearing Guam, the boat's seventy-seven enlisted men and nine officers celebrated what they hoped would be their last wartime Christmas. The skipper whipped up a sampler of eggnog from an improvised recipe of powdered milk, eggs, medicinal rye whiskey, and nutmeg. The cook prepared seven gallons for the holiday. "In our own small way we're trying to make Christmas seem like something, even way out here in nowhere," Fluckey wrote in a letter home to be mailed from Guam. "At times we all look awfully sad and moody and everyone seems to take turns snapping the others out of it. Really, Christmas Eve is the hardest to take. One of the men's mothers had sent me a phonograph record of his little sister singing a few songs for him and the rest of us. What a pleasant surprise it was for him when I put the record on. She had such a sweet voice. It was quite touching."

The boat arrived at Guam on 27 December to top off fuel and make minor voyage repairs. There, the *Barb* rejoined Loughlin's Loopers and continued west, the *Queenfish* and *Picuda* leading. Engine repairs while under way forced the *Barb* to lag behind.

Four days out from Guam the two forward submarines shelled a Japanese naval weather picket, leaving it holed and on fire. Commander Loughlin radioed the *Barb* to sink the vessel at Fluckey's discretion. Closing, the skipper noticed that two fires had been extinguished forward and aft and that no flooding was apparent. He assumed the ship's crew was hiding. With grapnels, the sub pulled alongside the hundred-ton ship and a well-armed boarding gang jumped aboard. For fifteen minutes they scoured the vessel, scooping up a sextant, charts, rifles, books, a compass, a barometer, and a radio transmitter. The submariners avoided searching the crew's quarters, where a gunfight might break out. The sub cast off and commenced shelling the ship. Nine sailors who scrambled on deck were killed by gunfire. Assuring the ship sank, the *Barb* resumed its run to the west.

Arriving at the northern reach of the Formosa Strait in the predawn of 7 January, the *Picuda* and *Barb* made contact with a convoy of seven ships sprinting east from Shanghai to the port city of Keelong on the northern tip of Formosa. Though rough seas, rain squalls, and haze foiled the *Barb*'s attempt to attack, the *Picuda* heavily damaged a 10,500-ton tanker and sank a cargo ship. Afterward the wolf pack headed for the Chinese coast.

For several days all three subs patrolled the coast without success. It soon was clear the enemy had adopted new tactics. Enemy convoys—"mudcrawlers" to the submariners—now traveled only during daylight hours, when planes could protect them as they hugged the Chinese coast in shallow seas where they believed submarines wouldn't operate. At night they holed up in shallow bays or river mouths behind mine fields and roving patrol boats. These anchorages were established all along a six hundred-mile stretch of coastline—from northernmost Shanghai to Fuzhou in the south, where convoys had to run the submarine gauntlet across the Formosa Strait to reach bases on the island and points south in the Philippines. The coastal route was characterized by inland waterways, rocky outcrops, and islands too numerous to count. The East China Sea was so shallow along the coast that the twenty-fathom curve—that point where the ocean was deep enough for subs to dive to avoid detection—was at least twenty miles offshore. Each of the China anchorages was within a day's run of each other. Americans became aware of what the Japanese were up to thanks to intelligence supplied by the little-known U.S. Naval Group China. The outfit operated a secret network of coast watchers based at an abandoned Buddhist temple, a vacated oil company dock, and other sites along the

Chinese coast. Reports of convoy activity were relayed to China Air, a central command, which then relayed them to Navy forces and Army air bases in liberated areas deep inside China.

Of the three Loopers, the *Barb* patrolled closest to the shoreline, following the twenty-fathom curve. Loughlin gave Fluckey the inward position because of the distinctive silhouette of the older *Barb*'s conning tower. From the distance, it easily could be mistaken for a Chinese fishing junk, which were numerous along the coast. Perhaps the sub could blend in.

Shortly after noon on 8 January the *Barb* was the first to report smoke from a southbound convoy of large ships beginning the daylight run across the 111-mile-wide Formosa Strait to the safety of the Japanese naval base of Takao on the southern tip of the island. The largest of the ships, the 9,256-ton *Anyo Maru*, was loaded with troops, kamikaze pilots, and military supplies destined for the Philippines. Aft of the *Anyo* were smaller freighters and tankers containing horses, vehicles, weapons, ammunition, aviation fuel, and more than a thousand combat soldiers.

With the Loopers in pursuit, Fluckey made an end-around while plotting the convoy's zig pattern and speed from radar bearings and observations from the bridge. Once ahead of the approaching ships, Fluckey waited for either of the other two subs to make contact. Confirmation came within half an hour from *Picuda*. The *Barb* dived and moved in on the starboard flank. Echo ranging and periscope sightings detected at least eight heavily laden freighters and tankers escorted by at least eight destroyers. Fluckey decided to attack the largest of the vessels, the *Anyo Maru*, with three bow torpedoes at 2,700 yards, then target a smaller cargo carrier before swinging around to launch stern torpedoes at another freighter. The attack, the skipper reasoned, would create enough havoc on the inboard edge of the convoy to turn the ships seaward into the path of the wolf pack.

Within the span of sixty-five seconds six torpedoes streaked away from the bow of the *Barb*. The boat turned to the third target just as two of the torpedoes exploded. Then a third, so violent it staggered the submarine, shattering light bulbs and loosening insulation on the compartment overheads. Fluckey was so intent on witnessing the destruction of the 6,892-ton munitions ship *Shinyo Maru* through the periscope that he hardly noticed. "The expressions on the faces of the fire control party snapped me out of my fixation and the full force of the explosion dawned upon me," Fluckey noted in his patrol log. "The boat had been forced sideways and down, personnel had grabbed the nearest support to keep from being thrown off their feet, cases of canned goods had burst open in the forward torpedo room."

"Now that's what I call a solid hit!" chortled the captain to no one in particular. He heard a muttered reply, "Golly, I'd hate to be around when he hears a loud explosion."

Amid breaking-up noises and the sound of high-speed screws, the *Barb* went deep, then made its way back to periscope depth. Fluckey took a peek. He could see the bow of a large freighter jutting up out of the ocean at a thirty-degree angle, its stern mired in the mud at thirty fathoms. Another ship was on fire. Smoke hung over the convoy. Amazingly the escorts had gone to the far side of the convoy without dropping depth charges. There, the *Queenfish* and *Picuda* initiated their attacks, sinking a few more ships over the next two hours as the sun set.

A moonless night prevailed as the *Barb*, its torpedo tubes fully reloaded, surfaced behind the remaining convoy. Fluckey decided on a radical new method of attack, one he termed "continuous attack"—come up from aft of the convoy on the surface at flank speed to overrun the ships and torpedo them, hoping to be mistaken for one of the enemy's escorts. "We did not have enough time going wide around the convoy to attack from in front before they reached the safety of their minefield pass [off Formosa]," the skipper later noted.

In the darkness the *Barb* joined the escort destroyers weaving back and forth aft of the starboard column, then turned in slightly and angled three torpedoes at each of two ships in the near starboard column. Both sank while the convoy maintained its course and speed. Rounding the destroyer ahead, the submarine turned in toward a tanker and fired three more torpedoes. The target blew up with such force that the pressure wave pulled shirttails of those in the conning tower over their heads. On the bridge, Fluckey stood transfixed. "The target resembled a gigantic phosphorus bomb," he noted. "The volcanic spectacle was awe inspiring. Shrapnel flew all around us, splashing on the water in a splattering pattern as far as 4,000 yards ahead of us. Topside we alternately ducked and gawked. The horizon was lighted as bright as day."

Escorts near the target had disappeared, consumed in the explosion. Fluckey could see only one ship left and a few scattered destroyers as the craggy cliffs of Formosa drew near. Chasing the remaining ship could bring the boat within range of shore batteries or mines. Still, at the urging of one of his officers, Fluckey decided to try. But the *Queenfish* got there first, sinking the target. Simultaneously artillery on Formosa opened up, lobbing shells that exploded on impact seven thousand yards from the *Barb*, too far away to have any effect. With the entire convoy eliminated, the Loopers turned back toward China.

The next day all three subs assumed lifeguard duty in the East China Sea as two waves of American bombers attacked northern Formosa. With no reports of downed aircraft, the wolf pack resumed its patrol of the Chinese coast. The *Barb* moseyed northward on the twenty-fathom curve. Meanwhile, the *Queenfish* came upon a tanker with two escorts. Loughlin launched eight torpedoes in three onslaughts. But they all missed. Out of torpedoes, the commander headed for Midway. Cdr. Ty Shepard in *Picuda* assumed tactical command of the remaining wolf pack.

The *Barb* continued operating close to the coast, with the *Picuda* patrolling well offshore. The ever-inquisitive Fluckey, now sporting a red beard, investigated mysterious discolorations of the ocean along the twenty-fathom curve. The boat dived into one, which proved to be a freshwater spring boiling vertically from the mouth of a tremendous underground river. For more than a week, the *Barb* cruised up and down the coast, looking for targets without success while avoiding "blind zones" established by China Air. American pilots were authorized to bomb any vessel, friend or foe, in these zones off-limits to all Navy submarines. On 18 January the *Barb* was cruising near one of the zones when a night flier caught it on the surface, strafing it and dropping four bombs over the submerging conning tower. The bombs lifted the stern. It was a close call but no damage was incurred.

Barb lookouts became familiar with the movements of the vast fleet of Chinese junks using nets to fish coastal waters. Fluckey decided to experiment. If the sub maneuvered in among the fishing boats manned by Chinese who had no love of Japan, would they sound the alarm? *Barb* eased in. The gamble succeeded. No planes appeared, convincing Fluckey there were no Japanese spies aboard the boats.

In the late afternoon of 20 January the *Barb* received multiple reports of a southbound convoy about to pass through Fluckey's patrol sector. For two hours lookouts maintained a careful surveillance but saw no sign of the enemy. The captain was baffled. The ships had to be using an unknown route. That evening the skipper called a meeting of his officers around the wardroom table, where they laid out topographical maps of the coast. The captain ran his finger along the mile-wide Haitan Straits leading south toward Fuzhou and shrouded from view by numerous rocky islands. Cartographers noted that the strait was too shallow—only six feet—for major ships to navigate. But had the Japanese dredged the passage? The *Barb* radioed China Air for an answer.

Throughout the next day, the *Barb* and *Picuda* made a fruitless search for ships in the Formosa Straits. At dusk, the *Barb* returned to the coast, where the captain received a reply from China Air. Yes, large ships, including at least one battleship, had used the Haitan Straits—the passage had been dredged. That clinched it.

The next day the *Barb* ventured ten miles inside the twenty-fathom curve, where it mingled with dozens of junks in order to get a clear view of the coast fifteen miles farther. If a convoy steamed through the straits, the *Barb* would see the smoke. At noon the boat trolled at one-third speed near the coastline. Fluckey joined the lookouts above the bridge against the shears. About two hours later smoke revealed at least six large ships moving in a single column south at ten knots through the straits. Fluckey calculated from the convoy's speed that the *Barb* could intercept the ships after dark on the southern egress of the channel at Sandu Inlet opposite Fuzhou. Fluckey set a course for the intercept point by heading out to sea while rounding coastal islands to the south to Sandu Inlet. It would take about five hours. "With a hundred miles to go, let's start galloping," ordered the captain.

The plan was for the *Picuda* to remain offshore in case the convoy got past the *Barb*, which arrived right on time and moved in tight to the coast. Fluckey positioned the boat between two deserted islands on the inland side of the shipping channel. The sub sat on the surface in just thirty feet of water at a dead halt in darkness, a heavy overcast hiding the moon. The captain hoped the *Barb* would be mistaken for a large rock as the convoy passed. The plan was to torpedo the ships as they went by, then dash past them to safety.

In steely silence the sub sat in the darkness. The captain remained on the bridge with the lookouts, breathless, straining to make out objects that might be ships. Down below radar operator John Lehman maintained a vigil for anything approaching from any direction. Crewmen elsewhere stood ready at battle stations, gripped by a sense of excitement mixed with foreboding, knowing there was no place to hide once the shooting started. Two hours passed. Still no convoy. Either the ships had taken refuge in an unknown harbor or somehow escaped. Fluckey grew impatient. Waste of time sitting still, he thought. "Notify *Picuda*," he said to Lt. James Webster, his new executive officer. "No joy at this posit. Let's gallop!"

The surge of the diesels powered the boat out of its hiding place the way it came in. Webster wondered what was next. "Captain, when we reach the twenty-fathom curve, where's the galloping ghost of the China coast going to gallop tonight?"

Fluckey had decided not to go out as far as the twenty-fathom curve. Rather, he wanted to backtrack to the shipping channel and follow it north.

Somewhere close by, there had to be a secret harbor between the *Barb*'s position and Seven Stars Islands eighty miles to the north, where the convoy had been spotted the previous day.

The captain went below and convened a meeting of his officers around the wardroom table. Webster spread out the map. Fluckey, using dividers set for ten-mile increments, stepped off a potential course for the *Barb* along the inland passage. Lt. Max Duncan, the TDC operator, pronounced the route reasonably unobstructed, aside from rocky promontories here and there. The captain reasoned that it was unlikely the Japanese would mine any areas used by the fishing fleet. The *Barb* could assume their routes would be safe to follow. When asked how the sub would detect a ship anchored off the beach, the skipper had someone retrieve a piece of clear plexiglass the size of the radar scope and trace the known coastline, shoals, and islands onto the plastic. It was then placed over the radar scope. Lehman, the radar operator, was to report any contacts that didn't correspond to the overlay. At that point the sub would investigate.

The skipper fully expected to sneak in undetected on the surface to attack a sleeping convoy of six or seven ships. The *Barb* would launch eight torpedoes—four forward and four aft—in one tremendous salvo, leaving just four torpedoes aboard, all in the after torpedo room. "Believe me," Fluckey told the officers, "he won't know what hit him. When he finds out, we'll be gone."

To the captain, the *Barb* would make an unprecedented attack, matched in its daring only by the Nazi submarine U-47, which in 1939 negotiated a narrow channel that guarded a British harbor in Scapa Flow to surprise and sink the anchored English battleship *Royal Oak.*

Fluckey radioed Captain Shepard in *Picuda,* inviting him to join the action. But he declined, thinking it was foolhardy and telling Fluckey to "drop dead!" The skipper was undeterred. Executive Officer Webster suggested handing out life jackets for the approach—just in case. The skipper thought it might frighten the men. He'd rather have them concentrate on the tasks ahead. He decided to address them over the intercom, to prepare them for what was to come. "Shipmates, we've got this convoy bottled up along the coast. We're going to find them and knock the socks off of them," he said. "This surprise will be *Barb*'s greatest night, a night to remember. If you have any questions, I'm coming through the boat now."

He started in the forward torpedo room, where he directed crewmen to reposition their torpedoes in the top four tubes so the fish could run at six-foot depths to prevent them from running aground. As the skipper passed aft, crewmen and officers were tense. Conversation was muted. The men simply signaled a "V" for victory with their fingers or thumbs up to the captain as he went by. The control room—the nerve center of the boat—was a morgue. "It was very businesslike—and had to be," said Dave Teeters, the electronics officer who was running the tracking party.

The *Barb* began its run before midnight, powering back to the coast and moving up the inland passage, following the track of the fishing fleet. Using radar and visual sightings, the boat maneuvered past several dozen darkened junks. On the bridge depth soundings were made every five minutes. The fathometer registered just forty feet. Lt. Richard Gibson, assistant gunnery officer who was standing on the bridge alongside the skipper, was worried. "It's the wrong place for a submarine to go," he confided. Fluckey expressed confidence. "The odds are with us, believe me."

Visibility lessened in a lowering overcast as the sub continued up the coast. Radar kept the boat from colliding with fishing boats as well as running aground. After forty-five minutes the radar operator reported a large smear that didn't correspond with the chart fifteen miles ahead. It was too large to be a single ship or even a couple of ships. Fluckey, Teeters, and Lehman, the operator, studied the oscilloscope and concurred the spiky images were typical of ships, in this case many ships! But doubt lingered. Never before had radar detected saturation pips at such long range.

The sub continued north toward Incog, seven small islands that stood in a circular group off a bottle-shaped bay that the Chinese knew as Nam Kwan. The smudge on the scope seemed to be located in that bay guarded by Incog and its darkened lighthouse. The boat's chart warned of "rocks awash," "not surveyed," "position doubtful," and "unexplored" among its notations on access routes to the bay.

The boat slowed on the seaward side of Incog after contact was made with a destroyer patrolling the inland side to prevent any attempt to enter the harbor. Webster, on the bridge, tracked the destroyer as it began a turn to the south. "Let me know just before she disappears," the captain said over the intercom to his exec. "We'll go ahead emergency and skin around Incog when she's on the other side of the island, shoot, and shove off."

At 0300 Webster confirmed the frigate had gone behind the island. "All ahead emergency!" demanded Fluckey. The sub picked up speed and rounded Incog, where radar imaging quickly revealed what was in the harbor. The skipper, Teeters, and Lehman were astounded. A two-mile line of ships at anchor in three columns, five hundred yards apart, and other vessels closer to the shore between the columns. "The Japs don't have that many ships!" Fluckey exclaimed, staring at the radar screen. But Teeters confirmed lots of ships, at least thirty by radar count. A torpedo attack couldn't possibly miss.

What the *Barb* had discovered was the overnight portage of two convoys—northbound Takao-Moji 38 and southbound Moji-Takao 32. The challenge for the *Barb* was two destroyers on patrol to the north of the anchorage.

"Okay," announced the skipper, "it is now time to take one of our well-known calculated risks."

Those who had been with Fluckey on previous patrols knew what that meant. "You know all the odds are against you and figure a way they won't happen," explained Chief Gunner's Mate Paul "Swish" Saunders. "Ahead of us on the bow were small escort ships, like our destroyer escorts, and we know they have depth charges. We know the water is sixty feet deep or less, and we know the place is mined, three miles wide. But Gene has charts, and they show a couple of stretches marked 'unexplored" and others 'rocks awash at high tide,' and other places 'rocks, position doubtful.' So the skipper says we'll make our attack and then retire to where it says 'unexplored' and 'rocks, position doubtful,' because probably the Nips won't follow us there. That's the calculated risk."

Fluckey assumed that once torpedoes started exploding, all hell would break loose. "Inasmuch as our attack position will be six miles inside the 10-fathom curve and nineteen miles inside the 20-fathom curve, we will require an hour's run before being forced down," noted the captain in his patrol log. "Consequently our attack must be a complete surprise and the force of our attack must be sufficient to completely throw the enemy off balance . . . a speedy, darting, knife thrust attack will increase the probability of success."

The skipper assumed the Japanese would employ searchlights, gunfire, and hot pursuit by the destroyers in the counterattack. The boat would countermand that with its remaining torpedoes plus 40mm and automatic weapons from the gunnery crew on deck. The sub would use radar to scan for obstructions like rocks and the fishing fleet during the speedy retreat. By dashing between the anchored junks, the sub would avoid mines while using the fishing boats as a barrier to pursuit by the destroyers. The escape route also would pass through the "unexplored" area to further dissuade an escort. By the captain's calculation, the sub would take a direct route perpendicular to the harbor and to the twenty-fathom curve, a surface run at high speed that would take at least an hour.

As the sub passed Incog, the captain announced on the intercom that the *Barb* had successfully entered Nam Kwan Harbor and the greatest target of the war was sitting dead ahead of the sub. "Make ready all tubes. I figure the odds are 10 to 1 in our favor. Man battle stations torpedoes!"

The gongs of the battle stations alarm brought cheers. But Fluckey had forgotten the order to put four cases of beer on ice. Gunner Saunders took care of that, ordering a couple of crewmen to ice down the beer to calm their nerves.

The boat steadily moved toward the anchorage, anticipation building. The outer doors of the torpedo tubes were opened. Everything stood in readiness. The men were going to either pull off the biggest sub raid of the war—or die trying. Saunders was breathless in the control room. "We creep in. You can't hear a thing but the fathometer pinging, and she says six fathoms. We could almost get out and walk. Everybody's heart is doing flip-flops. The pickles are all set."

The boat neared its firing position undetected. Fluckey darted up the conning tower ladder to the bridge to assure the sub was not tossing up a phosphorescent wake. With binoculars he also gave a quick glance forward. He could make out the ghostly silhouettes of the ships. They overlapped each other. One side of the harbor to the other. The trick would be to widen the trajectories of the torpedoes so that each would strike a separate ship to maximize damage and surprise.

Fluckey ducked back into the conning tower for a final bearings check. Two minutes later, "Fire 1! Fire 2! Fire 3! Fire 4!"

The *Barb*, shuddering, heeled about with a right full rudder to bring the stern tubes to bear. It took sixty seconds.

"Fire 7! Fire 8! Fire 9! Fire 10! All ahead flank! Let's get out of here!"

The sub bolted away, all four diesels on line. A flash of light lit the night sky. Then a second. And a third. The loud rumble of explosions. Saunders described the scene. "A big freighter goes up, and another. Then an ammo ship blows and sets the whole harbor off like a string of firecrackers. What a show, what a show! Tracers, rockets, the works. Ship after ship catches fire. Searchlights are streaking the sky looking for bombers, because nobody figures a submarine got inside."

Few noticed the *Barb* racing away. However, one of the destroyers patrolling northwest of the harbor got a bead on it from six thousand yards and took up the chase. Fluckey demanded more speed. The boat dashed for the area on the map marked "unexplored." The frigate steadily gained, cutting the distance by a third. Fluckey passed the order to the after torpedo room to load the boat's last four torpedoes and prepare for action. He also got on the squawk box. "Engine room, tell Chief [Franklin] Williams to crank up every revolution he can squeeze out. We must have more speed!"

The boat was flying—twenty knots. Was the frigate still narrowing the distance? Teeters got on the horn. "Thirty-six hundred yards, closing."

Fluckey ordered the crew to start the low pressure blower and keep it going. The blower would keep water from leaking into ballast tanks, thus pushing the boat higher on the surface and reducing drag. "I need more speed!" the captain implored Williams in the engine room.

"Sir," the chief replied, "the engines are at their top speed now. Any more and the governors will cut the engines out."

"Well, tie down the governors and put 150 percent overload on all engines!" ordered the skipper.

There was no choice. The governors, designed to shut down the engines to protect them from overheating, had to be overridden. It was the only chance of escape.

Teeters reported the destroyer still closing at 3,200 yards. But at a slower rate. "We're making 23.5 knots—a record for submarines," he added.

With urgency in his voice over the intercom, Williams reported the bearings were getting hot. "Let them melt, Jim!" came the retort from Captain Fluckey.

The skipper doubted the destroyer would open fire until it was within two thousand yards. He expected the ship to flip on its searchlights, at which time he would fire two stern torpedoes and turn in toward a rocky area, hoping the warship would wheel around for a broadside and go aground.

Teeters sounded an alarm. "Junks ahead nine hundred yards!"

"God help them!" the captain shouted. Teeters coached helmsman Bill Brooks on a serpentine course by radar through the fleet. "The *Barb* is now high balling it for the 20 fathom curve," Fluckey noted in the patrol log. "Expect to see a junk piled up on the bow at any second."

Startled fishermen waved as the sub flashed by.

Astern, gunfire could be heard from the direction of the destroyer. The warship's radar couldn't distinguish between the sub and the fishing boats. "Some poor junk's getting it," noted the captain. The keeper of the lighthouse turned on a beacon. The illumination allowed the sub to steer clear of rocks and shoals in the unexplored area.

The destroyer, in hot pursuit for thirty minutes, finally gave up. The submarine pulled away. Soon Fluckey slowed to seventeen knots and motor macs unstrapped the governors, permitting the bearings to cool down. A half hour later the *Barb* crossed the twenty-fathom curve into deep water. In the patrol log, Fluckey jotted his appreciation. "The Galloping Ghost of the China Coast crossed the 20-fathom curve with a sigh. Never realized how much water that was before. However, life begins at forty (fathoms). Kept going."

At dawn on 24 January Fluckey radioed the *Picuda* to report the *Barb*'s successful attack and escape. The captain also sent a message to China Air to acknowledge the intelligence on dredging Haitan Straits: "YOUR LATEST INFO RESULTED EIGHT HITS IN POT OF GOLD X FOUND YOUR CONVOY PLUS OTHERS AND POSSIBLE LARGE WARSHIPS ANCHORED AT NAM KWAN HARBOR LAST NIGHT X THREE SHIPS KNOWN SUNK X TERRIFIC EXPLOSION."

Fluckey ordered his officers and crew to stand down and extended congratulations. "Be proud of a night none of us will ever forget. *Barb* did it and will live it forever." The submarine dived for six hours to give exhausted crewmen a chance to rest, after which the captain announced they would break open the beer to celebrate.

For the next five days the wolf pack resumed its patrol of the coast, the *Barb* looking for a chance to expend its last four torpedoes before returning home. It got its chance at dawn on 29 January, when one large and one medium-sized cargo ship led by a destroyer came within radar contact. Heavy rain and seas obscured the convoy as the *Barb* moved in for a stern attack. From a range of 2,010 yards, Fluckey fired his last torpedoes. All apparently missed. The convoy proceeded on course, unaffected.

Out of torpedoes, the *Barb* and the *Picuda* set a course for Midway. The *Barb* arrived on 9 February to find the harbor closed for the night. The boat had to linger off the entrance channel to the atoll, risking attack by Japanese submarines known to patrol close to U.S. bases. The next day the boat entered the harbor to a hero's welcome. On 11 February it headed for Pearl Harbor and the completion of its 59-day, 16,509-mile mission. No one was at liberty to discuss the attack on Nam Kwan Harbor or any other action. And no one except Fluckey could have guessed the boat would become a ballistic missile submarine and sink a train on its next mission to Japan.

Mom Chung

News of the Nam Kwan Harbor attack would be withheld from the public for months. Fluckey could only hint about it, as he did in a quick letter he airmailed to his wife from Hawaii. The *Barb* was there only briefly, shoving

off for its long-awaited overhaul at Mare Island. "To sum our run up suc-
cinctly, the Japs are stercoricolous. Dropping my cloak of modesty, I believe
we've hung up a record that no one will ever beat with the same number
of torpedoes."

Arriving off the coast of California on the afternoon of 27 February
1945, Gene Fluckey's boat passed the Farallone Islands heading for San
Francisco Bay. Soon the Golden Gate Bridge appeared like a mirage, hanging in the Pacific mist in orange splendor. Hundreds of motorists on the
span pulled over and honked, waved, and cheered, bringing traffic to a
complete halt as the sub passed beneath with its dark blue battle flag fluttering mightily from the periscope shears. Outbound ships, including a convoy, whistled triumphantly, sailors crowding the rails for a glimpse of the
Barb as it entered the bay.

By the time the sub tied up at Mare Island, the Silent Service was electric
with the news of the sub's eleventh war patrol. For the attack in Nam Kwam
Harbor, the Navy credited Fluckey with sinking or damaging nearly ninety
thousand tons of enemy shipping, a record for a single mission. President
Roosevelt, who was in declining health, received the news, as did English
Prime Minister Winston Churchill, who sent word that he intended to award
a medal to the *Barb* for the rescue of British and Aussie prisoners in the
South China Sea. Accolades poured in—"one of the finest fighting submarines this war has ever known" . . . "this patrol should be studied in detail
by submarine personnel" . . . "history-making" . . . "remarkable accomplishment" . . . "devastating losses to the enemy" . . . "the all time all timer" . . .
"one of the great stories to come out of this war when it can be told."

Commander Fluckey, knowing his officers and men were to receive
a Presidential Unit Citation for the boat's eighth, ninth, and tenth war
patrols, thought the boat's eleventh might earn a second such citation—
unprecedented for a boat under a single skipper. Another sub captain had
interceded, however, to keep that from happening. Robert "Dusty" Dornin,
a former All-American football player at the academy, was the personal
aide to Fleet Adm. Ernest King. When he heard of the *Barb*'s tremendous
achievement, he retrieved the citation before it could be signed by Roosevelt
and added the eleventh to the commendation. Earlier in the war, Dornin
had earned a Presidential Unit Citation as commander of the USS *Trigger*
(SS-237) after it sank ten ships in two patrols. In Fluckey's mind, Dornin,
who was very familiar with the awards system, had "robbed" the *Barb* of any
chance of getting a second citation. Dornin, feigning ignorance, radioed
Fluckey the news, saying he had "no problem in convincing the board to

include the *Barb*'s eleventh patrol with the others so all your patrols in command will have such citation. Gene you owe me one for this. Dusty."

Fluckey was flabbergasted. "I just couldn't believe what I had read," he said. Yet there was nothing that could be done. He decided to give Dornin "a good kick in the backside" when he saw him and then "we'd still be good friends."

By the time of his arrival at Mare Island, Commander Fluckey wrote Marjorie that the red beard he had grown on patrol had been reduced to a "rakish" mustache as a defensive measure. "I intend to keep it for the moment as a measure of self-defense . . . the boys haven't seen a female for two hundred days and they are wild. Wolf wouldn't even begin to describe any one of us. So I wear my moustache."

The men divided into two groups for thirty days' leave each. The captain, heading the first group of married men, caught the first plane out for Annapolis and a joyful reunion. He hadn't seen his wife and daughter Barbara in more than a year. Back home, the nation had rebounded from the Great Depression. "The great Arsenal of Democracy," as Roosevelt had put it, was churning out munitions at a phenomenal rate. Factories were in full production. Seemingly endless streams of tanks, artillery, and troop carriers moved by train to ports on both coasts for shipment to the front. The economy was booming. Yet personal reminders of the cost of war were ever-present—long lines for rationed food and fuel, blackouts at night, and the continuing drumroll of battlefield wounded and dead. In towns and cities spanning the nation, news of casualties arrived in telegrams, in telephone calls, in conversations overheard. Those who would not be coming home left a pall over the living.

Nowhere was that more evident than in the Submarine Wives' Club in Annapolis. Marjorie Fluckey was one of thirteen in the support group, five of whom had been informed their husbands were "overdue and presumed lost." One evening Marjorie and Gene invited the group to join them at the North Severn Officers' Club for a bit of socializing and dancing. For Gene, the gathering was heartbreaking. "As each snuggled close, dancing with me, my heart did flip-flops. I knew four others were widows but they had not yet been notified. Damn the war! Already over half my submarine school classmates were buried in steel coffins at the bottom of the ocean. The horror those women had yet to face brought tears to my eyes as they danced with their eyes closed, dreaming of dancing with their husbands."

Toward the end of the furlough, the Navy's Bureau of Personnel notified Fluckey that he was to receive the nation's highest distinction, the Medal of Honor, for his heroics in Nam Kwan Harbor. President Roosevelt wanted to present it personally at a ceremony in mid-April. The skipper was flattered but informed the bureau that the Medal of Honor was for "dead men," that he was turning it down. Besides, he said, the *Barb*'s attack wasn't as hazardous as the Navy was making it out to be. He also noted that if he flew back from California to accept the award, it would interrupt his exec's furlough. He didn't want to do that.

Two days later he was summoned to appear in Washington before Admiral "Shorty" Edwards, vice chief of naval operations, who quickly came to the point. The nation was in need of "live, smart heroes" to inspire others in the Navy. The Medal of Honor had been awarded to five submarine commanders since the war began, two of whom—Richard O'Kane of the *Tang* (SS-306) and Lawson Ramage of the *Parche* (SS-384)—were very much alive. Fluckey should drop his objections. He was getting the medal whether he wanted it or not. He should accept it in the spirit with which it was to be given in the name of Congress. The admiral noted the ceremony would be moved up so the skipper wouldn't have to fly back from Mare Island. Secretary of the Navy James Forrestal and Admiral King would stand in for the president. The next day Fluckey posed for Navy publicity photos for use when the *Barb*'s story had been declassified. On 23 March, at a midday ceremony with no reporters in attendance, Forrestal presented the award, just twenty-one days before the president's death from cerebral hemorrhage. A beaming Marjorie Fluckey draped the star-studded blue ribbon and gold medallion around her husband's neck.

Later the couple went to see Gene's ailing father to show him the medal; he had never seen one before. Afterward the Fluckeys took Barbara out of school, obtained enough gas coupons from the Annapolis ration board to get across country, packed some belongings and their cocker spaniel Miss Nibs, and headed west in the family's five-year-old Plymouth sedan, which they planned to sell after arrival. The family would return by train. They passed through Yellowstone National Park on the way to Mare Island, arriving at the end of March. Max Duncan and his wife, Trilby, arrived by car from their home in North Carolina as did Phyllis and Dave Teeters from Oregon. The couples and their families settled into Quonset huts at the base while the overhaul continued. Weekends were spent enjoying San Francisco, particularly Fisherman's Wharf and the Top of the Mark Hopkins Hotel. The Fluckeys received an invitation to a Sunday night dinner party hosted by a fifty-six-year-old San Francisco physician.

Dr. Margaret Chung, born in the United States of Chinese ancestry, had established the first medical clinics in the city, where she was known as "the angel of Chinatown" in the 1920s. After Japan's invasion of China in the 1930s and the attack on Pearl Harbor, "Mom" Chung became famous by drawing national attention to the exploits of the Flying Tigers, three hundred American volunteers who flew for the Dutch from bases in Southeast Asia. Piloting P-40 fighter planes with sharks' teeth painted on their fuselages, the squadron took on the vaunted Japanese air force in the skies over Burma and China in the summer of 1942. As the war progressed, the flamboyant physician created a circle of "adopted" war heroes. They included "fair haired Bastards" (her moniker for aviators, soldiers, and sailors; she said she couldn't call them sons because she was not married), "Golden Dolphins" (for submariners), and "Kiwis" (her name for those in the performing arts, politicians, and business leaders who supported the war effort). The club included Pacific Fleet Adm. Chester W. Nimitz, Adm. William F. Halsey Jr., commander of the Third Fleet, and actor and future president Ronald Reagan.

The physician's large townhouse on Masonic Street became a gathering place for as many as a hundred guests at a time. Attendance was by invitation only, with the rule being that senior military and famous people wash the dishes. One submarine officer recalled his visit early in the war: "Lily Pons was singing, Admiral Nimitz was dishing out the chow, and Harold Stassen [former Minnesota governor and future presidential candidate] was among his assistants."

Word had gotten back to the doctor that Fluckey had earned the Medal of Honor and was at Mare Island. So she issued an invitation for him to join the Golden Dolphins. Fluckey insisted that Max Duncan go with him. "The parties were always on Sunday night and Mom Chung's walk-in refrigerator and liquor cabinet were well stocked by merchants, celebrities, and wealthy friends," recalled Duncan. "I was privileged to be made a Golden Dolphin. My wife, Trilby, and I went to Mom's with Marjorie and Gene at least twice, maybe three times. Mom made me Golden Dolphin 106 and gave me a ring with the number on it."

At that first gathering the Fluckeys and the Duncans enjoyed kibitzing with Lily Pons, Hollywood maestro Andre Kostalanetz, and Broadway and film star Helen Hayes. During the evening the conductor taught Fluckey how to drink a Nickolayev cocktail. The irrepressible skipper engaged Pons in a discussion of the finer points of her stagecraft.

Across the bay the *Barb* had entered the final stages of its overhaul. Among the refinements were installation of radar in one of the boat's two periscopes for more precise range finding during submerged attacks and anchoring a more powerful 5-inch gun aft of the conning tower. The 4-inch forward gun was removed. An after gun was more practical, as Fluckey learned while being chased from Nam Kwan Harbor. Officers and crew spent the last few days of the overhaul outside the Golden Gate practicing with the deck gun and making test dives. The boat also tied up to a pier in San Francisco for a day of degaussing—removing magnetic properties to make the sub less vulnerable to floating mines.

Fluckey, having made an incredible ten war patrols, graded the overhaul average. The *Barb* had always been exceptionally clean and sound, a tribute to its veteran petty officers who had completed war patrols in *Barb* and other boats. Saunders, the chief gunners mate, had made eleven war patrols. Gordon Wade, the chief electricians mate, had made ten, and the two chief motor mates—Franklin Williams and Thomas Noll—had five and seven respectively. Lieutenant Teeters, having been aboard for four runs, keened to the boat's tidiness. "It's the reason I went into submarines," he recalled. "I don't like dust."

On 16 May the wives saw the *Barb* off for its return to Hawaii. Afterward they packed their belongings and began the long journey home. Gene had asked Trilby Duncan to drive his family since the Duncans lived not far from Annapolis and she had planned to make the road trip on her own. She asked Phyllis Teeters to come along to help with the driving. The women drove a southern route, passing through Yosemite, Las Vegas, the Grand Canyon, the Petrified Forest, the Painted Desert, and New Orleans. Along the way Marjorie suffered a diabetic seizure at a hotel; fortunately Trilby noticed in time. A glass of orange juice reversed the effects.

Arriving at Pearl Harbor on 24 May, Commander Fluckey prepared for a variety of unique sub operations that had been rolling around in his mind since the seventh war patrol. Back then he wanted to use a rubber boat to smuggle saboteurs ashore in Formosa to blow up a railroad bridge, a plan turned down by the skipper. Likewise, he conceived using the sub as "a perfect platform" to launch missiles at land targets. Tuck Weaver thought it was an interesting concept but Captain Waterman rejected it as farfetched; he thought the sub's 4-inch gun was far more accurate than missiles. On the eighth patrol, Fluckey had been bothered by the inability of the *Barb* to destroy the strategic cable station in the Kuriles with the 4-inch gun. A rocket attack might have succeeded. "The torpedo has fulfilled its purpose. Its day, in this war, is passing," Fluckey wrote at the time. "Those of us, not specially equipped for the last good area [of sub operations], must stagnate and slowly slip into oblivion, or look to a new main battery—rockets. The rocket is not a toy. Its possibilities are tremendous, strategically and tactically, but not beyond comprehension."

ComSubPac gunnery officer Cdr. Harry Hull, who shared Fluckey's enthusiasm, pursued the skipper's request for a hundred spin-stabilized rockets tipped with nearly ten pounds of explosives, all of which would be stacked in the forward torpedo room at the expense of a few torpedoes. A mobile pipe rack launcher was bolted to the forward gun mount. The launcher could be raised to a forty-five-degree angle and pointed dead ahead to fire simultaneously a dozen of the four-foot-long MK10 missiles to their maximum range of about five thousand yards. Such a rocket salvo would far surpass the impact of the boat's 5-inch gun in Fluckey's estimation.

The skipper also brought aboard a new class of acoustical homing torpedoes—four Mark 27s and three larger Mark 28s for use on heavy targets. The Mark 27s were light enough to "swim" from a torpedo tube on their own without the normal boost of compressed air.

As June rolled around, news of the attack on Nam Kwan Harbor finally broke. The *Honolulu Star-Bulletin* reported in a screaming two-deck, page 1 headline, "U.S. Sub Barb Sneaks Into Enemy Harbor, Has Field Day." The *Los Angeles Times* led with "U.S. Sub Blows Up NIP Convoy," and papers back East declared, "Incredible . . . But True" and "Jap Sea Convoy Destroyed by Lone U.S. Submarine." The Navy, in disclosing Fluckey's Medal of Honor and the *Barb*'s Presidential Unit Citation, termed the attack on Nam Kwan Harbor "virtually a suicide mission—a naval epic." The United Press International crowed, "It is the sort of thriller with which boys series books about war are filled but which sound too incredible really to have happened," adding, "From the bridge of the surfaced ship Commander Fluckey could see Japanese ships erupting in the night like a nest of volcanoes."

There was no time for the skipper or his crew to bask in the limelight. The *Barb* was ready to go. All that was needed were the promised rockets. When they didn't show up as scheduled, Fluckey refused to leave without them. Finally a boat pulled alongside the sub and off-loaded the seventy-five-pound rocket launcher and seventy-two missiles. No others were available.

On the afternoon of 8 June the submarine cast off without fanfare. But lookouts had raised a makeshift flag to the pinnacle of the periscope shears. Emblazoned on the cloth were the words "Fluckey's 8th Fleet." As the black, unmarked submarine proceeded through the Pearl Harbor channel, battleships, carriers, and other subs sent a steady stream of blinker-signals and flag messages encouraging "Good hunting!" and "Good luck!" Commander Fluckey couldn't believe all the sailors waving and taking photos as the submarine motored past. Then another message arrived, this from Admiral Halsey: "GOOD LUCK BARB AND FLUCKEY X GOOD HUNTING AND GIVE THEM HELL X HALSEY." The skipper realized something was up, finally noticing what was written on the flag overhead. Completely embarrassed, he ordered it lowered and handed over but took no punitive action.

The skipper set a course that passed through Midway in a return trip to northern Japan and the Okhotsk Sea, where he soon would demonstrate the awesome future of submarine warfare.

Graduation (Twelfth Patrol)

With the war winding down, Commander Fluckey knew the pressure was on. In a letter to his wife, he sized up the task ahead:

> Shipping is very thin all over, yet everyone [in the undersea navy] seems to keep an eye on the *Barb*. That's why I asked for this on my own hook. If I'm proven wrong and we have a dry run, it will be my own doing and I can take the snickers. On the other hand, if my crystal ball pans out and the other boys dry up, I'm in like Flynn, again. After a hullabaloo at the barn I succeeded in getting some special experimental equipment installed which I believe will renovate submarine warfare. You'll enjoy hearing about this, and probably will get it via the grapevine before we return. . . . I intend to throw everything we have at the Japs till they rue the day the *Barb* was born—if not regret they ever started this war.

As the sub passed through the lower Kuriles into the Okhotsk, an "eyes only" message arrived from Admiral Lockwood directing Fluckey to make his presence known, to "raise a rumpus." Three wolf packs of nine submarines in the Sea of Japan were due to transit La Perouse Strait into the Okhotsk en route to Guam over the next few days. By drawing away air and surface patrols from the twenty-five-mile-wide passage, the *Barb* would enable the subs to slip through undetected.

Raise a rumpus? No problem. Fluckey would use all his bells and whistles—three kinds of torpedoes, more than seventy missiles, a larger deck gun, and saboteurs. He would create such havoc the Japanese would think the whole rim of the Okhotsk was under siege.

On the morning of 21 June the *Barb* attacked and sank two small, well-armed ships in the lower Kuriles northeast of Hokkaido. The sub continued down the coast, daring the Japanese by staying on the surface close to land in the daylight. The boat bore steadily toward the mining and lumber city of Shari on the northern coast of Hokkaido. Two hours after midnight on 22 June the *Barb* crept into the harbor as the city of twenty thousand slumbered. At Fluckey's order, "Swish" Saunders and his gunners scrambled out onto the forward deck, where they unstrapped the missile launcher, raised it to a forty-five-degree angle, loaded the pipes with a dozen missiles, and connected an electrical cord to a firing switch in the conning tower. The men then went aft alongside the conning tower. The captain, on the bridge, flipped his polarized goggles to their darkest setting and barked the order, "Rockets away!"

An explosion of blue-white flame lit the deck. The missiles lifted off in less than five seconds and disappeared into the night sky. It was the first ballistic missile strike by an American submarine in the history of warfare.

"Right rudder! All ahead two-thirds!" yelled the captain.

The *Barb* heeled about and made for the open sea. Thirty seconds passed until multiple impacts lit the city. Chunks of buildings flew into the air as the sub began a high-speed, twenty-hour run across the Okhotsk to the eastern side of Sakhalin Island north of La Perouse Strait. Fluckey was pretty sure the attack on Shari would divert Japanese ships guarding the strait, enabling the wolf pack to scoot through. Confirmation arrived in an ULTRA from ComSubPac: three Japanese destroyers had departed La Perouse to sweep the north coast of Hokkaido in search of a reported wolf pack off Shari.

As the *Barb* entered Patience Bay (Taraika Wan) on the eastern side of Sakhalin, the sub made radar contact with a diesel trawler. Its seven-man crew saw the sub coming and tried to escape. But a burst of 40mm gunfire and 5-inch shells brought the ship to a dead halt, on fire and sinking. Enemy crewmen looked like they wanted to be saved. Fluckey decided one might be useful; he couldn't spare enough men to guard additional prisoners. A wounded sailor swam for the sub and was pulled aboard. The *Barb* abandoned the rest to the frigid Okhotsk. But two hours later the boat returned. "We wanted to give the survivors some food and water as well as direction to land if they had found a raft or something to get up on," said Max Duncan, officer of the deck. There were no survivors.

The *Barb* resumed its coastal run north toward the city of Shikuka in Karafuto Province, the Japanese-held lower end of Sakhalin. Radar revealed a large number of pips on the city's waterfront, perhaps the remainder of the once powerful Japanese fleet. Fluckey envisioned a second Nam Kwan since the anchorage lay twenty-two miles inside the twenty-fathom curve.

The submarine closed to five fathoms where, to the crew's great disappointment, there were no ships—just numerous smokestacks. The boat returned to the open sea.

For the next two days the Barb journeyed north along the foggy upper half of Sakhalin, controlled by the Russians. Amid seals and ice floes the submarine sailed as far as the port of Urkt, where Fluckey thought the Soviets might be selling fuel oil to the enemy. No such activity or targets were encountered. But on the late afternoon of 26 June, during the return voyage, lookouts saw a southbound convoy dead ahead. When radar detected nothing, Fluckey realized it was an atmospheric anomaly. The skipper guessed the ships were about twenty-five miles over the horizon and initiated an end-around.

It took hours to get ahead of the convoy—two medium freighters, a smaller transport, a modern sub-hunter destroyer, two frigates, and two patrol boats. As was his habit while tracking ships on the surface, Fluckey sat on the bridge with his feet propped up, very relaxed, doing the math in his head. "He would ask his exec on the scope, 'What's the range and bearing to that ship that was bearing zero three zero at 4,800 yards five minutes ago?'" explained Duncan. "And you'd have to keep up with him in your mind in order to do that. If you didn't, he would ask me what the current distance to the target was. And I would say, 'Oh, about 2,200 yards.' And he would say, that's pretty good. It's 2,600 yards better than five minutes ago."

Night fell under a full moon, too risky for a surface attack. The captain submerged to periscope depth ahead of the convoy and waited. The setup seemed ideal until the convoy turned sharply west away from the sub into Patience Bay. The only chance was an "up the kilt" shot at the lagging destroyer using one of the boat's new Mark 28 acoustic torpedoes. Fluckey had to act quickly.

"Open outer door tube four! Range—mark! Final bearing—mark! Fire 4!"

A blast of compressed air sent the torpedo on its way at thirty-two knots. It locked onto the sound of the ship's propellers and curved toward the target. The Barb's sonar operator counted down the approach. One minute, fifty-three seconds. One minute, twenty seconds. One minute. Forty-five seconds. Thirty-five.

Silence. The torpedo's motor quit short of the target.

Frustrated, Fluckey brought the sub back to the surface for a new approach. He cleared the bridge of all but he and Duncan as the flash of gunfire lit the horizon. The whine of shells flying over warned the sub away. Fluckey set a zigzag course seaward, then headed farther down the coast. The convoy anchored overnight, and at sunup on the 27th resumed its southward trek. The submerged *Barb* was waiting. Morning haze had burned off, however, giving the convoy's aviators a perfect view of the sub's black hull etched against the shallow sea bottom. As Fluckey raised the periscope, two bombs exploded. Close. Then two more, followed by the thump of depth charges—getting closer. The boat made for deeper water as the destroyer raced forward, its spotter plane circling. The warship's side-throwing catapults hurled depth charges with abandon, clearing the ocean in a pattern never before faced by the *Barb*. Teeters plotted each detonation. Well above. One below. One astern. Another on the port side. The destroyer was off target, however. "Captain," Teeters shouted. "Plot indicates she has lost *Barb,* probably attacking some poor seal or a whale heading north. We're in the clear."

An hour later the submarine surfaced unseen. It was mid-morning and there was yet one more chance to do some damage before the convoy rounded the southern cape of Karafuto and disappeared through La Perouse Strait. Fluckey made another end-around, keeping the smoke of the convoy in view. The *Barb* arrived off the cape at dusk. There was no sign of ships. Again they had anchored somewhere up the coast. A sixty-mile search throughout the night was fruitless.

At dawn on the 28th the boat returned to its earlier position and submerged. A frigate appeared at one point, then departed. Also a plane flew over. But no convoy was sighted. With oxygen running low, Fluckey brought the sub back to the surface at dusk to recharge batteries and air out the compartments. Again the captain sought the anchorage without success before returning to the boat's submerged guard post at dawn.

At noon on the 29th a float plane flew past the sub's raised periscope. Startled, Fluckey had a good view of the pilot, staring straight ahead fifty feet off the glassy surface. Thirty minutes later, the skipper took another look. "Man battle stations torpedoes! Here they come!" he shouted. The sound of gongs mixed with cheers from below. The long wait was over.

The *Terutsuki,* with its scout plane, led the way. The *Barb* positioned itself for a stern shot. Fluckey took a look. "Angle on the bow still zero with plane weaving across his bow. This boy looks menacing. Coming left to give him a down the throat with stern tubes."

Up above, the plane did figure-eights ahead of the hunter-killer. Pinging from the destroyer combed the ocean for the submarine. The destroyer maintained a steady course at 10 knots. Range closed to 1,700 yards . . .

1,000 yards . . . 960. . . . Then, without warning, five bombs exploded over the boat, so powerful the periscope acted like a whip antenna. Flecks of insulating cork broke loose, creating a dust storm in the compartments. Light bulbs shattered. Crewmen clung to any fixed object to stay upright. Fluckey, maintaining periscope depth, took aim with a Mark 28 homing torpedo.

"Fire 10!"

The torpedo bolted away. But the motor again failed. Another dud. "Damn it!" cursed the skipper. "Open the outer doors on tubes 7, 8, and 9! Max! New setup!"

A depth charge exploded, then another well below the boat—perhaps the torpedo exploding on impact with the ocean floor.

Fluckey raised the periscope and fed coordinates to Duncan at the TDC. The destroyer continued lobbing depth charges.

"Fire 7! Fire 8! Fire 9! All ahead full!"

Three conventional electric torpedoes sped away. The *Barb* accelerated for twenty seconds, ending with a large knuckling of seawater as the boat turned sharply, giving enemy sonar the impression the cavitation was the submarine. All stop. The boat coasted silently away from the water disturbance.

Sixty seconds passed.

The three torpedoes converged on the warship—and passed under it without exploding. "It can't be!" Fluckey anguished, issuing the command to close watertight doors between the compartments. "Hang on, everyone!"

The *Terutsuki* sped up, coming in fast to finish off the *Barb*. The shriek of the destroyer's twin propellers rose audibly, as if they would cleave their way through the boat's hull. Crewmen braced, ears tuned to the overhead. They could hear the heavy splash of countless depth charge canisters, followed by the sharp clicks of detonators. The depth charge direction indicator in the conning tower lit up like a runaway computer. Explosions ahead. Above. Below. Port. Starboard. Somehow the submarine remained watertight.

It was Fluckey's turn.

This time he would narrow the distance. Another Mark 28 couldn't miss. The skipper raised the scope. "Thrilling. The ship's doing a St. Vitas dance!" he shouted, describing the rocking motion of the destroyer, slinging depth charges side to side. "Geysers are flying up from a stream of charges shot from her side throwers."

Someone in the crowded conning tower yelled back, "Captain, for God's sake, get that periscope down!"

"Fire 4!"

With a jolt, the torpedo left the bow. Moments later its motor also failed, and it fell harmlessly into the depths.

The destroyer paused out of range, listening and pinging. It turned and throttled up, bearing straight for the boat. Fluckey knew the *Barb* was in big trouble. "Open the outer doors on tubes 1, 2, and 3! Max! New setup!"

Screws of the speeding *Terutsuki* rose to fever pitch. Crewmen held their breath, pulses pounding. The sound man counted off the approach. "He's at 1,000 . . . 600 . . . 400 . . . 100." The swish of the warship passed overhead. Then the splashdown of canisters, lots of them. Sledgehammers waffled the boat. Explosions too numerous to count.

Fluckey's evasive tactics again saved the boat.

He prepared to counterattack. "This time we'll let him come close so we can't miss," he said to Duncan. Max calculated six hundred yards—it would give the boat's conventional torpedoes a twenty-second run, just enough time to arm them.

The captain quickly raised and lowered the periscope. The destroyer turned, straightened out, and came charging. A plane circled over its bridge.

One last check.

"Up scope. Angle on the bow five starboard. Range—mark. Final bearing—mark. Down scope."

The telemetry checked. Six hundred twenty yards and closing.

"Fire 1! Fire 2! Fire 3!"

All three bore a hot, straight course. A minute later sonar reported them again passing under the destroyer. No explosion.

"Damn the torpedoes!" roared the captain.

Fluckey, his mind racing, put another knuckle in the sea, stopped, started, backed down, came up to eighty feet. The *Terutsuki* laced another carpet of explosives. Concussions whipped the boat. The pressure hull groaned.

With no means of reloading, the only remaining option was to find an escape route. Not easy. The sub was trapped between the destroyer and the beach and more escorts were joining the fray. Fluckey was desperate. He ordered Duncan to jettison the boat's mechanical decoys—bubblers, gassers, and swim-out beacons. Duncan counted seventy-six. "Fire them all!" When Duncan questioned the directive, the captain replied cryptically, "I said all. I need them now before he attacks again." Max carried out the instructions as the sub made a few more high-speed knuckles, twists, and turns. Fluckey kept a wary eye on the distance to the beach. Only 5,500 yards. The *Barb* maneuvered wildly in a series of stops and starts and radical turns, all the while ejecting decoys that filled the depths with loud noises.

The sonar operator announced there would be no way to pinpoint the sub's position in such commotion. "Great!" said Fluckey as the boat wiggled its way to the open seas undetected. There, the skipper breathed a sigh of relief, happy to have come away with a draw.

The skirmish was hardly the end of the patrol. The sub moved up the coast of Karafuto, where the skipper had his men test the sub's inflatable rubber boats to see if they could steer a straight course. Satisfied, he planned to invade a large processing plant on Kaihyo, a tiny island at the eastern end of Patience Bay. The factory converted seal carcasses into oil and jackets for aviators. Every enlisted man volunteered to be in the landing party. Only eight could go, however, four to a boat. Fluckey selected them, depending on their skills.

The sub approached from the north on 1 July. Persistent fog, however, shrouded the island; the skipper wanted a full view. The *Barb* waited until dawn of the next day when the weather cleared. As the sub circled the island, lookouts were surprised at the large number of barracks, warehouses, and buildings on the western side—a much larger concentration than expected. As the captain sounded the battle stations alarm, the *Barb*'s gunnery crew poured on deck to man 20mm, 40mm, and 5-inch guns. Ashore, the Japanese saw the boat approaching and began running. The first rounds destroyed a 75mm gun emplacement on a cliff overlooking the plant. Return machine gunfire fell well short. Within minutes all opposition ceased. The sub closed to within eight hundred yards, where it came to a complete halt and opened fire. The captain couldn't be more pleased. "The ideal submarine bombardment—huge fires burning, sections of buildings flying up in the air, sampans destroyed, oil drums tumbled and split, a field piece overturned, and a machine gun hanging loose, unattended."

The *Barb* backed well offshore for three hours in anticipation of enemy aircraft. When none appeared, it moved back in to launch the invasion force. Lookouts noticed a pillbox on the hillside on the way in. Fluckey and Duncan made a quick sweep with binoculars and noticed three more fortified sites. The *Barb*'s 40mm gun destroyed the largest. Given the possibility of resistance and having reduced the plant to flaming wreckage, the skipper chose to withdraw, terming the skirmish "Little Iwo Jima." Indeed, the Japanese army would later report that three American ships had dropped six hundred bombs on the plant, destroying it.

The *Barb* sped to the northwestern side of Patience Bay, with plans to bombard the large city of Shikuka and its factories and big aircraft base. The boat would have to venture fifteen miles inside the ten-fathom curve however—a much greater distance in shallow seas than the Nam Kwan transit. The captain was confident. No search was under way for the submarine. Total surprise was on his side.

At midnight on 3 July 1945 the submarine approached under a heavy, overcast sky and a steady drizzle—"perfect for rocketeering," as the skipper put it. Radar revealed high smokestacks, the point of aim for the missile strike. "Swish" Saunders led his team onto the forward deck, unstrapped the launcher, adjusted the angle, and loaded a dozen rockets, set for a range of 4,550 yards. After an initial short circuit, the missiles rose in a flash of light and disappeared as the submarine roared away. Behind, the thunder of impact could be heard, ravishing the air base. The Japanese would later report the attack as the work of five U.S. warships.

The boat continued down the coast and seven hours later encountered a thousand-ton Japanese freighter bound for Skikuka. From deep submergence, Fluckey attacked with one of the boat's four smaller Mark 27s, nicknamed "cuties," which could be fired only from very close range. The torpedo silently exited the stern on its own power and made a sweeping upward curve to intersect the target. The torpedo exploded, snapping the ship's keel and sending the ship quickly to the bottom, where it landed with a thud next to the submarine. The *Barb* surfaced in flotsam and coal dust. There were no survivors. From the bridge, Fluckey noticed a floating pilothouse and rolls of bobbing charts. With grapnels crewmen snagged the charts. Duncan stepped onto the roof of the pilothouse to retrieve more charts. They were a goldmine, providing the locations of minefields in the Okhotsk and La Perouse Strait.

The crew celebrated the *Barb*'s fourth sinking with cake and beer as the sub set a course for the southern end of Karafuto to patrol Aniwan Bay, a small body of water that opens like a crab's claw on the strait. Large train ferries linking Karafuto with Hokkaido routinely sailed the bay and strait, as well as Japanese frigates. Late on the morning of 5 July Fluckey sank an enemy freighter with conventional torpedoes. A subsequent plan to stage a missile attack on the city of Shimoyubesu on the north coast of Hokkaido was canceled after surveillance revealed it to be a poor target. The sub returned to Patience Bay and on 8 July sank a cargo ship with 40mm gunfire.

New orders arrived, shifting the *Barb* five hundred miles south to the east coast of Hokkaido for lifeguard duty during a bombing strike by Admiral Halsey's Third Fleet Carrier Task Force 38. En route the submarine sank a large diesel sampan with gunfire. The air bombardment began on 14 July, setting large fires on the mainland that burned all night. In the morning fifty planes returned and leveled everything ashore. The submariners listened in on the pilots' frequency as the aviators looked for anything to attack. "There's a horse. I'm going after him," radioed one of the pilots. "You leave that poor horse alone," came the reply from the flight leader.

All planes returned safely to their carriers, freeing up the *Barb*, which set a course back to Aniwa Bay, where two days later it torpedoed a frigate whose cargo of depth charges blew up. Out of torpedoes except three Mark 27 "cuties" in the stern tubes, the boat returned to Patience Bay.

Many times during the patrol the "Galloping Ghost" of the east Karafuto coast had witnessed steam locomotives hauling freight and passengers along the shoreline. Troop trains moved at night. What Fluckey had in mind was smuggling commandos ashore to blow up one of them. Planning for the mission had been in the works for three weeks. Lt. William Walker, the boat's engineering officer, would lead the invasion in one rubber boat while "Swish" Saunders would command another. Several of the men had been Boy Scouts, experience that Fluckey thought could come in handy if something happened and they had to live off the land. Neal Sever, a second-class signalman, was among the chosen for his scouting and communications skills. Also Larry Newland, a first-class cook, was to go ashore. Saunders and Billy Hatfield, a third-class electrician's mate, devised a fifty-five-pound bomb from missile warheads. They loaded the explosives into a large pickle can with wires leading to three dry-cell batteries in their own waterproof tin. The men dubbed the demolition a "land torpedo." Commander Fluckey wondered how it would be triggered since the saboteurs didn't have the time to wait to detonate the explosives; blowing up the tracks without taking a train didn't seem worth it.

To study the issue, the skipper convened a meeting in the wardroom attended by enlisted men. Hatfield, a former railroad worker in his native Kentucky, knew exactly what was needed. A micro-switch. Bolted to a wooden wedge, it could be pushed up under one of the iron rails. The weight of the locomotive would cause the track to sag, pressing down on the switch and detonating the bomb. Fluckey was ecstatic, slapping Hatfield on the back. Max had a question, however: "Do you have a micro-switch?" Hatfield replied no. But Lieutenant Teeters, the radar officer, might. He did. That clinched it. The mission was a go.

Fluckey and the officers chose a sandy beach in the lower portion of Karafuto, a stretch dotted by many waterfront homes but with clear access to the railroad. The sub would approach to a thousand yards of the beach and launch its boats. The landing party would be equipped with red lens flashlights, watches, knives, D-rations, inflatable life jackets, cigarette lighters, a signal gun, a Very pistol for firing flares, binoculars, electrical wire, wedges, and the demolition charge. Carbines, tommy guns, and hand grenades would be loaded onto the boats. Teeters came up with another idea—affixing pieces of tin to the boats so radar could track them. Once they reached the beach, Signalman Sever and Newland would remain with the boats while the rest of the squad proceeded across a highway to the railroad. There, two guards would split off fifty yards up and down the rail line. A third would be posted twenty yards inland. The remaining three men, including Lieutenant Walker, would plant the explosives in a hole between the tracks using improvised picks and shovels. The bomb would be wired to the dry-cells, buried in a second hole. Another set of wires would lead to the switch.

The skipper wanted everyone back aboard within three hours—fifteen minutes before the first glimmer of daylight. Talking would be kept to whispers during the mission. Fluckey had the men practice bird calls. A whistle mimicking a bobwhite would be used when encountering each other in the dark. A sound like a whippoorwill would mean the men should come together. A mechanical whistle would represent an emergency—run for the boats. A blinker gun would signal the *Barb* that the boats were returning. Two flares would mean the commandos were in trouble; gunfire was needed in the direction indicated. A single flare, on the other hand, would mean the boats couldn't locate the sub. A single flare fired from the sub would mean it had to leave and would return every night.

What was needed now was a dark, moonless night. It arrived on the fourth night, 23 July.

With the sub at a halt on the surface 950 yards from the beach, the invaders climbed into their boats, packed with gear. Fluckey, on deck, had rehearsed a sendoff, something like, "Synchronize watches" and "Slip-Keep"—one slip and it's for keeps, the *Barb*'s slogan for stay alert. But he didn't. Instead, "Boys, if you get stuck, head for Siberia 130 miles north—follow the mountain ranges, good luck."

Radar followed the boats all the way in. It took thirty-five minutes.

Fluckey had anticipated problems. In fact, there were. "I was in the lead boat with my back to shore and the compass between my feet," explained Sever, the signalman. "I held a light on the compass so Lieutenant Walker could see it. The many metal objects in the boat compromised the magnetic feature. That, coupled with poor visibility, caused us to land elsewhere than planned. I could see a lighted window, a dwelling about two hundred yards from the beach. I heard a single bark of what sounded like a small dog, then silence. I signaled the *Barb* and received one flash in acknowledgment. Newland, the cook, brought meat in case dogs bothered us. He stayed with the boats while I scouted the beach for a hundred yards or so to the north of our landing place."

The saboteurs skirted the house and sprinted two hundred yards across what they thought would be grass. Instead, it was waist-high bulrushes that crackled with every step. Lieutenant Walker was the first to reach the road, where he tumbled headfirst into a four-foot drainage ditch. Warning the others, he got up and bolted across the highway, only to plummet into another ditch. The men finally reached the tracks, where the three guards fanned out. One of them, First-Class Motor Machinist Mate John Markuson, went to investigate something that looked like a water tower. He soon came racing back, breathless and unable to mimic a bobwhite. "Jeepers, that thing is a lookout tower with a man inside asleep," he whispered to Walker. The lieutenant told him to stay put. Walker, Saunders, and Hatfield bent to the task of digging two holes between the ties in the rail bed, preferring to do so with their hands to avoid noise.

Before the job could be completed, a northbound locomotive came barreling out of the dark. The saboteurs dived for cover behind low bushes and gullies as it rumbled by, the engineer leaning far out of his cab and looking down on the Americans, who lay flat and frozen. Hatfield, who had jumped into a depression, thought he had been shot. Fortunately the sharp noise proved to be the discharge of carbon dioxide cartridges attached to his life vest.

With renewed urgency, the men hollowed out room for the bomb and the batteries and carefully covered them with stones. The most critical step was attaching the switch. Fluckey wanted all but Hatfield to move away in case the bomb went off. But all five stood over him to make sure the switch was wired correctly. The work completed, they made for the boats in a noisy retreat. It was up to Sever and Walker to wade out with the loaded boats to launch them against the cresting waves and climb in. "You can appreciate our efforts in getting those erratic rubber boats out beyond the surf," said Sever. "By the time we got the boat out to where the paddlers could hold it, Lieutenant Walker and I were waist-deep or more in water. With foul weather gear soaked, we really struggled to pull ourselves aboard."

The saboteurs were halfway back to the *Barb* when a northbound express train appeared trailing wispy white smoke. On the bridge of the *Barb*, Fluckey saw it too and broke the silence with a megaphone: "Paddle like the devil! We're leaving!"

Seconds later the bomb went off under the locomotive, rupturing its boilers. The explosion threw wreckage two hundred feet into the air. Cars piled into one another and lurched off the tracks in a mass of twisted, rolling metal.

The saboteurs scrambled aboard the *Barb*, which turned and disappeared into the bay.

Back at sea the crew celebrated what they considered the high point of Fluckey's graduation patrol. But the skipper was not about to rest. Over the next few days, he directed a fiery wave of destruction. North of the smoldering train wreck, the sub launched thirty missiles at the city of Shiritori and its factories, starting two large fires, including one in the Oji paper factory, the largest in Japan. The inferno spread three miles through the industrial area. The sub launched its last missile salvo at the town of Kashiho, forty miles south. Offshore, the *Barb* sank four sampans in separate gun actions, boarded one, and took a prisoner. Next were canneries in the coastal city of Chiri in the upper reaches of Patience Bay, obliterated with twenty rounds of 5-inch shells. The Japanese were convinced an invasion by Halsey's fleet was imminent and scrambled reinforcements to northern Japan.

Returning to the lower Kuriles, the sub attacked a sampan shipyard and lumber mill at Shibetoro on the island of Kunashiri. Bombardment with 40mm and 20mm gunfire destroyed thirty-five sampans. The sub kept firefighters away with bursts of gunfire.

During the action, Commander Fluckey watched with dismay the pitiful sight of an older man, stripped to his waist. The owner of the lumber mill carried a bucket in each hand. Duncan saw him and ordered a ceasefire. Everyone watched as the solitary figure followed a path to the shoreline, shook his fists at the submarine, then stooped to fill the buckets. He turned and lugged the water slowly uphill. When he saw his mill engulfed in flames, he dropped the buckets and turned to face the submariners. Distraught, he threw up his arms, all hope lost. Defeated, he walked away and disappeared into a forest. Fluckey could feel his pain, muttering to himself, "War is such hell."

In its last act, the sub attacked a trawler, took two prisoners, and set the vessel on fire. When it would not sink, the submarine put its nose against the hull and rolled it over. Fluckey then turned for home. It was 27 July 1945. Gene Fluckey's war with Japan was over.

The submarine arrived at Midway on 2 August to a triumphant reception. It was the completion of yet another amazing voyage. Submariners throughout the Pacific had gotten a hint of that in ComSubPac's nightly news broadcast a week earlier. In a roll call of boats at sea, most of which reported little or no action, Gene's boat stood out. COMSUBPAC BREEZY NIGHTLY NEWS X BARBAROUS BARB REPORTS SINKING ONE LARGE AND ONE SMALL FREIGHTER AND THREE LUGGERS ONE TRAWLER FOUR SAMPANS

IN ADDITION TO ONE ISLAND SMASHING BOMBARDMENT AND TWO ROCKET MASSAGES GIVEN IN EXCHANGE FOR BOMBS AND DEPTH CHARGES RECEIVED X DUTCH SUBMARINE O-ONE NINE REPORTS ITSELF AGROUND ON LADD REEF WITH COD SPEEDING TO AID X.

Now, in Midway harbor, all eyes were on the submarine and its massive battle flag streaming from the periscope shears. Six feet high and as many wide, it was covered with more than sixty colorful swatches made by crewmen to commemorate each Japanese ship sunk and damaged, the missile strikes on Japan, the sabotage of the sixteen-car train, the numerous gun attacks, and the rescue of Allied prisoners of war in the South China Sea. The sub's guy wires from bow to stern also were decorated with fifty red ball pennants indicating the number of vessels of all types sunk or destroyed ashore in the boat's just concluded patrol.

The captain, smiling broadly from the bridge, could bask in the great satisfaction that, despite an estimated four hundred shells, bombs, and depth charges lobbed over the *Barb* in its five patrols under his command, the boat had endured every punch and returned to safety time and again without a single casualty. In a final accounting, the Navy credited the skipper with sinking twenty-five ships—second only to Richard O'Kane and his *Tang* (SS-306). The *Barb* also had the distinction of participating in the sole landing by American military forces on the Japanese homeland and the first ever ballistic missile attack by a submarine. Fluckey, his officers, and his crew had earned an astonishing 6 Navy Crosses, 23 Silver Stars, 23 Bronze Stars, a Navy Unit Commendation for the 12th patrol, the Presidential Unit Citation for the 8th, 9th, 10th, and 11th patrols, and the Medal of Honor for the 11th. The *Barb* had emerged under Fluckey's innovative leadership as one of the great submarines in an undersea offensive that had much to do with winning the Pacific war. American submersibles, just 2 percent of the Fleet, sank approximately 55 percent of all Japanese naval and merchant marine shipping. Of the 288 Navy submarines that fought in the war, 52 were lost—a rate of almost one out of every five. Out of an operating force of 16,000 men who made war patrols, 3,131 crewmen and 374 officers perished. The casualty rate of 22 percent was the highest of any branch of the American military.

In his official report of the *Barb*'s twelfth war patrol, Captain Fluckey paid tribute to his men:

How difficult it is to close this chapter of the *Barb*. What wordy praise can one give such men as these. Men who, without the information available to the CO follow unhesitatingly when in the vicinity of mine-field so long as there is the possibility of targets. Men who offer half a year's pay for the opportunity to land on Jap land, to blow up a Jap train with a self-trained demolition team. Men who flinch not with the fathometer ticking off 2 fathoms beneath the keel. Men who shout that the destroyer is running away after we've thrown every punch we possess and are getting our ears flattened back. Men who will fight to the last bullet and then want to start throwing the empty shell cases.

On 9 August 1945 an atomic bomb exploded over Nagasaki. The following morning, the Presidential Unit Citation was presented to the entire crew assembled in uniform at Midway. "The ceremony was held on the *Barb* and the Beautiful 'B' was lovely," wrote Gene to his wife.

The crew was in whites and our battle flag waved itself so proudly in the breeze. The dock was filled with formations of men sent by every submarine and tender present. The commodore gave a short speech summing up the prowess of our results and you could just feel the thrill that went through the crowd when he boomed out our total devastation upon the Japanese—destruction in sunk and damaged ships amounting to one quarter of a million tons. Oh honey! Then he had me step forward and read off the citation. Upon its completion he handed it to me, the band played 'The Star Spangled Banner' and our Presidential Unit Citation flag was run up on one of the periscopes. My chest nearly burst.

Officers and crew celebrated through the afternoon and into the night. At midnight news arrived that the Japanese had surrendered. Within minutes enlisted men were awakened and there was dancing in the streets until dawn.

Admiral Nimitz, commander in chief of all forces in the Central and North Pacific, was in Guam when the surrender was announced. He greeted the news with little more than a serene smile as officers around him leaped joyously. For four years vilification of the Japanese as subhuman fanatics had fanned ruthless combat throughout the Pacific. Now Nimitz, a great admirer of famed Japanese Admiral Togo, whose fleet destroyed the Russian Navy in the Battle of Tushima in 1905, wanted the racial slurs to stop. In a congratulatory announcement to be broadcast to the Fleet, Admiral Nimitz reminded naval officers that "the use of insulting epithets in connection with the Japanese as a race or individuals does not now become the officers of the United States Navy."

Fluckey received orders to relinquish command and report to the sub base at Pearl Harbor. The new skipper, Lt. Cdr. Cornelius Patrick Callahan, acceded to the captain's request to forgo the traditional transfer of command. "I didn't have the courage to have a formal relieving aboard ship with the crew at quarters—I would have blubbered," Gene wrote his wife. Instead, he assembled the sub's officers in the tavern at the Gooneyville Lodge. Everyone stood at attention as first Fluckey, then Callahan, read orders, formally transferring command.

With a plane standing by to fly him to Pearl Harbor, Fluckey made his way to the submarine pier one last time. The *Barb* was preparing to shove off for Guam, where it would be stationed as a precaution. The skipper lifted the last line mooring his boat and tossed it to deck hands, crewmen with whom he had shared so much—a life-and-death journey none would forget. Gene wished them well. On the bridge was the new executive officer, Max Duncan, returning a steady, poignant salute. Tears clouded the former captain's eyes as the boat made its way through the shipping channel and out into the Pacific. Sitting on a mooring bollard in his khaki uniform, Fluckey steadied his gaze, following the submarine until it disappeared from view over the horizon.

PART THREE

At my age, thirty-four, don't you think I'm too old a submariner
to be baking potatoes in the woods?

—CAPT. EUGENE FLUCKEY *to Boy Scout officials, who begged
him to become an Eagle Scout, Groton, Connecticut, 1947*

Nimitz

The flight to Hawaii was rougher than expected. The heater was out of
order and there were no blankets aboard. Gene Fluckey resorted to pac-
ing in the belly of the transport to stay warm and contemplate his future
as the plane droned on high above the Pacific. At Pearl Harbor a media
frenzy awaited him. Newspaper reporters scurried for interviews, now that
the story of the *Barb*'s last two war patrols had been released. *Time* magazine
scored a one-on-one interview, and NBC radio went live with the skipper.
The Navy encouraged him to go with the flow. "Public relations here wants
me to sell submarines," he wrote of the hubbub in a letter to Marjorie,
whom he addressed as "Mrs. Dogfish." As he had hoped, his new orders
were to report to the sub base at Groton, where he was to put into commission the USS *Dogfish* (SS-350), one of the first postwar submarines and
thought to be the most advanced in the world.

At least, that's what the Navy thought. But with the surrender of Japan
and Germany, the realization was setting in that both wartime enemies had
undersea boats that surpassed American technology in many ways. The first
look inside astounded Admiral Lockwood. Nazi subs could attain better surface and submerged speed than their American counterparts. They had better sonar, optics, diesel engines, and batteries. They could dive deeper and
faster. Japanese torpedoes were far superior and vastly more reliable than
anything produced by the Navy. Axis nations also had subs with snorkels,
breathing pipes enabling them to operate submerged on diesel engines.

The Navy set to work to adapt many of the refinements, including streamlining the hulls of fleet boats and installing tall, sleek conning towers with snorkels. The Navy called these air-breathing vessels "GUPpies"—an acronym for Greater Underwater Propulsion. The *Dogfish*, being built at the Electric Boat Company, eventually was to be one of them.

With his family relocating from Annapolis to New London in the fall of 1945, Fluckey arrived in September to participate in the launch of his boat. Before he could take command, however, he received orders in November to join the staff of Secretary of the Navy James Forrestal, the man who had presented him with the Medal of Honor. At President Truman's behest, Forrestal was trying to unify the armed forces. Though the war had been prosecuted successfully by an independent Navy and Army, there had been bureaucratic wrangling throughout the conflict because of differences in organizational structure and national strategy. How to mold the two branches into one unified command was daunting. Furthermore, it came at a time when Truman was intent on drastic cuts to the defense budget. The president embraced a deep conviction that excessive military spending could be ruinous to the country. Knowing what was coming put the Army and Navy in competition for shrinking federal dollars.

Forrestal, facing congressional hearings on what could be done to bring the branches together, decided to bring along Medal of Honor winners. He tapped Fluckey to represent the Silent Service. Realizing the Navy wouldn't resist all change, the secretary was hopeful a little tweaking could bring consensus. But he hadn't anticipated the impact of James Doolittle. The Army brigadier general had earned the Medal of Honor for leading a squadron of bombers on a successful one-way bombing mission over Tokyo from the aircraft carrier USS *Hornet* in 1942. Of the sixteen B-25 twin-engine bombers, four crash-landed in China and one landed in Vladivostok, Russia, where the crew was imprisoned for more than a year. The others either ran out of fuel or were hit by enemy fire, forcing the pilots to parachute from their crippled bombers. Of the eighty men who participated in the mission, three died during the raid and four were critically injured. Eight others were captured by the Japanese. Of them, three were executed and one starved to death. Doolittle, who landed in China, went on to command Army squadrons in Europe before moving back to the Pacific to direct B-29 strikes against Japan toward the end of the war.

Now, before Congress, Doolittle demanded independence for the Air Force. "It all ended in a big mess," explained Fluckey. "Jimmy Doolittle made some very bitter remarks about the B-29ers will be turning over in their graves if they didn't get a separate Air Force—what do you think the B-29ers were fighting the war for? Period. Forrestal's reply to this was to turn and tell the four of us that it was going to be a mud-slinging fest, this unification business, and he was not going to have any bright junior officers mixed up in this type of politics, so we were all excused and would receive orders the next day."

The next morning seven sets of orders arrived—Fluckey's choice. None appealed to him. Then a new one arrived, canceling the previous seven. Fluckey was to embark on a thirty-day promotional speaking tour for the Navy during the Christmas holidays—without his wife. The commander was beside himself. Just home from the war, just reunited with his family, and now to be separated once again during a holiday period he hadn't enjoyed in years—what a setback. He longed for a return to the *Dogfish*, now impossible since a new skipper had been named. Deep in gloom at the naval operations headquarters in Washington, he had no choice but to follow orders. Then a call came in from Admiral Nimitz's office upstairs. He wanted to see the young officer.

Twice during the war Nimitz had come into contact with the skipper of the *Barb*. The first was when he, General MacArthur, and President Roosevelt visited him at the Royal Hawaiian where the president had insisted on meeting him. The second meeting was near the end of the war, when Fluckey suggested the admiral deploy ten wolf packs to mine the coast of China, from the Yellow Sea to Amoy. Intrigued, the admiral studied the plan and agreed it was feasible. However, since Okinawa had fallen to American forces, there was no need for the mission.

Now, in the admiral's office, the two men—one of the war's greatest submarine commanders and the man who had commanded five thousand ships and two million men at war's end—stood face to face. Fluckey, thirty-two, was a good six inches taller than Nimitz, fifty-nine. Gene's red hair, boyish complexion, and beaming smile were quite a contrast to the stoic, chiseled features of the slightly built white-haired admiral. Nimitz came to the point. He had just been named chief of naval operations and he needed a personal aide for the next two years. Would Commander Fluckey be interested? The offer was a godsend. Such a prestigious assignment would give him the inside track on future promotions in the Navy. But what did he know about being an aide? "I don't know anything about this particular business but I'm sure I can learn," he opined, adding, "Are there any special orders that you'd like to have, mistakes that your previous aides have made possibly?"

Only one thing, replied the admiral. "I'm going to give you one order, and this is the last order I give you: never offend anyone."

Nimitz was a pioneer in the undersea fleet dating all the way back to 1907, when he served in the *Plunger* (A-1). He successively commanded the original *Snapper, Narwal,* and *Skipjack* until 1912 and was the first commanding officer of the submarine base at Pearl Harbor. It was through his efforts at age twenty-six that dangerous gasoline engines were replaced by diesels beginning with *Skipjack.* Like Fluckey, who had saved the life of a friend by swimming to his aid when he was a child, Nimitz was honored by the Treasury Department for saving the life of a naval fireman who couldn't swim and was swept away from his ship by a strong tide. Nimitz, commanding officer of the E-1 submarine at the time, dove into the sea and swam to W. J. Walsh's side, keeping him afloat until both were rescued.

During World War I Nimitz was chief of staff to the commander of Atlantic submarines and eventually rose to command of the heavy cruiser USS *Augusta* and chief of the Bureau of Navigation. On Christmas Eve 1941—seventeen days after the attack on Pearl Harbor—Nimitz secretly flew to Hawaii to take over the Fleet to restore confidence. Fittingly, he was sworn in as commander-in-chief on the deck of the submarine *Grayling* (SS-209) on 31 December. He brought a very personal touch, insisting on greeting incoming ships as often as possible, not only to debrief the commanders, but, as he put it, "to size up the men"—to get a sense of their fighting caliber.

In the latter stages of the war, with the Navy poised to defeat Japan, Truman and Nimitz had a falling out over the president's intention to drop the atomic bombs on Japan. The admiral also disagreed with Truman's idea of instituting a universal military training program of six months. Nimitz thought the latter was a waste of government money, and believed there was no need to drop the two atomic bombs, that it wouldn't save that many American lives at the cost of two Japanese cities. Due to the admiral's intransigence, the president adamantly opposed Nimitz becoming chief of naval operations despite his immense popularity throughout the country. "If it hadn't been for such a blunt man as Admiral King [the outgoing chief of naval operations], he probably wouldn't have been promoted," explained Fluckey. "But from what I understand, Admiral King told Truman personally, 'You either make Nimitz chief of naval operations, or you explain to the American public why not.' "

The president caved in. But he appointed Nimitz to a two-year term— not the customary four.

For Fluckey, the role of personal aide demanded long hours and a blur of activities. The routine was start work at 7:30 in the morning until 7:00 at night, seven days a week. Afterward the admiral and his aide usually attended social events until 11:00, when they called it quits. Fluckey handled the admiral's appointments, helped with his speeches, accompanied him wherever he went, and was his liaison to the public. It wasn't unusual for three hundred or four hundred telephone calls to come in every day, as well as lots of letters. "The mail was just phenomenal," said Fluckey. "Any time Admiral Nimitz did something that was out in the newspapers or something, the mail just came in by sackfuls." The admiral often made three speeches a day, each laid out by Fluckey on cards put in Nimitz's pockets. The admiral had a knack for using humor and narrative stories, especially useful when dealing with the press. Recalled Fluckey, "He taught me to be a pretty good storyteller because, at press conferences, when we were moving into questions and fields that were not quite ready to be publicized, then he would start to tell a story. He'd say, 'That question reminds me of a story . . .' and he would start to tell the story. This broke the chain of thought."

Nimitz was careful about those he depended on for advice. "He didn't like yes-men around him, and he used me constantly to bounce ideas off," recalled Fluckey, an idea-a-minute man himself. "The bounce was usually quite good. If I didn't believe in them, he expected me to speak up and I wouldn't hesitate."

To Fluckey, Admiral Nimitz was a leader, not a driver. Either style could work, illustrated by the difference between Nimitz and Admiral King, known for his incendiary temper. "It's the difference in whether people will work their hearts out for you," said his aide of the gentle-spirited Nimitz. "The driver had a job getting this done, whereas the people just want to do the very best they can for somebody they like. Admiral Nimitz usually made people so ashamed of themselves, of their narrow, bigoted, parochial wheeling and dealing viewpoint or outlook," said his aide. "He would never lose his temper, in spite of what people were trying to foist on him. And then his calm patience would spread like the sea. When conferees were getting angry, he would halt everything by saying, 'No further decisions will be reduced today. Now talk it out.' The next morning they would reconvene and decisions came out one, two, three as quickly as you can snap your fingers. His leadership was amazing in this regard."

Nimitz had a cordial working relationship with Congress but didn't trust lawmakers to deliver on promises. In an appearance before an appropriations panel, for instance, the lawmakers fawned over him while going over the Navy's budget, assuring him of support while asking, "Are you sure you have enough, Admiral?" Nimitz replied the budget was sufficient. Later Fluckey expressed surprise at the generosity shown by the lawmakers. Yes, replied the admiral, but they should be ignored. "The party line this year is to cut, and cut they will, and it's very sickening when people—there they are reasonable while they're listening to you, but the minute you're away, they'll go ahead back and adopt the party line. So now we'll go back and plan for the cuts." Three weeks later the cuts were announced and Nimitz was ready with a plan to deal with them.

The admiral and his aide became quite fond of each other. "He grew on me so rapidly that really he became closer to me than my own father, and I could see his effect on everybody else in much the same way," said Fluckey. Indeed, the admiral drew loving throngs just about everywhere he went. "I used to carry handfuls of autographed cards in my pockets," explained his aide. "Women would kneel in front of him, grab his pants leg, kiss the cuffs of his pants. They'd kiss the sleeves of his uniform, just stop him, absolutely stop him dead in the street and he couldn't move."

One such occasion was at a governors' conference in Kansas City, where Nimitz gave the keynote address. Afterward he and Fluckey were coming down the stairs of the capitol before thousands of visitors who had come to get a glimpse of the admiral. "The crowds broke through the police lines and started running up the steps to get a hold of him," recalled Fluckey. "I had another group of policemen I kept on the side that came charging in to form a circle around him. They broke through them, and I grabbed Admiral Nimitz by the hand and dragged him back up the steps, because I really thought he would just be trampled to death. I'm talking about thousands of people, if you can imagine it. I just kept pulling him up the steps as fast as we could, with a few people clawing at him, and right back into the capitol, and finally pushed him into a men's restroom. Here were all these ladies outside and they broke right past me and went right into the restroom." The admiral had to stand on a toilet seat in an enclosed stall to keep from being seen. Later he and Fluckey slipped out unnoticed through a basement entrance to the capitol.

In Washington Nimitz's popularity made it virtually impossible for him and his wife to go out together in public. Seeing a movie was impossible; patrons would interrupt constantly or stare at the couple. According to Fluckey, the Nimitzes resorted to dressing up in old gardening clothes with slouch hats and leaving their home at the Naval Observatory through a backyard garden gate in the evening, crossing Wisconsin Avenue unnoticed on the way to a movie theater.

The seven-day pace as Nimitz's aide was tough not only on Gene but on his family. At a dinner for the Fluckeys at the Nimitz home, Mrs. Nimitz asked Marjorie how "shore duty" was going now that her husband was home from the war. "Well," she replied, "if you can call this 'shore duty,' I see less of my husband than I saw of him during the war practically and certainly less than at any time he's been on sea duty before." Mrs. Nimitz wasn't surprised. She'd been trying to pare down the admiral's hours without success. The price of being a Navy wife.

Since she liked Marjorie immensely, Mrs. Nimitz later scolded the admiral for the "lousy life" he was imposing on the wives. He decided she was right. There would be no more working hours on Sunday. He also began dismissing his staff at 4:00 PM on Saturdays.

The Fluckeys and the Nimitzes found common ground in a most unusual way four months into Gene's new assignment. It was late March 1946 and the admiral and Army Gen. Dwight Eisenhower were invited to speak at the University of Richmond, where they were to receive honorary degrees. Nimitz and his wife had invited Marjorie to come along to make a foursome. She felt ill that morning and declined. After the ceremony, historian Douglas Scott Freeman hosted a noontime reception at his antebellum mansion. Mint juleps were served amid much laughter as the two military leaders shared humorous vignettes from the war. When the early afternoon reception broke up, Nimitz suggested that he and his wife repay the courtesy call that Marjorie and Gene had made to their home in the observatory. The admiral suggested his aide take along a fresh mint julep for Marjorie.

What could he say? "Wunderbar!" remarked Fluckey. "Marjorie certainly will be feeling better by now."

Mint julep in hand, Gene and the Nimitzes climbed into the couple's chauffeured Marine car. Fluckey, holding the drink steady, sat on the front seat next to the driver all the way back to his snow-draped Virginia neighborhood near Washington. When the car turned onto Gene's street, the passengers were startled at the sound of a radio blaring full blast. "What crummy neighbors," Gene thought. To the commander's great chagrin, the door to his home was wide open with the sound of the radio pouring from inside. Flustered, he jumped from the car, still holding the mint julep, and ran up the steps while calling out his wife's name, leaving the driver to assist the admiral and his wife. Marjorie wasn't there. Further, the normally immaculate living room was a mess, with children's coats and newspapers scattered everywhere. Gene quickly shoveled off a place for the Nimitzes to sit while tossing the rest of the junk behind a sofa. As the Nimitzes entered, he suggested Marjorie was at a neighbor's house.

"While we're waiting, what libation would you like?" he asked. "Iced tea," replied the admiral. "But isn't that water coming from under the door into the kitchen?"

At that moment Fluckey turned and heard the swish of running water. Running for the door into the kitchen, he pushed it open to find daughter Barbara and all the neighborhood kids hosing down mud on the floor.

"Out—all of you! And take your hose with you!" demanded Fluckey as the children scattered through a back door.

Hearing the commotion, Nimitz called out to eight-year-old Barbara, who squeezed past her father before he could catch her and ran to the admiral, plopping on his knee. As they chatted, Fluckey noticed mud from her snow outfit sliding down the trouser leg of the admiral's best dress uniform. Gene pointed to it but Nimitz waved him off. Fluckey went to get a towel and returned with the iced tea just as Marjorie walked in, calming her frantic husband. The Nimitzes expressed complete understanding.

After a brief visit, Fluckey escorted his guests back to their car, where the driver stood at attention next to the open rear door to the plush 1941 Packard. Unfortunately the kids who ran from the Fluckey backyard had left the gate open. The family's two cocker spaniels were loose in the yard next door, rolling around on a fresh coat of fish bone fertilizer. Gene, whenever he wanted to take the dogs for a ride, would open the door of his sedan and they would jump in. Seeing the admiral's door swing open, the dogs came running, bounding inside the car and onto the back seat before the driver could react.

"Smoky! Nibs! Come here!" yelled Gene, completely mortified. Marjorie, in the background, yelled at her husband, "Don't yell at Smoky!" Too late. Both dogs exited the car in fright, leaving a puddle of urine on the seat. Mrs. Nimitz entered the car and sat down, let out a yelp, and scrambled back out. Urine mixed with fish bone dripped from the back of her silk dress. Commander Fluckey, embarrassed and turning redder than his hair, pulled out a wad of tissues and began wiping the backside of Mrs. Nimitz's dress. "Gene," said the admiral, taking the Kleenex from his hand. "I think I had better take care of that part of her anatomy."

Marjorie, who appeared with a towel, apologized profusely, as did her husband, leaning into the car to sop up the puddle while noticing the pungent odor of fertilizer permeating the car. Shaking his head, he stood up and lifted his hands to the heavens in remorse. By that time the Nimitzes were doubled over in laughter, tears in their eyes. Catching her breath, Mrs. Nimitz said, "Gene, please don't worry. We've brought up four children."

Fluckey, seeing no humor in the moment, offered to drive the couple back to the observatory in his car. But they wouldn't hear of it. Said Nimitz to the driver, "Cozard, open up all the windows—we'll ride up in the front with you." Still laughing and waving, off they went.

The Fluckeys sat down in a daze. "We thought we might receive orders the next day to one of the three S's—Siberia, Saudi Arabia, or the South Pole," recalled Gene.

The following morning Fluckey arrived at work ahead of Nimitz so he could call Capt. John Davidson to report the admiral might be looking for a new aide and that Gene would appreciate Davidson's effort in finding a submarine for him. A half hour later Nimitz arrived, smiling. Fluckey offered to resign. But the admiral waved him off, saying that he and his wife had never had such a "uniquely enjoyable call" in their entire career.

Fluckey called Marjorie to report all was well and then phoned Davidson. Cancel the submarine request.

As it turned out, the Nimitzes and the Fluckeys became best of friends. Whenever the admiral wanted to refuse a dinner, he'd get his aide to invite him to his house. "The neighbors were always amazed to be invited in to play poker with Admiral and Mrs. Nimitz and have a potluck supper," said Fluckey. "He was an excellent player. It was always amusing, because he had a lot of card tricks that he knew."

The admiral was also a skilled horseshoe tosser. He used that ability, among other things, to soften up crusty Harry Truman. Nimitz had established a Little White House in Key West where the president could relax. "The admiral provided submarine rides for him there, even on some of the old German submarines that we had. He also went out personally with him aboard some of the carriers, to show him what carriers could do, and I think he really had Truman becoming more and more Navy-minded."

One day Fluckey got a call from the reigning world horseshoe champion who planned a visit and wanted to know if he could get an autographed photo of Admiral Nimitz. Fluckey was sure the admiral would want to meet the champion, which he did, engaging him for an hour after canceling all appointments. During that session the admiral phoned the president. "Mr. President, I've got the champion horseshoe pitcher of the world over here. We'd like to come over to the White House and show you how he can pitch horseshoes." Truman, who loved the game, was delighted and canceled his own appointments. Fifteen minutes later the president, the admiral, the famed sub captain, and the world champion were all at the White House doing all kinds of tricks pitching horseshoes.

During Fluckey's eighteen months with Nimitz, the admiral successfully downsized the Navy. Secretary Forrestal also worked out a military unification plan. Rather than alter either the Army or the Navy, the plan stressed coordinating military, diplomatic, and economic aspects of national security in a more systematic approach. The plan created a presidential advisory board—later to be known as the National Security Council—which consisted of representatives from each of the armed forces, the State Department, and various civilian agencies chosen by the president. Augmenting the advisory board was a Central Intelligence Agency to ensure intelligence operations throughout the government were well coordinated. A third component was creation of a new independent branch of the military—the Air Force—to direct land-based strategic bombing campaigns against foreign enemies. The Army and the Navy retained their specialized air forces—ground troop support for the Army and aircraft carriers for the Navy to protect the Fleet.

By the end of 1947 Nimitz became special assistant to the secretary of the navy in the western sea frontier, a post he held for little more than a year before becoming a roving goodwill ambassador for the fledgling United Nations. Commander Fluckey, meanwhile, had returned to the Silent Service. He relocated with his family back to New London, where he assumed command of the submarine *Halfbeak* (SS-352). There he renewed old ties with the submarine community, stung by news from the Joint Army Navy Assessment Committee (JANAC).

JANAC had been at work since the end of the war trying to verify through copious Japanese records all sinkings credited to the Silent Service. Admiral Lockwood had long claimed his skippers had sent 10 million tons of shipping to the ocean bottom. The committee ultimately agreed that 10 million tons of shipping had been sunk—but only half was due to submarines. Japanese records could verify only 5.3 million tons—1,314 ships—sunk by submarines. The announcement proved to be an embarrassment for sub skippers. Top-ranked Richard O'Kane of the *Tang* had been credited with 31 ships at 227,800 tons during the war. The official JANAC tally, however, came to 24 ships at 93,824 tons—a considerable fall but still ranking him number one in numbers sunk. Fluckey, who was the second leading skipper at the end of the war with 25 ships at 179,700 tons, fell to fourth with a JANAC-confirmed total of 16.33 ships sunk at 94,409 tons, still making him number one in tonnage sunk. What really rankled him was JANAC crediting him with a single sinking in Nam Kwan Harbor.

In their defense, submarine commanders could only estimate total tonnage of target ships and often had to rely on "breaking up noises" after an attack to confirm a sinking. Visual sighting of a ship going down was the only reliable barometer of a successful attack. Poor surface conditions, swift counterattacks, and darkness often prevented that. Admiral Lockwood and the skippers also pointed out that JANAC didn't credit them with any ships under five hundred tons—and they were numerous. Nor did the committee tally ships that were beached and effectively put out of the war—there were many. JANAC also nullified credit when an enemy ship had been attacked and sunk by more than one submarine. Still, by any measure, the submarine force had done a remarkable job, given the unreliability of its torpedoes. The subs sank a Japanese battleship, six large aircraft carriers, six escort carriers, seven heavy cruisers, thirteen light cruisers, and numerous destroyers. Many in the Navy believed the blockade was so effective that it literally could have starved Japan into submission without dropping the atomic bomb. But the United States was in no mood to wait after four years of combat. Nor was there time to dawdle on what-ifs at the close of the war. The A-bombs were a message to a new and potentially more deadly foe—the Soviet Union. And Gene Fluckey soon would serve on the front lines of what was to become the Cold War.

The Fluckey Factor

It was a dreary, cold November afternoon in 1947 when the Boy Scouts made a surprise visit to Gene Fluckey at his home in Connecticut. He and his family had moved into new quarters seemingly for the umpteenth time, this time to the tiny hamlet of Groton at the big sub base. It was typical for naval visitors to meet often with the captain on business in his den. But this was unusual. Tom Keane, national public relations director of the Boy Scouts of America (BSA), and two BSA executives had arrived from New York City. They had learned from a speech by Admiral Nimitz at Scouting's national convention in October that Fluckey was a former Scout who had dropped out as a teenager. Keane explained how Scouting was in trouble. A growth spurt anticipated after the war never materialized. Quite the opposite was happening: thousands of youths were abandoning the organization. An internal investigation determined teenagers had begun ridiculing Scouting. The FBI, asked to investigate, concluded that communist sympathizers were trying to undermine the organization and were pushing the line in the nation's schools, "Don't act like a Boy Scout, don't be a sissy!"

Keane, in laying this out for Fluckey, wanted to know why he had dropped out just two Merit Patches short of becoming an Eagle Scout, Scouting's loftiest ranking. "I remember that our Boy and Girl Scout troops met in the Congregational Church on Friday evenings," explained Fluckey, perplexed at the question. "When I turned fifteen, the Girl Scouts became very attractive. So I started dating. Also I had graduated from high school and was off to prep school at Mercersberg Academy. But probably it was girls that caused me to drop out. Why?"

"Well," replied Keane, "how would you like to become an Eagle Scout?"

Fluckey was taken aback. "At my age, thirty-four, don't you think I'm too old a submariner to be baking potatoes in the woods?"

The remark drew laughter. But the Scouts were serious. The organization had enlisted Admiral Nimitz and General Eisenhower as honorary Scouts—Silver Buffaloes—to serve as roving ambassadors. Fluckey, the youthful wartime submarine hero, becoming an Eagle Scout would do even more to boost the image of Scouting. With little further coaxing, the commander agreed to do what he could.

The first step was to qualify for those last two Merit Badges. The *Halfbeak*'s skipper took to the task with typical Fluckey zeal. He went down to the local headquarters of the Boy Scouts and bought study pamphlets covering Merit Badges he had missed. He chose a favorite subject—civics. And since his hobbies were "dogs, birds, and boats," as he often put it, he also decided on a bird study. The latter became a labor of love.

"For Christmas, my wife gave me a jig saw and lumber for bird houses and feeding stations," he explained. "Soon we had all the birds in the neighborhood. I thought I was a great success. But I hadn't counted on my daughter's friends. They objected, for all the wild birds had left their houses and were at ours. So we bought more lumber, established a production line, and outfitted the whole neighborhood with bird houses and feeding stations. Everyone was happy."

By the end of February Fluckey had completed all the requirements and appeared at a local auditorium filled with young Scouts, ready to be examined by a Court of Honor in curtained booths in the center of the room. "I awaited my turn along the wall sitting on a folding chair, a bird feeding station perched on one knee and a bird house on the other," said the commander. "I wasn't embarrassed in spite of the more than a few quizzical glances my way, for I was contemplating my responses to the expected questions of the examiner."

A small Scout sitting next to the six-foot Navy captain could stand it no longer. "Sir, aren't you a bit old to be a Boy Scout?" Fluckey was at a loss for words at first, but then replied, "Son, once a Boy Scout always a Boy Scout. It just takes some of us a little longer."

When he got his turn before the examiners, the sub captain nailed the requirements for two Merit Badges and was inducted as an Eagle Scout. In the years to come he would become a sought-after speaker at Scouting events throughout the nation as an ardent foe of communism.

Commander Fluckey's first responsibility remained the submarine *Halfbeak*. But he would not be skipper for long. By May 1948 he moved up to assistant reserve coordinator in nearby New London, where he honed his considerable speech-making skills. One year later he was promoted to flag secretary on the staff of Rear Adm. James Fife, commander of the Atlantic submarine fleet during a time of rising enmity between the Soviet Union and the United States.

The Soviets, flexing their military muscle, had tested their first atomic bomb in 1949 and had imposed an overland blockade on routes leading to Berlin, requiring the United States to airlift materiel to a city deep inside Russian-controlled East Germany and divided into Russian, British, French, and American sectors. A mutual defense pact signed by communist leaders of China and the Soviet Union exacerbated international tensions. An invasion of democratic South Korea by the communist regime of North Korea also ushered in the Korean War.

Meanwhile, a cat-and-mouse competition was under way between the Soviet Union and the United States under the seas. The U.S. Navy bubbled with all kinds of radical new ideas under a $4.4 billion budget for submarine warfare. Being studied were boats several times larger than the standard Fleet-style submarine with an ability to carry jet-propelled planes and a Marine landing force . . . attack submarines capable of launching guided missiles that the *Barb* had pioneered . . . undersea cargo ships for supplying overseas bases in the eventuality of an atomic war . . . small submersibles for reconnaissance of rivers and harbors, or planting atomic explosives in an enemy port.

During his time as Admiral Fife's flag secretary, his leadership and concern for personnel was brought into sharp focus with the loss in 1949 of the USS *Cochino* (SS-345). In a strong gale off the coast of Norway, her snorkel got carried away, resulting in flooding, electrical fires, and the explosion of the boat's batteries. The USS *Tusk* (SS-426), sent to rescue the crew, lashed itself to the side of the sinking sub and saved all but one of the *Cochino* crewmen at the cost of six of its own. A naval court of inquiry recommended letters of censure and disqualification for *Cochino* officers and crewmen. Asked to comment on the findings by the commander of the Atlantic Submarine Force, Fluckey disagreed with the court. In a four-page appraisal of the testimony, the captain pointed out that there was no clear way to handle the multiple calamities aboard. He recommended that no one be disqualified and that no letters of censure be issued. Ultimately the Navy agreed with him and no punitive actions were taken.

In 1950 Gene Fluckey began a three-year stint as naval attaché at the American Embassy in Lisbon. There, life slowed down for the family.

Gene was no longer on extended missions at sea. He, his wife, and their daughter found more time to be together, enjoying the sights of Europe and getting to know the ancient and beautiful capital of Portugal. "My memories go by the school I was in and where we lived," recalled his daughter Barbara of the many relocations in her early childhood. "Dad just came and went until the war was over and we finally settled down for three years in Portugal. He was a bit of an influential mist until then. Portugal was the time that I really fell into step with Dad."

Gene and Barbara, entering her teen years, ate breakfast together nearly every weekday and he normally drove her to school rather than make her take the train. "So for three-plus years we had time to talk. He was interested in educating me as his parents did him. Discussions of important current events at dinner or touring factories. He molded me into a news 'junkie' forever and factory tour-taker ever since."

The family owned a 1948 Buick convertible, which they much enjoyed on vacation in Spain, Southern France, and Switzerland after securing an international drivers license and gasoline coupon books issued by the Embassy. The Fluckeys immersed themselves in Portuguese society and customs, learning to speak the native language as well as French. They often entertained visiting VIPs, who marveled at the couple's energy, enthusiasm, and attention to making those around them comfortable. The Fluckeys' fun-loving nature in Lisbon attracted lots of friends and acquaintances in a city they called "heavenly."

But within a short time, Commander Fluckey became acutely aware of the politics of Lisbon in regards to foreigners. "There is a continual flood of deliberate wafting of Spanish-Portuguese friendship. However actually it is a cold, stilted, kid-gloved friendship with the Spanish looking down on the Portuguese and extremely so vice-versa," Fluckey wrote in a letter to Rear Adm. R. F. Stout, assistant director of Naval Intelligence in Washington. The captain warned of the difficulty the Navy might face in choosing future naval attachés: "As a test, I asked a reliable Portuguese naval officer friend what his feeling would be if an officer of Spanish, Portuguese or Italian extraction was the new naval attaché. His reply was, 'If Spanish, many people would feel that the U.S. considers us a part of Spain. If Portuguese, he thought it would be acceptable. If Italian, he more or less threw up his hands then said, 'Why don't they send an American.' I carefully explained that America is a melting pot of all nations and races and that we were all

Americans. He agreed but added that basically Americans were considered to be of British or German extraction."

Four or five times a year the Fleet would pay a courtesy call on Lisbon. Fluckey was counted on to make all the arrangements, including hotel and restaurant accommodations for officers and frequently their wives. A Fleet visit produced a carnival-like atmosphere throughout the city. In August 1952 Battleship Division Two commanded by Rear Admiral H. R. Thurber from his flagship, the USS *New Jersey* (BB-62), anchored in Lisbon. A month beforehand, Fluckey sent a letter to the admiral to inform him of differences in protocol in Portugal, while assuring him of adequate police protection and that 27,000 naval personnel visited the previous year without incident. The attaché asked that the admiral do one thing before the Fleet arrived, however: "I would appreciate your putting out an order that no cushions or other missiles be thrown into the bull ring during, or at the end, of the bull fight. We had this happen once last year, which to the Portuguese was a sign of extreme disapproval. Actually it was skylarking, in very poor taste, and was finally explained to the Portuguese that it was an approving type of rowdyism occasionally seen at baseball games in which the Brooklyn Dodgers were involved."

Occasionally officers brought their own automobiles aboard ship so they could tour the countryside. Fluckey provided information about planned itineraries—as well as warnings. When Capt. F. D. McCorkle, of the *New Jersey*, announced that he planned to drive around Europe in his English Austin, the attaché cautioned him regarding bandits in the mountains and driving at night.

The Fluckeys returned to the United States in 1953, relocating to San Diego, where Gene assumed command of Submarine Division 52. The boats operated between San Diego and Hawaii, where they successfully developed countermeasures to acoustic torpedoes by deploying an electronic beacon on a tow line 450 feet astern of a submarine (Project Jimgene). In March 1955 Captain Fluckey became skipper of the sub tender *Sperry*. Five months later he was promoted to commander of Submarine Squadron Five, consisting of more than eighteen boats based in the Western Pacific. The commodore's first action was to tour submarine bases in the Western Pacific to resolve minor command problems at the behest of ComSubPac. Along the way he cautioned officers to step up security to thwart illegal currency transactions, black marketing, and the narcotics trade. Of particular concern was a visit he and his wife made to a Japanese orphanage in the port city of Yokosuka that ComSubPac supported with cash donations.

Missionaries affiliated with the American Soul Clinic in Los Angeles operated the home. Submariners raised two hundred dollars a month to support the children and paid for a new wing to house a total of twenty orphans. Medical treatment and food were provided by the Japanese government. Realizing that previous visits, made with advance notice and fanfare, painted a rosy picture, the Fluckeys decided on a surprise inspection. "It was a horrible shock," he wrote in his report. "The children were unkempt, in rags, the yard was strewn with broken glass and absolutely filthy as was the interior."

Fluckey ordered an audit and reorganized the management and care of the children with input from Marjorie. He also recommended strenuous efforts to find adoptive families for the children—"2 imbeciles, 10 Negro-Japanese, 4 Jap Japs and 19 Caucasian-Japs." As a result of the visit, staffing of the orphanage was increased to eleven workers, conditions were much improved, and an adequate, balanced diet for the orphans was established.

Captain Fluckey had hoped—without success—that he would be tapped to become the skipper of the nation's first nuclear-powered submarine after its launch in 1954 but that went to a younger man. Nevertheless, Fluckey spoke enthusiastically of the *Nautilus* as a Jules Verne vision come to life. "At last every submariner's dream is fulfilled," he told a television audience. "We have in the *Nautilus* the first true submarine. A submersible that can stay submerged for weeks at a time and circle the world at thirty miles per hour without refueling or surfacing. What a political muscle she is! Imagine a combatant ship that can roam the seas at will probably undetected. Imagine the threat of her lurking in the untrod silence of the prehistoric abysmal depths beneath the polar ice cap from which she could dart out on her savage forays. A ship that may pass from the Atlantic to the Pacific via the North Pole. Can one deny the vast possibilities?"

Asked how long the *Nautilus* could stay submerged, Fluckey beamed. "Well, I understand they intend to bring her up to the surface every four years so the men can reenlist."

Fluckey predicted that submarines like the *Nautilus* would in the near future be equipped to launch guided missiles long advocated by the captain. In a message to Cdr. C. D. Nace of ComSubPac in Pearl Harbor in 1956, he noted, "The guided missile business seems to involve at least 75 percent of my time catching up with the reams of material that have been written, visiting missile shootings and conferences, both in and out of town." Fluckey was present during test flights in the Hawaiian archipelago of the Navy's *Regulus II* missile launched by Submarine Squadron Five. Under development since 1947, the missile was based on captured German V1 missile designs with a swept wing design and could deliver a three thousand-pound warhead to a target five hundred miles away. It was the forerunner of the *Polaris, Poseidon,* and *Trident* ballistic missiles as well as the Navy's *Tomahawk* cruise missile.

When there seemed to be resistance in some quarters of the Navy to embrace the future of missile-carrying submarines, Fluckey voiced concern to Secretary of the Navy Charles S. Thomas, who was visiting the *Tunny* (SSG-282) to see its missile-launching capability in April 1956. Fluckey arranged for a short presentation on plans for a submerged launch missile. Thomas was astounded, unaware of such possibilities. In a note to a confidant, Fluckey later summarized his private meeting with the secretary:

> I managed through prearranged plans to capture him without guests for twelve minutes in the *Tunny* missile center and gave him a lecture on the imbalance of the Navy, our desperate need for guided missile subs and the submerged launch missile, our accuracy, our present capabilities close to enemy coasts, and our tracking ability to points inland which I am pushing to the maximum. Finally I pointed up our shining future with *Slim, Reg I, Reg II, Triton,* topped off with submarines built around the IRBM [Intermediate Range Ballistic Missile] which immediately thereby transform it into an ICBM [Intercontinental Ballistic Missile].
>
> Now is the time to hop on the IRBM bandwagon for subs before we get shut out of the picture—and we can build subs to deliver it. Thus we take over the number one offensive position in the Navy. The Navy needs us for optimum delivery and we've got to hop in the ring and start swinging now. . . . In this connection I am forming a society called Martyrs for Missiles—and am looking for volunteers who will "go for broke" and possibly terminate their further promotion in order to seize every opportunity to jam submarines and guided missiles down the Navy's gullet until our potential is factual and of proper proportions.

Captain Fluckey had long believed the American public was underestimating the subversive threat of communism to democratic institutions. "We allow Reds to convert 'free speech' into weapons sure to be used against us," he often told an audience. "Living with Commies in our free democracy is like hiring a kidnapper to baby-sit. We must outlaw communism." To Fluckey, the threat was pervasive.

A visit to Santa Monica gave Fluckey a chance to discuss with a movie mogul something that had been gnawing at him for some time—the frequent use in movies of the line, "Don't act like a Boy Scout, don't be a sissy!" The line, according to the movie industry, was to gain a few laughs. "At lunch with Gene Zukor, the Crown Prince of Paramount [movie studio], I broached the problem," Fluckey recalled later. "He informed me that they had a watch dog committee to pull this line out of films. They were cognizant of the Scout problem. Scripts passed through many hands. Infrequently even when they had yanked the line out, movies would be distributed and the line had reappeared. Everyone disclaimed the line."

Despite it all, Scouting had rebounded and was to double its enrollment from pre–World War II levels to more than two million in just a few years.

In 1956 the Fluckeys relocated to Annapolis, where Gene headed the electrical engineering department at the academy. The couple left Barbara behind to attend the University of California at Berkeley.

As Gene settled in to his new responsibilities, Rear Adm. William R. Smedberg, III, became superintendent of the academy. He was aware that the Naval Academy Athletic Association owned 101 acres west of the campus on which it hoped one day to build a football stadium. The association, founded in 1892, had collected $1.5 million over the years to put toward it. In the mid 1950s college football was growing in popularity and the Navy team was poised to challenge for national championships. Smedberg calculated that the time was right to build the stadium and that another $2.2 million was needed for a facility that would seat thirty thousand spectators. He thought the money could be raised with a dedicated fundraising effort and approached Navy Secretary Thomas S. Gates for his support. Gates, however, thought it was impossible to raise the money privately and that no money could be expected from Congress. When the admiral persisted, the secretary finally gave in. "Well, Smeddy, okay, I'll give you a trial, but do you have any idea how much $2.2 million is in ten-dollar and fifteen-dollar and twenty-dollar and twenty-five-dollar amounts?"

What Gates didn't know was that Smedberg had a secret weapon. "Fortunately, I had this most magnificent head of department, Gene Fluckey, who was a great submarine wartime hero, one of the greatest, I think, we ever had, Congressional Medal of Honor winner in submarines, who was the head of my fund drive."

Fluckey approached the task with meteoric fervor. "He had a brilliant idea a minute," said the admiral. "I was constantly being pushed and prodded to do things I wouldn't really ever have done myself." Things like putting a Cadillac and a Ford Thunderbird sports car in the middle of the

academy to be raffled off. And a brand-new speed boat. A sail boat. And a
Piper aircraft. All Fluckey ideas. Volunteers stood long hours, day after day,
selling tickets beside each of the raffle items set up all over the campus.
Only one prize would be awarded. Net proceeds: $75,000. That was just the
beginning.

Fluckey's full-court-press put Smedberg on the griddle occasionally.
"One day I got a call from Don Felt, who was the vice chief of Naval Operations, and he said, 'Smedberg, what the hell are you trying to do?' I said,
'What do you mean, Don?' He said, 'This whole Pentagon is filled with midshipmen selling raffle tickets for your god-damned stadium. Get them out
of here. Don't you know it's against the law?' "

Which it was in D.C. but not in Maryland.

Commander Fluckey forged ahead, soliciting contributions from cor-
porations, movie studios, and advertising agencies. Billboards, car bumper
placards, radio spots, TV commercials, and newspaper stories sprouted
everywhere. Columbia recording artist Mitch Miller and the Naval Academy Choir cut a special wax recording of "Anchors Aweigh" backed by the
"Marine Corps Hymn." One million discs were distributed to 3,700 deejays
across the United States and a thousand local naval districts. A contribution
of one dollar earned a patron a record, all proceeds going to the stadium
fund. Fluckey also lined up testimonials, all the time soliciting new ideas.
He enlisted the help of Endorsements, a public relations firm in New York,
and studied such articles as "Ten Rules for Believable Testimonials" from
Advertising Requirements magazine. The captain arranged for Admiral Smedberg to appear on a national TV broadcast of "Person-to-Person" hosted
by Edward R. Murrow, on which the admiral made a pitch for the stadium.
Checks for a hundred dollars, two hundred dollars, five hundred dollars
soon began rolling in. Fluckey also persuaded a Hollywood studio to film
a movie skit with Burt Lancaster, Clark Gable, and Smedberg for use at
halftime during football games, encouraging more contributions. The cam-
paign percolated with energy and ideas. One was for memorial chairs in
the new stadium for a hundred dollars a pop. Captain Fluckey was assertive,
looking for donations in every possible place. When he was in Washington with the secretary of the navy to convince flag officers to contribute a
hundred dollars each, he turned to the secretary and said, "Mr. Secretary, I
don't have your check." Gene got the check.

Fluckey coined the term "Concrete with Heart" in a four-paragraph
appeal to Navy sailors and Marines everywhere to get behind the push.
"The Navy-Marine Corps Memorial Stadium," he wrote, "is much more than
just a football field. It is the only single memorial to the Navy and Marine

Corps. The facade will be adorned with memorial plaques. State flags will fly from its highest points. Its balconies facing the field will be emblazoned with famous battles, such as Belleau Woods, Midway, Tarawa, Coral Sea, Iwo Jima, Inchon, etc. It will be an inspiration to every American who passes though its portals."

The appeal evoked an outpouring of contributions. Said one Marine sergeant in San Diego, "I'm the biggest dang Marine in the U.S., so here's my whole big pay check for the biggest memorial we've needed for so long." Another donor sent in what he could, with this note: "Dear Admiral. I'm 11 years old. I earned this dollar shoveling snow. I hope someday to play in our stadium."

Fluckey campaigned relentlessly, taking his quest international with ads in foreign periodicals. He made a personal pitch to Navy commanders at sea. He conceived a competition among them to raise the most money. Gates to the stadium were to be named after winning fleets. The rush was on—sometimes to the extreme.

Adm. Wallace C. Beakley, commander of the Seventh Fleet, got into a fierce rivalry with Adm. Charles R. "Cat" Brown's Sixth Fleet. Beakley was determined to win, even sending his men into the stores and "joy houses" in Singapore and Hong Kong to get contributions. The Rev. George N. Gilligan, a Catholic priest who ran a mission for visiting sailors in Hong Kong, was appalled and complained, terming the effort "polite blackmail" of Hong Kong merchants and wanted it stopped.

Though Adm. Arleigh Burke, the chief of naval operations, and other flag officers thought Smedberg was going too far out on the limb this time, they stood on the sidelines. "They let me get away with it, because none of them really thought I was going to make it," said the superintendent. "But they all wanted the stadium."

The Seventh Fleet eked out a victory, but both Fleets earned their gates.

In all, Fluckey cashed out 300 memorial plaques, numerous gates, walls, and arches and more than 8,000 memorial chairs. The submarine fleet donated $10,000. Veterans of Fluckey's old boat, the *Barb*, pledged $1,000.

In the end, "the drive," as Fluckey and Admiral Smedberg termed it, easily eclipsed the goal. The fund went over the top in July 1958. Captain Fluckey was ecstatic, announcing to the news media that the Navy had not used the services of professional fundraisers. "Ninety-eight cents out of every dollar is going into construction," he declared.

Four other fundraising drives in 1957–58 for the USS *Enterprise*, the *Constellation*, the *Arizona Memorial*, and the Air Force Academy Stadium failed.

Navy Secretary Gates was amazed the academy's effort succeeded. "Smeddy, I didn't think you could do it. I don't know yet how you did it," he said to the superintendent. Replied Smedberg, "It was all due to Gene Fluckey. It wasn't due to me, it was due to this dynamic Fluckey."

Construction of the Navy-Marine Corps Memorial Stadium began in the summer of 1957 and the stadium was dedicated on 26 September 1959. That day, the Midshipmen pounded William & Mary on the gridiron, 29-2. Though the team finished the season 5-4-1, Joe Bellino emerged as a star running back under first-year coach Wayne Hardin. The next year the team posted a 9-1 regular season record, with Bellino winning the coveted Heisman Trophy as the best halfback in college football. The team appeared in the Orange Bowl, losing narrowly to Missouri, 21-14.

For Gene Fluckey, the dedication of the stadium seemed somewhat prophetic. In a letter to Admiral Nimitz in 1947 updating him on the Merit Badge quest, Fluckey made reference to the Navy's growing inability to draw recruits. "Would you inform Admiral Denfeld [Nimitz's replacement as chief of Naval Operations] that the personnel situation is scraping the bottom of the barrel to such an extent that he had better convert the naval Air Arm into a sky-writing outfit for recruiting purposes. Can't you visualize the blue skies over a football stadium plastered with 'Join the Navy'?"

Twelve years later Gene Fluckey made that a possibility in Annapolis.

Flag Officer

NORFOLK—A small task force of three Navy ships slipped away from Norfolk piers Tuesday on a mission which will have far reaching implications in United States relations with newly emerging countries in Africa. The mission of the force, under the direction of Rear Adm. Eugene B. Fluckey, the youthful commander of Amphibious Group 4, is to quietly extend the hand of friendship of the Navy and the United States to the peoples of the African continent. . . . Fluckey, who has been called on to direct the operation, is a much decorated hero of World War II.

The Virginian-Pilot, 20 April 1961

It was called Solant Amity II (short for South Atlantic Friendship) and for Gene Fluckey the voyage to Africa would mark the beginning of a decade of remarkable events for him as a flag officer in the Navy. The mission was to give the newly elevated rear admiral a chance to flex his leadership skills in an area of the world fast becoming a front line in the Cold War.

Gail Bove, Gene Fluckey's granddaughter, as a teenager in the 1970s. *Courtesy Fluckey family*

A prototype *Regulus* missile is poised for launch from the deck of a submarine in the mid-1950s. Commander Fluckey pioneered the use of missiles fired from the *Barb* in his last war patrol and conceived the idea of ballistic missile submarines as a deterrent to nuclear war. He was involved in the test program for the *Regulus*, which was the forerunner of *Polaris* and *Triton* missile systems. *Courtesy Fluckey family*

Capt. Eugene Fluckey after achieving what others in the Navy thought was impossible—raising more than $2.2 million to construct the Navy-Marine Corps Memorial Stadium at the Naval Academy in 1959. *Courtesy Fluckey family*

On promotion to rear admiral, Eugene Fluckey took command of Amphibious Group 4—the "Brush Fire Brigade"—stationed in the Caribbean in 1960. The admiral (*on the right*) learned to scuba dive and often joined commandos practicing undersea demolition techniques. *Courtesy Fluckey family*

Rear Adm. Eugene Fluckey sharing a peck with South Africa's "Lady in White" Perla Sidle Gibson prior to departure of the admiral's flagship USS *Spiegel Grove* from Durban during his Solant Amity II goodwill cruise of African nations in 1961. *Courtesy Fluckey family*

During the Solant Amity II cruise, Admiral Fluckey flew by helicopter to Lambarene, Gabon, on 15 August 1961 to visit Nobel Peace Prize winner Dr. Albert Schweitzer and deliver medical supplies to his hospital there. The admiral said the physician reminded him of Fleet Adm. Chester Nimitz with "the twinkle in his eyes and the pervading humility." *Courtesy Fluckey family*

The atomic attack submarine *Barb* (SSN-596) floats down the ways at the Pascagoula River in Mississippi after its launch from the Ingalls Shipbuilding Yard on 12 February 1963. Mrs. Marjorie Fluckey was the ship's sponsor. Her husband gave the keynote address on the occasion that included the first reunion of the original *Barb*'s crew. *Courtesy Fluckey family*

Rear Admiral Fluckey (*left*) boards a Navy A3J Vigilante supersonic bomber at the Naval Weapons Evaluation Facility in Kirtland, New Mexico, in 1962. Accompanying the admiral is pilot Lt. Cdr. Samuel R. Chessman. The two reached Mach 2 in a test flight arranged for Fluckey, then the president of the Navy Board of Inspection and Survey. Back on the ground, it was announced that the admiral was the first submarine officer to fly at twice the speed of sound. *U.S. Navy photo*

The couple pose in Oahu, Hawaii, prior to the admiral being detached to become director of naval intelligence in Washington in 1966. *Courtesy Fluckey family*

Gene Fluckey and his second wife, Margaret, cut the ribbon to open Fluckey Hall at the U.S. submarine base in Groton, Connecticut, on 17 November 1989. Vice Adm. John A. Tyree Jr. is in the background. *Courtesy Fluckey family*

Rear Admiral Fluckey (holding American flag) with Margaret Fluckey and an unidentified Russian submarine officer participate in the Russian Peace Victory Parade on 9 May 1992. *Courtesy Fluckey family*

Rear Adm. Eugene and Margaret Fluckey remained very active in events all over the world through the 1980s and 1990s. *Courtesy Fluckey family*

On 4 June 1991 Admiral Fluckey posed with two residents of Nam Kwan who, as teenagers, remembered the attack on two Japanese convoys by the *Barb* and confirmed that not one but many ships were either sunk or damaged by the submarine in 1945. *Courtesy Fluckey family*

Admiral Fluckey stands on a dock overlooking Nam Kwan Harbor where fifty years earlier he led an attack by the *Barb* on nearly thirty Japanese ships at anchor there. *Courtesy Fluckey family*

Gene waves goodbye to residents of Nam Kwan and departs on the Chinese junk that carried him into the harbor. *Courtesy Fluckey family*

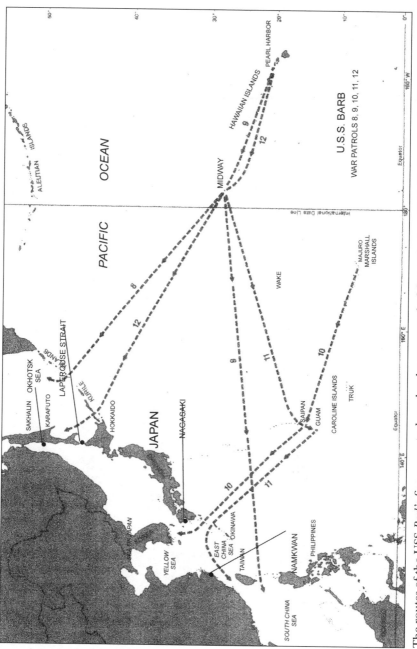

The routes of the USS *Barb's* five war patrols under the command of Gene Fluckey, 1944-45. *Genevieve LaVO*

Nationalism was sweeping Africa, toppling colonies ruled for two centuries by Britain, France, Belgium, Portugal, and Spain. Rioting had erupted in British Nyasaland and the Belgium Congo, leading to independence and more rioting. Republics had been proclaimed in Central Africa, Niger, Upper Volta, Ivory Coast, and Dahoney. In South Africa the English-speaking white government clung to power amid international condemnation and internal unrest over its institutional racism. The United States viewed the continent as ripe for communist expansion at a time when newly elected President John F. Kennedy grappled with a series of foreign policy setbacks. Within days of Solant Amity II's departure from Norfolk, two huge public relations disasters faced the president. On 12 April the Russians won the race to place the first man in orbit around the earth. Five days later a small force of rebels supported by the CIA landed at the Bay of Pigs in Cuba in an attempt to overthrow the communist government of Fidel Castro. Soviet-armed troops backed by tanks crushed the invaders. Kennedy accepted full responsibility for the failed plot to a howl of worldwide scorn. The fledgling president was in need of any bit of good news—the kind vested in Gene Fluckey.

Coming off the euphoria of the stadium drive in 1958, he had moved quickly toward flag rank by attending the National War College at Fort McNair in Washington followed by a year-long assignment to the National Security Council. On Fluckey's selection as rear admiral in July 1960, Arleigh Burke sent congratulations but warned of how all-consuming his new duties would be: "Being a Flag Officer is much more difficult than anyone anticipates until he is faced with it. Your successes and failures will become well known quickly to many persons both inside and outside the Navy. Your responsibilities will increase tremendously and examples you set will have much greater effect than you as an individual perhaps realize now."

Fluckey's first assignment was command of Amphibious Group 4, the so-called Brush Fire Brigade that guarded American interests in the Caribbean. The rear admiral learned to scuba dive and practiced undersea demolition techniques with his commandos. In January 1961 he had operational tactical command of a naval Task Fleet comprising sixty-five ships off the tip of Puerto Rico during a naval parade for forty-seven generals and admirals from Central and South America.

Returning to Norfolk after months at sea, Gene was hopeful of a little shore duty that might extend into the summer. If that wasn't possible, he and Marjorie anticipated the amphibious group being shifted to the Mediterranean, where she could relocate to an overseas base, allowing her to be with her husband at least some of the time.

But that was not to be.

The Solant Amity II mission was part of a broad initiative by the Kennedy administration to collect intelligence and curry influence in Africa south of the Sahara. An earlier voyage—Solant Amity I—had visited South America and the west coast of Africa between November 1960 and May 1961. Fluckey's objective as commander of Solant Amity II was to venture to the turbulent east coast of the continent to establish friendships with new governments.

The task force of Solant Amity II consisted of the amphibious dock landing ship USS *Spiegel Grove* (LSD-32), a tank landing ship, two destroyers, and a small refueling tanker. The ships carried 1,670 officers and men, including a company of 450 Marines and 6 helicopters aboard *Spiegel Grove*, Fluckey's flagship. The idea was to host dignitaries in each country visited, open the ships to tours to show off the Navy's equipment and personnel, participate in parades, stage performances by task force musicians, and distribute supplies and gifts. It took almost six weeks to fill the holds of the ships with food, candy, sporting equipment, souvenirs, toys, magazines, packets of seeds, Polaroid cameras, and fourteen tons of medical supplies.

Fluckey had hoped to make it an all-inclusive visit to Africa, including stopovers in Portuguese territories. But the Navy declined. "Everyone turns down my request to visit the Portuguese Colonies to avoid widening the U.N. breach [with Portuguese colonial policies] which I argue endangers our primary foreign policy of maintaining NATO intact—and the Portuguese commanding there now are old friends from Lisbon," Fluckey groused in a letter to retired Admiral Nimitz. The Navy, however, was in a dilemma. Portugal, one of the founding members of NATO and staunchly anticommunist, was determined to hang on to its African colonies. Resulting bloody clashes between Portuguese soldiers and African rebels had cost numerous lives on both sides.

With visits to the Portuguese colonies of Angola and Mozambique off limits, Fluckey set to the task of popping in and out of ports around the horn of Africa and up the east coast. From 1 May to 1 September Solant Amity II visited nineteen African countries and twenty-eight ports-of-call. The commander frequently went ashore to visit dignitaries or made helicopter visits to remote villages. He was a natural with his cheery disposition and willingness to engage people everywhere, young and old. He was a striking visage alighting from his helicopter in a short-sleeved, tropical white uniform in the remote deep bush village of Tsevie in Togo to present athletic equipment, candy, and medical supplies to tribal chiefs. In the former French colony of Gabon in west-central Africa, he did the same thing, winging into Lambarene in helicopters loaded with two thousand pounds of medical supplies for Dr. Albert Schweitzer. The Nobel Peace Prize-winning physician and humanitarian lunched with the rear admiral and escorted him around his hospital and the village for 4 hours, posing for photographers and discussing conditions in Gabon. Schweitzer was concerned independence had come too soon for a society not prepared to govern itself. "[Schweitzer] reminded me of Fleet Admiral Nimitz—that twinkle in his eye and the soul-pervading humility. What a man!" Fluckey later recalled.

In the South African port of Durban, South Africa's "Lady in White" serenaded Solant Amity II on its arrival. Throughout World War II, as troopships embarked from Durban to support the British, soprano Perla Sidle Gibson would appear on the North Pier with a megaphone to sing patriotic and farewell tunes that the sailors could hear as they passed. She never wavered from a vow to see off every single troop carrier. Now, as Solant Amity II prepared to depart, she stood dressed in her symbolic white dress on North Pier to give Rear Admiral Fluckey a ceremonial kiss before he climbed aboard his flagship. "She was warbling 'God Bless America' as she had done on our arrival," wrote Gene in a letter home. "Thousands lined the decks all the way out to the end of the jetty and I counted 39 persons who waded out on the mud flats, fully clothed, waving goodbye to us and singing with the band, 'Auld Lang Syne.' What a parting! It's enough to make Admirals weep."

In French-speaking Madagascar the rear admiral attended a ceremony in which live game was fed to sacred crocodiles, supposedly descended from humans. He also visited Catholic and Protestant churches and a mosque, where he joined five hundred barefooted Muslims. He took off his shoes and stood in his socks on the dirt floor. The iman gave a twenty-minute speech. "It made it necessary for me to respond with a ten-minute impromptu speech in French; they were so thrilled by my French speech that the Iman requested my permission to say a prayer in my behalf, and 500 voices droned away for me and cleansed me of all my sins past, present, and future; then when I thanked them for this soul stirring prayer they became so happy they chanted a prayer for all my ships; late that evening I washed my dirty socks which I fear will never come clean."

In Madagascar Fluckey stood before the press, which threw him a curve. "If you have an Amity visit to a colored Republic such as this, don't you think you should have one to your own colored people in Alabama who are being beaten?" asked one reporter, referring to civil rights demonstrations in the United States. The admiral answered with grace and humility. As he recalled, "I think they were a bit surprised when I admitted we weren't perfect, that great progress had been made, that we have a great American dream of equality which we believe can be achieved, that 95 percent of our schools are integrated, and that we have over two hundred thousand Negroes in our colleges and universities."

The task force moved on to the Seychelles, a British dependency of ninety largely uninhabited islands scattered across the western Indian Ocean north of Madagascar. Solant Amity II anchored at Port Victoria on Mahe Island, which Fluckey termed "a nice sleepy port set in the Garden of Eden." The republic was governed by Sir John and Lady Thorp, who hosted a state banquet in their Victorian mansion. "Pancahs swinging back and forth over the table provided the equivalent of air conditioning," Fluckey later noted. "A pancah is a heavy drapery about ten feet wide and four feet in depth attached to a yardarm rigged athwart the table and well above it. Through a system of rigging, the three pancahs spaced over the table are joined by a single rope that runs out through a hole in the wall, over a pulley, and down into a section of the kitchen, where a servant sits tugging on the rope to set the pancahs swinging back and forth. The resultant breeze is delightful."

The following morning Lady Thorp taught the rear admiral how to surfboard at the couple's beach residence, then had him join her in snorkeling over nearby reefs. "It's the most beautiful skin-diving in all the world—a myriad of unbelievably-colored fish that make all aquariums appear drab," he wrote Marjorie. He described a return visit at daybreak. "At that time the fish are so dormant one can bring his finger tips within an inch of the fish, attempting to caress them before they lazily move away. As the sun bursts over the low mountains the underwater world breathtakingly changes from subdued light grey hues to a kaleidoscope of sparkling, animated, crisscrossing rainbows."

From Port Victoria the task force steamed to French-speaking Reunion Island, then to Zanzibar for refugee relief, and on to Mombassa and Aden, before returning to Cape town in South Africa. It was there that Fluckey received orders to fly across Africa to Liberia to be the U.S. naval representative for the 114th Independence Day Celebrations. The Navy had diverted the USS *Valcour* to Monrovia to be Fluckey's flagship during his stay.

Among the many events he attended was an all-night ball. "Did I get integrated!" reported Fluckey in a letter home.

Never having danced with an African before, my destiny as the only Caucasian at the President's table was obvious. Kindly they offered to get me a good-looking African partner, but being a bit dubious even of Caucasian blind dates, I assured them that I preferred to dance with their lovely wives. Having thrown the gauntlet down, I quickly looked around the table for the best looking target for my first experience, and settled on the Attorney General's wife. They were all beautifully gowned and she was most attractive. Yet when I nervously held her in my arms, I could feel my scalp starting to perspire from the crown of my head down. She remarked that it was very warm and perhaps it would be cooler if we danced around the edge of the floor. After a while it was like putting your feet in hot water, once in it's nice and comfortable and the perspiration stopped. I must say these Africans have a built-in rhythm.

The next dance was a 'High Life'—this is very popular on the East Coast of Africa. It's sort of a cross between a shuffle, rock and roll, the mamba and the bunny hop. This time I reached higher and asked the Vice President's wife to dance. Unbeknownst to me she is known as being a good strong dancer. She whisked me around the floor like a graceful camel with me doing something akin to a hula while I swear she was doing an Egyptian belly dance. I just couldn't do the forward and back-ward grinds and keep in time with the music. All I could think of was "if they would just take a movie and send it back to Admiral Burke, he'd recall me from Africa post-haste." . . . During the night I danced with all their wives, all of whom were charming, delightful people. Consequently my thinking and philosophy have changed considerably. Having had my eyes opened, I am led to believe that Americans, on the whole, are the biggest racial snobs in the entire world.

Generally events were well organized and went off without incident. But occasionally a problem developed, sometimes with humorous consequences.

In the former French colony of Dahomey, the admiral hosted a dinner aboard *Spiegel Grove* for the nation's first president, Herbert Maga. An enormous man, he came alongside the ship in the admiral's barge and, in heaving seas, almost lost his balance twice and nearly toppled into the sea. Two seaman were able to get a firm hold and finally heave him up a ladder to the ship's deck. As he was piped aboard, another big roller caused him to lose his balance and knock over the officer of the deck and several seamen like bowling pins. Recovering his dignity, Maga went below, where Fluckey apologized.

During Solant Amity II's visit to Gambia, the rear admiral described in a letter to Admiral and Mrs. Nimitz a sporting event he had attended.

You would have enjoyed the Native Wrestling Matches they put on in my honor. . . . There was a fire at opposite ends of the wrestling ground (no mats) and a couple of witch doctors had been brewing herbs, crocodile heads, etc. all afternoon. This they then bottled. The wrestlers put on strings of amulets around their chests, arms and necks, took a good slug out of the bottles and squared off. Now the witch-doctors, bottles in hand, sprinkled their boys (acting as seconds), put hexes on their opponents, erased the hexes on their own lads, sneaked around and stole their opponents' footprints and rushed over to the fire to burn them. The wrestling started. After the first fall the loser quickly ran over to the sidelines to change his amulets (the last ones hadn't worked) and the gals rushed out to give the winner small bits of money with many huzzahs.

In both Togo and Dahomey Fluckey's plan to offer visitors helicopter rides created pandemonium. William B. Hussey, Foreign Service officer in Togo, recalled the scene. "In both countries the helicopter rides were a disaster, with the operation getting quite out of hand with crowds surging aboard, the overload finally being dispatched only to have new faces and hands pushing, grasping at any part of the helicopter. In Togo I also remember people crawling from timber to timber underneath the long pier trying to avoid the lone lines waiting their turn to board the running boats for ship visits."

Despite the logistic problems, Solant Amity II's visit was quite a success, which was noted in a letter to Fluckey from Hussey. "You know how valuable the overall effect of the visit in Togo was for the entertainment provided, the endless number of repairs effected [by Navy mechanics] from locomotives to equipment of every sort. Then there were the athletic contests in many sports. From President [Sylvanus Epiphanio] Olympio down to the fellows in the street, the visit was highly appreciated and thoroughly enjoyed." Indeed, Fluckey drew great satisfaction from what had been accomplished. Marine helicopters had taken 3,358 visitors aloft. Eleven Navy and Marine musical ensembles had entertained an estimated 230,000 citizens. Helicopter displays, amphibious exhibitions, drill team performances, and soccer, basketball, baseball, volleyball, softball, and tennis matches between Amity crewmen and local citizens drew nearly 300,000 spectators along the way. Another 112,000 guests visited the ships—VIPs in the morning and the general public in the afternoon. There were also parachute jumps and judo wrestling exhibitions by the Marines.

The rear admiral came away with a sobering view of Africa's new nations.

> Contrary to our concept of democracy, one is startled to run into a situation like Zanzibar—a perfectly legal, honest election was held, but the losing party, which was the majority party, became incensed at being outsmarted and wouldn't accept the election results. So, many reverted to savagery, broke out their machetes—and started hacking. Some sixty-three people were killed and over 250 maimed—babies, girls, old ladies, men, it didn't matter—had ears or limbs hacked off. Frequently your faith is shaken in the present course of events. In many suburbs of nation capitals the drums are beating all night long. You watch tribal dancing with the earth truly shaking under the pounding feet. . . . In pushing democracy we push the decay of the tribal system which means the decay of a built-in social security system. We must have something solid, ready to provide social security or Communism may offer a better answer.

Solant Amity II left Africa at the end of August, sailing for Brazil and Trinidad before returning to Norfolk on 8 September. There, Admiral Fluckey caught up with events he had missed, especially the marriage of his daughter Barbara to dentist Charles Bove in July. During the long separation, Marjorie kept up a heavy correspondence, often expressing great loneliness that deepened after Barbara's marriage. The forced separation couldn't have come at a worse time. Before Gene departed, she had fought her way back from cancer after an initial misdiagnosis. Chemotherapy treatments had taken her to death's door before she rebounded just in time to say good-bye to her husband. "Right now I have as much use for this man's navy as an old shoe," she wrote while her husband was away. "Better than five months' separation at this stage is too much for me and frankly I'd be ready to call it quits if this is what the future holds . . . life as an Admiral isn't all it's cracked up to be. Darling, I know this letter seems to be, for the most part, nothing but grumbles. But loving you so much, this being apart seems to be making me a chronic complainer. I'm trying to be happy but without you life holds very little to make me so."

By the end of July there was speculation on the wives' grapevine in Norfolk that Gene's new orders would be to Washington, a thought that gave Marjorie pause. "I've never seen such a lot of old and tired people as these Pentagon sailors," she wrote Gene. "From the lowest to the highest they all looked as if they had aged ten years. It certainly is a rat race of the first water."

Boomers

It didn't take long for Eugene Fluckey to make history as an admiral—and it wasn't in a submarine.

Rather than being assigned to the Pentagon as his wife feared, the admiral became president of the Navy Board of Inspection and Survey from November 1961 to March of 1964. As such he was responsible for evaluating each new weapons system and making a recommendation to the secretary of the navy to either accept or reject it. The board put each advance through a thorough and rigorous trial, a practice that dated to 1868, when Congress established the group to ensure Navy ships were properly equipped to defend the nation.

When Fluckey was appointed, the *Polaris* ballistic missile system was coming to fruition. The Navy also was pushing boundaries with a supersonic nuclear attack bomber, the largest combat aircraft ever launched from an aircraft carrier. The A3J Vigilante came off the drawing board in 1955 and entered the service in June 1961, intended to replace Navy's A-3 Skywarrior. The Vigilante was extremely advanced electronically. Its pioneering digital computer could run all its systems, including multimode radar that could map topographical features below and ahead of the plane, inertial navigation, closed-circuit television under its nose, and a computerized attack system that incorporated one of the first heads-up displays for the two-man crew. The plane could fly very high and at great speed. In 1963 it would set a new world altitude record of 91,450 feet. Despite all its advantages, maintenance problems, balky bomb jettison equipment, and high landing speed on aircraft carriers made it a challenge for the most experienced pilots. It also was susceptible to a new breed of Soviet ground-to-air missiles.

In 1962 the challenge for the Board of Inspection was not so much overcoming the technical hurdles as much as finding an adequate role for the plane. It seemed clear that *Polaris* missiles would satisfy strategic bombing requirements for the Navy. Being a hands-on officer who liked to experience weaponry and tactics up close, Fluckey decided to take a ride on one of the new bombers. Arriving at the Naval Weapons Evaluation Facility in Kirtland, New Mexico, he boarded the swept wing jet with Lt. Cmdr. Samuel R. Chessman, the pilot and project officer for the Vigilante test series. The plane lifted off and quickly surpassed Mach 2 as it streaked over the Southwest deserts to Fluckey's great delight. Back on the ground, Capt. David G.

Adams Jr., commander of the Kirtland facility, presented the rear admiral with a "Mach 2" pin for being, as he put it, the first submarine officer to fly at twice the speed of sound.

Ultimately the Board of Inspection and Survey recommended the *Polaris* system replace the Skywarrior, leaving the Vigilante with no mission. The jets eventually would be deployed on reconnaissance missions during the Vietnam War. Eighteen were lost in combat, more than any other Navy aircraft.

Gene Fluckey's exploits in World War II were never very far from his mind as he studied new weapons systems aboard nuclear submarines. He often thought about his old diesel boat. By 1963 new attack nuclear submarines that dwarfed the *Barb* were coming down the ways in American shipyards. The Navy had decided to name them after famous boats that had fought in the Pacific War. One was SSN-596. The Navy arranged a reunion of the old *Barb* crew for the launch of the new *Barb* at the Ingalls Shipbuilding Corporation yard in Pascagoula, Mississippi, on 12 February 1963.

A crowd of more than eight hundred spectators, including thirty-five *Barb* veterans, gathered at the shipyard to witness the launch of the nation's twenty-ninth atomic submarine—its eighteenth nuclear attack sub—on a pleasant sixty-degree afternoon. Mrs. Fluckey, the ship's sponsor, sent a ceremonial bottle of champagne smashing against the hull, where it exploded in a cascade of bubbly froth that flew skyward above her husband and sister, standing behind her. The big vessel lurched backward, gaining speed as it slid down the ways into the Pascagoula River to the strains of "Anchors Aweigh" by a Navy band. Six months later Fluckey returned to Pascagoula for the *Barb*'s initial sea trials. The boat, fitted with the most advanced underwater detection equipment in the world and extremely quiet machinery, met every requirement and deployed to the western Pacific.

Following his stint on the Board of Inspection, Gene Fluckey served for three months on special assignment for the secretary of the navy before assuming command of the Navy's Pacific submarine fleet in June 1964, fulfilling a personal dream. After the world war, there were only two flag-rank billets in submarines—commander submarines Atlantic and commander submarines Pacific. Fluckey now had one of them. In a transfer of command aboard the flagship USS *Plunger* (SSN-595) at the submarine base in Pearl Harbor, Fluckey relieved Rear Adm. Bernard A. "Chick" Clarey, who moved up to vice admiral and deputy commander in chief of the U.S. Pacific Fleet.

The Fluckeys relocated to Oahu, where they entered a whirl of social activity. Marjorie, who enjoyed that aspect of the Navy, accented her husband well, knew where to draw the line in social drinking for both of them, loved to converse with people, had many friends, and expressed a good sense of humor. "She was the perfect Navy wife," said her daughter years later. "She knew the ins and outs of required protocol. She was a successful hostess, she attended what she had to—and that cheerfully. She could talk with ambassadors knowledgeably although she had to quit school at fourteen. She read the Time-Life history series, always had a novel in hand, and was absolutely up on current events. In fact, my recollection of her would be that of always having a book in hand."

Gene was in and out of Hawaii overseeing operations of more than ninety submarines, including the new *Barb,* and ten thousand officers and enlisted men in three flotillas based in San Diego, Pearl Harbor, and Yokosuka, Japan. Several of the boats were armed with deck-launched *Regulus* missiles that Fluckey had worked with during testing in the 1950s. They were being phased out during Fluckey's watch because the *Polaris* and Fleet ballistic missile submarines were on the way. The first of these mammoth boats, the USS *Daniel Boone* (SSBN-629), had arrived in Pearl Harbor shortly after Gene took command.

Following a tradition of promoting those who had worked with him in the past, the admiral chose Capt. Max Duncan to run the submarine base at Pearl Harbor. The former torpedo and gunnery officer in the original *Barb* was younger than others standing in line for promotion. But Fluckey was unfazed. "Gene was unusual in that he stayed in touch with officers and some of the crew members of the first *Barb,*" explained Everett "Tuck" Weaver, former officer on the old diesel boat. "He later told me that in a session on management techniques he was criticized by his peers for giving preferential treatment in the selection of persons for jobs to individuals who had worked for or with him in the past. Gene's position was that they were proven commodities, and there would be no unpleasant surprises."

Fluckey had long assumed that Vice Admiral Clarey, former skipper of the USS *Pintado* (SS-387) during World War II, was a friend and mentor who would help him become vice admiral when the time came. However, Clarey was a complex individual who tended to denigrate accomplishments of others. Rear Adm. Corwin Mendenhall, the former ensign in the USS *Sculpin* (SS-191), which had been in the thick of combat in the Southwest Pacific in the first year of World War II, was on the receiving end of Clarey's biting sarcasm when he met Clarey at the Navy's shipbuilding yard in Kittery, Maine, in 1943. Clarey had graduated from executive officer of the USS *Amberjack* (SS-219) to skipper of the newly launched *Pintado.* Mendenhall was his exec. "He somehow learned that I had been regimental commander at the Naval Academy and proceeded to make some cutting remarks to me about my position at the school," recalled Mendenhall in a memoir published in 1991. "He had his ego, could be temperamental, secretive, and hard for me to understand; and he had a sharp tongue, lashing out at inconsequential things. . . . As time went on, when a *Pintado* problem came up like one we had solved in *Sculpin*, I would offer the *Sculpin* solution. Chick would summarily dismiss the suggestions with disparaging remarks about *Sculpin* and her captain and exec. This was very unkind treatment, particularly in the presence of others, so thereafter I tried to keep *Sculpin* out of my vocabulary."

Similarly, Fluckey's pride in the original *Barb* drew Clarey's scorn whenever the rear admiral was not around. One day in Pearl Harbor the vice admiral was walking down a dock with an associate, not realizing Gene was trailing behind. He overhead Clarey say that he was sick and tired of hearing about the *Barb,* that he hoped never to hear about that boat again. "This totally surprised Gene," recalled "Tuck" Weaver. Fluckey hoped the remark would not have repercussions for his career. But there were hints. Said Duncan of those years in Pearl Harbor, "Anything Gene wanted to change was something Chick had put in place. Gene couldn't win."

In taking charge of the nuclear attack boats, the SSNs, Fluckey was unlike many predecessors in the way he met his responsibilities, even at great personal risk. Such was the case when he flew from Pearl Harbor to a Pacific Missile Range ship that was working with the *Plunger* to test the performance of the Navy's experimental SubRoc missile, a nuclear-tipped missile designed to be launched from a torpedo tube of a nuclear submarine.

From the test range ship, Fluckey and his entourage were lowered in a long boat for the crossing in heavy seas to the *Plunger.* Twenty-foot rollers prevented them from coming alongside, however. "I called over a megaphone to the submarine: 'If we swim over, can you pick us up?'" the rear admiral later recounted. "They manned the sail bridge with lines and one at a time we swam over and they picked us up."

Two days later, after the tests had been completed, Fluckey and his staff needed to get back to the mother ship. However, seas were still rough and again the long boat couldn't get near enough to the submarine to take on its passengers. Not to be dissuaded, the admiral got on the phone to the pilot of a helicopter hovering overhead. The group would dive into the ocean, where the aircraft would dangle a line to pick them up one at a time.

"I was the first one and I swam out about a hundred yards," recalled the fifty-one-year-old commander.

> I am a good swimmer so I was sure I could either survive or get back on board the submarine. I did have a life jacket on, but what I hadn't

appreciated was that when the helicopter came to pick me up, and he
dropped this horse collar down in the water, the high waves were beating it up and down and I couldn't find it with all the spray around. So
the pilot could see my dilemma and he dragged it back and forth until
it finally got near me. I put myself in the horse collar and got my arms
around it. I gave him the "up" signal.

He took off because he was endangered by the heavy waves. He was
about 150 feet in the air and I was swinging like a pendulum. I was winding and unwinding and watching this cord above me . . . and wondering, "If this ever lets go while I'm up here, this is going to be the highest
dive I ever made in my life."

The admiral made it safely to the ship, as did his staff.

To young submarine officers, the *Plunger* story contributed to the legend
of Gene Fluckey, the "Galloping Ghost of the China Coast." His reputation
for valor and ingenuity preceded him wherever he went. Many young officers looked on him with great reverence, having studied his war patrols in
classes at the academy. R. Michael Henzi, class of 1966, was one of them.

"I was attached to SubPac during my first class cruise in the summer of
1965," he recalled.

The middies were invited to a cocktail party a couple days after arrival
in Pearl Harbor. Our uniform was tropical whites, which consisted of
white shoes, white trousers, and a short-sleeved white shirt adorned
with shoulder boards. Admiral Fluckey arrived a bit late from some
other event at which the uniform was dress whites. His uniform was
white shoes, white trousers, and the high-necked white tunic. The tunic
was adorned with gold uniform buttons and gold admiral's shoulder
boards. He wore only two decorations: gold submariner's dolphins
and a pale blue ribbon around his neck, from which was suspended
the Medal of Honor. When he walked into the room, every one of
us gasped. This sight was nicely set off by his flaming red hair. We all
knew about the admiral and his World War II exploits beforehand, but
nothing could prepare us for the actual sight of this legitimate hero all
decked out in gleaming white, shining gold, pale blue, and that one
incredible medal.

Two weeks later Henzi was at the Pearl Harbor officers' club when he
noticed Fluckey in the pool with his granddaughter Gail, who had flown in
from Maryland for a visit. "The admiral was trying to teach his small granddaughter how to swim. I overheard him say to the little girl, 'No, no. You

have to make yourself *positively* buoyant.' The instruction was spoken like a true submariner."

The rear admiral's motto in his two-year command was "Think Deep." He broadcast it everywhere he went. At the launch of the Polaris submarine *Mariano G. Vallejo* (USBN-658) on 23 October 1965 at the Mare Island naval shipyard in California, the commander referred to it in a welcoming address to the boat's officers and crew. "The noblest thing that you and your life-giving crew can do is to serve the cause of freedom well. You will come to understand our submarine force motto: 'Think Deep.' Your deployment arena will be some 80 million square miles of ocean. Your survivability is assured, for no enemy can afford the size force, or even man such a force, to find you, as you intelligently rove the lonely dark abyss of the ocean in deepest secrecy."

It was this certainty of invulnerability that convinced Fluckey nuclear war between the superpowers was improbable. In an address in San Diego to three hundred Navy League guests at a submarine anniversary celebration in June 1966, he minced no words. "I have no fear of a direct confrontation with the Russians. We will have no full-blown nuclear war because there will always be the avenging angel, *Polaris.*"

The growing war in Vietnam, however, was another matter. He warned that communism was on the move in Southeast Asia. Referring to demonstrations against President Lyndon Johnson because of a peacetime draft and continuing buildup of U.S. military forces in South Vietnam, he listed the consequences of a pullout. Thousands of South Vietnamese would be massacred. Communist aggression would spread throughout the world, weakening smaller nations no longer trusting American promises. A "pincer" move would be made against India and Pakistan. Finally, "China would become the colossus of the East. The few remaining democracies would soon have their backs to the wall against this preponderance of the earth's population and raw material. We would be fighting for our very survival." He added, "I would like to know where the people who want us to withdraw would like us to dig in our new position—the Tijuana border? Vancouver? Niagara Falls?"

Fluckey drew a standing ovation.

Back in Hawaii, Admiral and Mrs. Fluckey attended a submarine officers' ball at the Kahala Hilton. The sub base and much of Hawaii awaited the arrival of the latest boomer, the USS *Kamehameha* (SSBN-642), named for Hawaii's most famous native king. Admiral Fluckey was relinquishing command the following morning to return to Washington. He and his wife entertained VIPs at a cocktail party in the presidential suite to say aloha to the many friends they had made. The suite was jammed to capacity with admirals, generals, colonels, captains, and civilians. Said one officer of the crush of well-wishers, "It looks a little like a submarine." Even the elevator was stuffed to capacity. Rear Adm. E. Alvey Wright, commanding officer of the shipyard, joked on the way up, "There's some pitch and yaw here!"

After returning to D.C., Gene Fluckey became director of naval intelligence for two years at a time when the Vietnam War was becoming a political quagmire and civil unrest was spreading at home. The admiral, the Navy's ultimate Cold Warrior, despised what he called "hippies, kooks, and peaceniks heavily aided, abetted, and tainted by the Communists." When they demonstrated outside the Pentagon in the fall of 1967, he waded into their midst to argue his point of view to no avail. "I went home and washed my dogs. Incidentally, while I was there, two of the hippies got married in a bathtub—it was a double ring ceremony," he later quipped in addressing the naval Reserve Intelligence Division in Atlanta, Georgia.

In that speech, Fluckey discussed the worldwide threat that Soviet naval power represented. "The Soviet naval war game is now a global fact of life. Wherever there is a demonstrably strategic sphere, wherever there is an obvious tactical area and another nation's reason for being there, there also is the Soviet navy." Fluckey drew particular attention to Russian operations in the Mediterranean Sea. "In the past four years Soviet operations in the Mediterranean grew from sporadic and seasonal small-scale appearances to the continuous presence of some thirty-five to forty naval ships in recent months. This force now generally comprises four to six submarines, some fourteen surface combatant ships, and a dozen or so auxiliaries and support ships. . . . This naval strength has taken on the appearance of permanence. You no doubt have read of their increasing visits to certain Arab ports as well as their constant attempts to shadow or harass units of the Sixth Fleet."

The cutting edge between East and West did appear to be the Mediterranean. For Gene Fluckey, that represented opportunity. He still sought to move up to vice admiral. The way seemed clear to do just that—by returning to Portugal as the first commander of NATO's expanded Iberian area Atlantic operations. But there was hidden risk for him as a target for assassination.

Sintra

Developments in Europe and the Mediterranean were ominous when Admiral and Mrs. Fluckey arrived in Portugal in 1968 after an absence of fourteen years. Mobile atomic missiles had been deployed in East and West Germany in an "I-dare-you" standoff between the Warsaw Pact and NATO. Soviet, Polish, East German, Bulgarian, and Hungarian troops had invaded Czechoslovakia to put down a separatist movement, and the Russian buildup of naval forces in the Mediterranean continued. The threat of a possible nuclear showdown between East and West seemed to be intensifying. NATO, reeling, issued a warning. "Clearly any Soviet intervention directly or indirectly affecting the situation in Europe or in the Mediterranean would create an international crisis with grave consequences," announced alliance Secretary General Manlio Brosio of Italy.

Part of NATO's response to all these events was to initiate a separate, consolidated command called IBERLANT to guard the strategic Strait of Gibraltar and important Atlantic shipping lanes running north and south along the Iberian Peninsula and North Africa. Admiral Fluckey's objective was to unify British, Portuguese, and American forces in an oblong box extending from Portugal's northern border five hundred miles west into the Atlantic Ocean, then south to the Tropic of Cancer—410,000 square miles of ocean. Through this sector passed most of Western Europe's oil supply as well as commodities from South America, Africa, and Mediterranean nations. Washington-based newspaper columnist Holmes Alexander described the importance of the admiral's mission after a visit to Portugal. "The Soviet and the Warsaw Pact nations have us out-manned along most of the land-borders, have us outgunned in intercontinental missiles and have us checkmated with a politico-military maritime crunch inside the Mediterranean basin. But just west of Gibraltar, where the Atlantic begins, it's still anybody's ball game." In response to questioning by Alexander, Fluckey replied, "There's been a change in NATO thinking. It was oriented toward the Iron Curtain but now it's swinging to the South Atlantic."

The most overt sign of this was Portugal's decision to build and pay for a sprawling, two-story NATO headquarters to house Fluckey's command on the site of abandoned eighteenth-century Fort Gomes Freire, situated on a rocky prominence overlooking the Tagus River southwest of Lisbon near the river's confluence with the Atlantic. The headquarters was to be Portugal's contribution to NATO, and would include a cobweb of subterranean intelligence bunkers. In the meantime, a temporary operations center with a skeletal staff of fifteen Portuguese, British, and American officers had been established within a leased walled villa in Sintra, a storied borough twelve miles west of Lisbon on the Atlantic Ocean.

NATO could not have found a more beautiful setting than Sintra, a mountainous dreamscape of fairytale castles, sky-blue lakes where black swans cavort, spectacular palaces and villas, incredible gardens, precipitous roads and lookouts, swirling mists, thick forests, and foliage, flowers and fauna of infinite variety long celebrated by poets and writers. Over the centuries a parade of conquerors—Romans, Spaniards, Moors, Lusitanians, and even a Norwegian king—had imbued Sintra with exotic architecture and art from Europe, Egypt, North Africa, and the Orient. Five extravagant palaces, a Moorish castle, and a peculiar monastery made entirely from cork and stone dominate the mountaintops. Flourishes of Italian glassware, Chinese screens, Austrian porcelain, marble fountains, blue Moorish tiles, and Gothic archways add to the enchantment.

The Fluckeys had discovered the beauty and gracious living of Sintra years earlier when Gene was naval attaché in Lisbon. To be back, to be in Sintra and standing in line to become a three-star vice admiral at the commissioning of COMIBERLANT's new headquarters would be a perfect capstone to his career—or so it seemed to Gene Fluckey at the time.

In Lisbon the Fluckeys were at the top of the social order and had renewed many friendships. They purchased a quinta (pronounced "queen ta")—a small farmette—on the drier southwestern face of the Sintra Mountains just below Pena Palace, a lavish medieval castle governing the crest. The quinta with its gardens and woods was owned by a widow who had fallen on tough times and couldn't keep up with maintenance. The domicile was remote despite its location near the castle, a popular tourist attraction. With help from local craftsmen, Gene envisioned restoring the estate to its former glory.

"That place was the love of his life, if that's possible with houses," said daughter Barbara.

> He loved views, and when there wasn't a cloud over the mountain, you could see all the way to the Ponte Salazar [the 25th of April suspension bridge] in Lisbon.
>
> Dad remodeled [the quinta] and tried to do it to American standards. He employed a retired stonemason and he tapped away each day, fitting the broken marble slabs Dad bought from a quarry at the bottom of the mountain, making gorgeous flagstone-type marble terraces and paths into the woods and other areas of the quinta. It was stunning. It was built on a series of marbled terraces where gardens of flowers grew. The house had a grand entrance hall, which led into a huge dining room and on to the living room, which had a rounded terrace overlooking "the view." Both rooms were on the right, and on the left was a chapel Dad converted to a bathroom for that floor. A huge

butler's pantry and kitchen finished it off. The lower level was a garage, maids quarters, storage, utilities, etc.

On the left of the entry was an enormous wide stairway with a major landing, where he put a large hi-fi, and then another stairway to a big landing that was his office. From that landing the size of a regular living room, there were the entrances to four bedrooms and marble baths. One room was used as Mom's sewing and crafts room. As the master bedroom was over the living room, it shared the same view toward Lisbon.

Mom had the most gorgeous custom Arioles carpets made up for the stairway, the hall, the landings, the living room, and the bedrooms, except she had a large white India tree of life carpet in the master bedroom. The hall and landings and stairs had the same spectacular pattern, navy blue gold, with Crusaders' crosses as the pattern.

To reach the house required driving up a steep cobblestone road, where the quinta was entered through two wrought-iron electric gates flanked by tall posts, each supporting a large dolphin, emblematic of the undersea service.

The setting was ideal for Mrs. Fluckey. Portugal's gorgeous scenery, mild climate, and sunny days proved to be the perfect tonic for Marjorie's fragile health. She loved the quinta, and she and her husband were determined to enjoy the good life there as long as possible.

Admiral Fluckey immersed himself in his role as NATO chief with customary energy. Strategic planning, conferences worldwide, and a social life in Portugal and Europe that didn't quit occupied him. Among his friendships was a warm bond with Portugal dictator Antonio de Oliveira Salazar, a lawyer and economist who had controlled the country since 1932. Salazar often confided that the dictatorship was necessary because he didn't trust the Portuguese to make good decisions. He alone controlled the police, the military, labor unions, banks, and schools. Citizens had no political freedom. Newspapers, books, and art were censored, and any negative comment about the government was forbidden. Salazar secured his reign with a secret police service that numbered more than twenty thousand, making dissidence very difficult. He kept his country largely isolated from the rest of Europe and rejected technological advances that might have made life easier for impoverished citizens.

What the Fluckeys saw, however, was a nation virtually crime free, orderly, with a climate and lifestyle—if you had the money—that was intoxicating. Salazar, whom the admiral had known since the early 1950s, was an unflinching NATO supporter, Portugal being one of the founders of the alliance. The dictator had agreed not only to cede land for the new IBER-LANT headquarters, but had underwritten the cost of building it.

Of course, Admiral Fluckey's consuming concern as commander was putting together a strategy to stymie the dreaded Soviet Union; Portugal's internal affairs were not his concern. But they soon would have an impact.

The nation seethed with unrest because of Salazar's determination to hold on to Portuguese colonies in Africa. More than a hundred thousand young men had been drafted and sent to Angola, Mozambique, and Guinea-Bissau, where thousands were killed or injured in a vain attempt to stifle rebellions.

In some ways Fluckey could empathize with Salazar's situation. He saw the parallel at home in the United States, where drafting of college-age students to fight in Vietnam was causing turmoil. Protests against the administration of Richard Nixon appalled the admiral, who viewed the president as the "sharpest guy I ever briefed" when he was naval intelligence chief. Fluckey, like many in the American military, thought of the war in Vietnam as the latest front in an ongoing struggle by democracies against Soviet-inspired international communism. In the ultra-right-wing culture of Lisbon in the late 1960s, President Nixon was highly praised for his conduct of the war and foreign policy. Lisbon newspapers regularly pilloried Democrats for criticism of the president. In 1969, when Senator Ted Kennedy left the scene of a fatal car accident in Chappaquiddick in New England, it got front-page treatment in Lisbon. Observed columnist Alexander at the time of his visit, "The Portuguese gloat when anything goes wrong with Democratic politicians. It was under Democratic Presidents that the U.S. started its policy of heckling the Portuguese for being imperialists and racist."

Many in Portugal assumed the fascist political climate in Lisbon would change after Salazar suffered a major stroke. He lingered for nearly two years before succumbing in 1970. Admiral Fluckey was one of his pall bearers. Salazar's long-time cohort, Lisbon University rector Marcelo Caetano, followed him and pledged to lead the country to more civil freedoms. However, he remained conflicted by the African question and was unable to change course. Many more young men were sent off to their deaths in Africa as families of would-be draftees emigrated from Portugal rather than risk conscription. An opposition movement existed, but because of the extensive secret police apparatus, it could not exert itself. But it would find a way.

Though Fluckey had been looking forward to a promotion with the commissioning of IBERLANT, news arrived in the spring of 1971 from Vice

Adm. Dick H. Guinn, chief of naval personnel, that Gene would be relieved *before* the commissioning. Having brought IBERLANT nearly to fruition, the rear admiral thought the decision was unfair. In an impassioned reply to Guinn, he argued for a delay until IBERLANT was operational. "If one wants action here, one needs connections otherwise you cry in a bureaucratic wilderness," he wrote of hurdles yet to overcome. "Certainly a few of the staff Portuguese can help, but they never reach above their level or move off the bureaucratic track. They and others laughed when I said we'd have IBERLANT fully underway in October 1971—the Portuguese because of Bureaucratic mire—others because no NATO project was ever built on schedule. Dick, we'll be underway if our U.S. personnel are on board. . . . I frankly believe I can cajole, wheedle, and influence the Portuguese military more, in the interests of NATO and the United States, than anyone I know."

Two weeks later Guinn relented, postponing Fluckey's relief until the summer of the following year.

Just as predicted, there were significant obstacles to be overcome as the new headquarters took shape. Sufficient numbers of adequately trained personnel were an early impediment. Contractors hired by Portugal to build the headquarters were under no time constraints to meet deadlines. Fluckey had to constantly remind them of the cost of inflation and the need to get the facility up and running. But still there was foot dragging. Finally, to force the contractor to speed up, Fluckey ordered his command to occupy the building in late September and set a 29 October 1971 date for commissioning as work continued.

It had the desired effect. The labor force in the building tripled. The rush to completion, however, had unwitting consequences. Among painters hired to detail the building were two men opposed to the Caetano regime. They had smuggled in large tins disguised as paint cans, each packed with explosives and timing mechanisms. The canisters were positioned just outside Fluckey's office. Additional explosives were planted at a receiver station at Fonte da Telha, about fifty miles from the headquarters. The terrorists intended to make a statement by killing the rear admiral, wrecking the NATO command center, and taking out the communications receiver on the eve of the commissioning.

The painters took an early dinner, telling guards they would be back to finish up. They never returned. Fortunately the timers did not go off until the rear admiral and his staff had left the building. Multiple blasts erupted after midnight, demolishing interior corridors, blowing out doors and windows, and destroying communication equipment below ground as well as the distant receiving tower. However, no one was injured or killed. The headquarters was largely vacant, patrolled by a few military guards.

Admiral Fluckey got the call at home and quickly returned, stunned that such an attack could occur in a country where it was unheard of. Rumors quickly spread that it was the work of Communists, perhaps with the support of Jesuit priests opposed to the African wars. After surveying the damage, Fluckey decided the commissioning could go on as planned after a Herculean cleanup. Using every available resource, Fluckey organized an all-night debris removal. Chunks of concrete, twisted metal, glass shards, and wiring were removed bit by bit from the headquarters. Shattered windows throughout the compound were completely removed. Since the commissioning ceremony would be staged outside away from the building on a clear morning, Fluckey hoped that from the distance the windowless frames might look like they had glass.

At daybreak the rear admiral sent an urgent dispatch to Jose de Sa Viana Rebelo, the Portuguese defense minister, to urge him not to cancel the ceremony. "As you know, the above ground administrative facility of the IBERLANT Headquarters received extensive damage from a bomb placed in the open portico," Fluckey wrote. "Though we deeply regret such a happening, I urge you to accept our recommendation that the Commissioning Ceremony continue as planned." Rebelo agreed.

Right on schedule at 0900 of 29 October—less than forty-eight hours after the attack—Portuguese Admiral Americo Tomaz, president of the country, commissioned the $6.5 million headquarters and conveyed it formally to Rear Admiral Fluckey and NATO. Among the dignitaries in attendance were NATO Secretary General Dr. Joseph Luns, Supreme Allied Commander Atlantic Charles K. Duncan of the United States, and West German Air Force General J. Steinhoff, chairman of the NATO military committee. Also attending were NATO chiefs of staffs from Belgium, Canada, Denmark, Germany, Greece, Italy, Luxembourg, the Netherlands, Norway, Turkey, the United Kingdom, the United States, and Portugal, as well as a French military liaison. Admiral Fluckey addressed the assemblage, outlining the significance of the new headquarters as a key defensive initiative to "the Russian wolf that passes ever closer to our door."

Guests marveled at the clean lines of the administrative headquarters and commented on how "spotless" the windows were. The international press made no mention of the bombing. But the blast set back operations for months. The receiver station had been so crippled that it would not be completed until the fall of 1972 at the earliest, according to an assessment prepared by Fluckey in March 1972. Portugal and NATO hushed up any references to the attack. The results of an investigation were never disclosed. And those within NATO who knew some details henceforth would only refer to the incident as "The Bomb." All the Portuguese public and the world at large knew was that IBERLANT's new headquarters opened on schedule and was fully operational—just as Admiral Fluckey had intended.

By March 1972 the headquarters reached its optimum staffing of 41 officers, 159 enlisted personnel, and 6 civilians drawn from the United States, Great Britain, and Portugal. In addition, a French liaison officer, a German naval officer, and a Danish civilian were posted at the headquarters, as well as a variety of Portuguese civilians employed as draftsmen, translators, printers, switchboard operators, and maintenance workers.

The long hours and challenges of bringing IBERLANT to fruition were now over for Gene Fluckey. Why he wasn't promoted to vice admiral was left to conjecture. Those who had followed his illustrious career were aware of a schism in the Navy leadership between those who much admired the "Galloping Ghost" and those who disparaged him. "There were pro and con Fluckey factions in the Navy," said Capt. Max Duncan, who had served with him in the *Barb* and in the admiral's Pacific submarine command. "I was tempted to ask a couple of very senior officers that I knew well about it but never did. Some of it may have been his friendly approach to everyone, officer and enlisted. In earlier times I didn't notice it; informality is usual in submarines. Submarine discipline is strong but informal. Not so in large commands. I know that from having command of a tender with 1,000 plus, a [Pearl Harbor] base with 2,500 plus, and naval Support Activity Saigon with 5,000. I know deep down he just liked people and very seldom had negative comments about anyone."

Former Navy Lt. (j.g.) Fred Sill, who served under Fluckey in Solant Amity II, said jealousy may have played a role. "My guess is that it started the very moment he became the youngest admiral in the Navy. He may well have leapfrogged over others, which always upsets some colleagues. And his youthful enthusiasm for everything he did could well have been considered unbecoming by his peers. The 'familiarity breeds contempt' concept had been ingrained into my officer's training, and I often felt that [Gene's] easygoing attitude with the enlisted personnel was going a bit too far. But that's the way he was. I think that it was he who led the conga line around the *Spiegel Grove* one evening during a shipboard reception in South Africa."

Vice Admiral Guinn reminded Admiral Fluckey in the spring of 1971 that he would have approximately one year of possible service remaining after IBERLANT was in full operation. "I am sure you can appreciate the difficulty of trying to arrange a meaningful one year assignment for you," Guinn wrote. "It would therefore be very helpful if we could have some indication as to your personal plans and/or desires at that time."

Fluckey and his wife discussed their options and ultimately decided to retire and stay in Portugal. They enjoyed their home, their Sintra neighbors, and the many friends they had made in Portugal and Europe. They had enough money to live comfortably and travel at will, including trips home to the United States.

On his last day at IBERLANT in August 1972, Fluckey studied the view from the window of his second-floor office. He could see the white dot on the distant mountain, the one just below Pena Palace. It was a clear view of home. The admiral's view of his career, his capabilities, and his goals had always been one of clarity. Life had been good. Physically he and his wife had triumphed over major impediments—Marjorie had successfully battled cancer and survived a lifelong battle with diabetes, and Gene had reversed severe nearsightedness to remain in the academy, become an ensign, and evolve into the most formidable submarine captain of the Pacific War. His leadership traits were nurtured by Admiral Nimitz when Fluckey was his aide, traits that stuck with him and enlarged their friendship. "The part of [Nimitz's] character I have absorbed has certainly made me a more effective and tolerant leader, so long as high standards are maintained," he would reflect years later in an interview. Fluckey was among the last to see the admiral at a hospital in San Francisco before his death on 20 February 1966 from complications following a stroke. The rear admiral visited with the Nimitzes at their home on Treasure Island in San Francisco Bay whenever he was in the area on Navy business. "The doctors would not permit me to see him in the hospital, and I said, 'You'd better tell him I'm here, because I think he might want me to cheer him up.' With these doctors he immediately said, 'I don't care whether I'm dying or not, come on in,' and he started telling me stories again. A great man has passed on."

Above all, Gene Fluckey stubbornly clung to the one mantra that had carried him through life, handed down to him as a teenager in the static of a distant radio broadcast by President Calvin Coolidge. It was a credo for a purposeful life that the Boy Scout, the midshipman, the submarine captain, the naval attaché, the sub fleet commander, the naval intelligence chief, and the commander of IBERLANT came to repeat throughout his life in tough times that sometimes became tougher: "We don't have problems, just solutions."

Epilogue

A life is like a ship afloat;
Image and status not withstanding,
Some will venture far, some just hug the coast.

Some, burdened with self, merely fill a void.
Others with goals to pursue, will flee all bonds
Of season or state of sea, their missions to fulfill.

At times, out of reach, but always in touch,
Forging ahead with imagination and vision afar,
With many a high tide, each achievement to mark;
Each risk, each goal to be shared.

With time, a bit threadbare, yet still enduring;
And by word and deed,
Creating a memory, knowing no age.

A life replete with glory, rare companionship and grace.

*—Cdr. David Teeters's Ode to Gene Fluckey,
written on the occasion of his selection as
Distinguished Graduate, United States
Naval Academy, 2003*

In His Light

Gene and Marjorie Fluckey devoted themselves to the care of orphans in Portugal upon retirement. The couple provided clothing, food, and other needs to the Catholic orphanage of Escola Santa Isabela, as did their daughter Barbara and her family, who sent regular shipments of clothing. Meanwhile, Gene stayed active in all things Navy.

10 July 1972—"I can still see the Barb *approaching"*
SINTRA, Portugal—Neville Thams of Australia today visited Gene and Marjorie at their quinta. Thams, among Australian and British prisoners rescued by the *Barb* while adrift in the South China Sea in 1944, expressed his thanks, noting, "I can still see very clearly the *Barb* approaching us . . . the rope to pull us on board . . . and the crew who watched over us . . . answering the frequent calls for water and with great patience attending to our needs."

15 October 1972—Sold for scrap
WASHINGTON, D.C.—The U.S. Navy announced today it had sold the *Barb* for scrap metal, raising $100,000. The boat, loaned to Italy after the war, had outlived its usefulness and was returned to the Navy. Admiral Fluckey said that had he and his shipmates known the *Barb* was headed to the scrap heap, they would have raised enough money to spare it and convert it into a museum submarine.

25 April 1974—Revolution of the Carnations
LISBON, Portugal—Soldiers aligned with Major Otelo Saraiva de Carvalho today seized control of the Portuguese government. Without opposition, troops occupied key intersections, bridges, and government buildings all over Lisbon and Portugal. Jubilant citizens swarmed the streets and put red carnations into the barrels of the soldiers' rifles. The new government decreed that all Portuguese colonies in Africa would be set free immediately.

26 February 1978—River Kwai
SYDNEY, Australia—American author Clay Blair Jr. arrived here today to interview former Japanese POWs for his book, *Return from the River Kwai.* POW Charlie Madden described for Blair the approach of Gene Fluckey and his submarine in the South China Sea: "It was the sound of an engine and we looked up at the sky. But there was nothing there and there still was the sound of the engine. It was coming from below us and we all thought

we had gone mad. Then beside us popped up this submarine. It was the USS *Barb*. The seas were getting up and we were the last ones to be rescued. We were lucky, as we had had no food or water for five days and were just about done."

17 August 1979—Passing of Marjorie Fluckey

CROFTON, Maryland—Marjorie Fluckey died today at the home of her daughter after battling cancer for more than a decade. The second recurrence of the disease was diagnosed after she arrived in Portugal, where her husband took over NATO's Iberian command. She returned to Bethesda (Maryland) Naval Hospital in the United States for massive radiation treatments. After a long period of quarantine, the doctors discharged her to return home to Sintra. "They thought she would die. But she fooled them," recalled her daughter Barbara. In 1972 she returned to the hospital for a checkup, where the doctors called her a "miracle."

Unfortunately, the cancer returned a few years later, getting progressively worse until 1976, when she mysteriously regained a long-term burst of energy. For more than two years she and her husband traveled extensively. "They traveled to Russia, down the Danube, and to other places," explained her daughter.

In January 1979 the disease took an aggressive turn. The Fluckeys moved into their daughter's home in Crofton, where they stayed until Marjorie's death in August. "My father rarely left her side," said his daughter.

Mrs. Fluckey's body was cremated. Her husband flew back to Portugal with most of her ashes and spread them in the gardens she so loved at their quinta and also on the grounds of the orphanage. The Naval Academy class of 1935 made a donation to the orphanage in her name.

20 August 1980—"Plucky Fluckey"

ISLE OF MANN, England—Gene Fluckey today married Eleanor Margaret Wallace. Nine months after his wife's death, the admiral met her at a luncheon arranged by her sister, who lived in Sintra. Margaret, a British subject with homes in Wales and the Isle of Mann, was going through a difficult divorce from prominent English civil engineer James McAlpine. With a penchant for sports cars, she embraced life as much as Gene. After their marriage, Margaret arranged for the admiral to meet two friends for lunch. She introduced her husband as "Eugene Fluckey." He added, "You won't forget my name, will you, as in lucky Fluckey?" And they sang in chorus to the admiral, "And she's plucky Fluckey." The newlyweds honeymooned by touring France's Bordeaux region by hot-air balloon.

Summer 1981—Homecoming

ANNAPOLIS, Maryland—Gene and Margaret Fluckey sold their homes in Portugal and on the Isle of Mann and relocated to a home near the Naval Academy. Both began a close relationship with the academy and the Brigade of Midshipmen.

13 November 1981—Gathering of heroes

PEARL HARBOR, Hawaii—Admiral Fluckey was among more than two hundred Medal of Honor winners gathered today at the submarine base in Pearl Harbor for a Medal of Honor Society convention. Four surviving World War II sub skippers were in attendance—Vice Adm. Lawson P. Ramage (USS *Parche*), Rear Adm. Richard H. O'Kane (USS *Tang*), Capt. George L. Street III (USS *Tirante*), and Gene Fluckey.

October 1983—Nimitz and Togo

TOKYO, Japan—The city's Togo Shrine was closed to tourists for a banquet in honor of Gene and Margaret Fluckey. Japanese officers and crewmen who had served in *Kurashio,* the former U.S. submarine *Mingo* (SS-261) loaned to the Japanese navy in 1955, hosted the event. Fluckey had trained the first Japanese crew to sail the sub.

During a pre-banquet tour of the shrine, the Fluckeys noticed many photographs of Admiral Nimitz. Fluckey was stunned, asking his Japanese escorts, "Why photos of Nimitz?"

"He did so much for Admiral Togo," explained a Japanese officer. "During our conflict he ordered that no Allied bombing was permitted to target the battleship *Mikasa,* Togo's flagship, when he sank the Czar's Baltic Fleet at the Battle of Tsushima Strait [in 1905]. After our surrender he had the mooring cemented between the piers so she can never sink. Furthermore he dedicated all his profits from his book *The Great Sea War* to the rebuilding of the Togo Shrine."

12 December 1983—Ronald Reagan

NEW YORK, New York—Admiral Fluckey today attended a special luncheon to honor President Ronald Reagan, who received the Patriots Award from two hundred surviving members of the Medal of Honor Society.

29 August 1986—Reunion

BALTIMORE, Maryland—Officers and enlisted men of the original *Barb* reunited for the first time since the launch and commissioning of the atomic attack sub *Barb*. Forty-three crewmen plus Admiral Fluckey, Adm.

Robert McNitt, Tuck Weaver, Capt. Max Duncan, and Reserve Cdr. Dave Teeters attended. All had been very successful in life. Admiral McNitt had served as commander of NATO submarines in the Mediterranean, superintendent of the Naval Postgraduate School, and director of the Navy Management Systems Center at Monterey, California. Upon retirement in 1972, he became senior professor and dean of admissions at the Naval Academy. Weaver became a business executive who traveled internationally and was the first *Barb* veteran to visit Australian Neville Thams, the POW rescued by the submarine in 1944. Max Duncan spent twenty-three years in subs commanding two submarines, a division, a tender, a base, and a squadron. He capped his career as commander of Naval Support Activity Saigon in 1968 and 1969. Dave Teeters, after the war, continued a very active career in the Naval Reserve, received his Ph.D. in physics from the University of California at Berkeley, was involved in the development of the touch-tone telephone at Bell Telephone, and eventually retired as professor of physics at Monmouth University of New Jersey. Also attending was Chief Gunners Mate Paul "Swish" Saunders, who was the *Barb*'s chief of the boat and one of the most decorated enlisted submariners in the Navy. Many crewmen graduated from college on the GI Bill and became successful in business and in various professions and governmental posts.

10 March 1989—Deactivated
SAN DIEGO, California—The USS *Barb* (SSN-596) was decommissioned today. Like the original *Barb*'s rescue of prisoners of war, the atomic attack sub saved four crewmen of a B-52 bomber that crashed off the coast of Guam on 10 July 1972. In waves cresting forty feet, *Barb* officers and crew located two rafts carrying survivors. Because of seventy-knot winds and an inability to come alongside the rafts as the sub rolled forty degrees, Chief Torpedoman Jon Hentz dived overboard and swam a line to the first raft. In the swim back, he almost didn't make it. It took a remarkable feat of seamanship for *Barb* crewmen to haul him and the aviators on both rafts to safety.

17 November 1989—Fluckey Hall (Connecticut)
GROTON, Connecticut—Gene Fluckey today addressed enlisted men and officers at the dedication of Fluckey Hall at the Naval Submarine School here. The ninety thousand-square-foot, six-story facility is designed to support advanced combat systems training for submariners into the twenty-first century. The school trains more than sixty thousand students annually. The admiral expressed how proud he was, comparing the sensation to the way his eight-year-old granddaughter Gail Bove felt on learning to swim

on a visit to her grandfather's house in Hawaii in 1965. "At the end of the summer she won the prize in a race swimming on her back while reading a magazine," explained Gene. "A trophy was presented. She asked if it was really gold. I told her no, it was more important than gold for it represented achievement. Her response: 'Granddad, I'm so proud of myself, I can hardly stand me.' "

30 January 1990—"Best part of war"
BRISBANE, Australia—*Barb* torpedoman Don Miller of Pittsburgh, Pennsylvania, arrived today to be reunited with Jack Flynn for the first time in fifty years. Flynn, seventy-two, was captured while fighting in Burma for the British and later was cast adrift on flotsam in the South China Sea. The *Barb* miraculously located Flynn and thirteen other survivors. Recalled Miller, "I'll never forget the Australians for how they looked when we picked them up—thin and with thighs like my wrist—and I'll never forget the Japanese for what they did to them. That's a part of the war I remember the best. That was the best part, getting to save somebody."

5 September 1990—Guests of honor
KISSIMMEE, Florida—It was an emotional reunion today between thirty-eight Barb crewmen and Jack Flynn and his wife Sandy, who arrived from Brisbane as the guests of the veterans. The Flynns were accompanied by Don Miller and his wife.

4 June 1991—Mystery
NAM KWAN HARBOR, China—Gene Fluckey arrived here today to determine whether the *Barb* sank more than a single ship in its daring attack on the port where a twenty-seven-ship Japanese convoy was at anchor. The Chinese government provided a van, a government interpreter, and a cashier to make the overnight drive to Nam Kwan over rock-strewn roads and jagged mountains with hairpin turns. In Nam Kwan, two elderly men who were teenagers when the *Barb* attacked confirmed that four ships were sunk and three damaged.

9 May 1992—Cold Warrior in Red Square
MOSCOW, Russia—Eugene and Margaret Fluckey today marched in the Russian Peace Victory Parade here. They were invited by the Russians to mark the end of the Cold War and the dissolution of the Soviet Union. The parade wound for four miles through Moscow, starting at the Parliament Building and ending in Red Square before the Kremlin. Dressed in uniform with his Medal of Honor suspended by its pale blue ribbon around

his neck, Admiral Fluckey greeted a Russian naval captain en route. Both locked arms in a warm embrace before thousands of cheering spectators.

1992—Next best thing

CLEVELAND, Ohio—Admiral Fluckey was the guest of honor for the rechristening of the USS *Cod* (SS-224) as the USS *Cod* Memorial on the Cleveland waterfront. The *Cod* is the last remaining World War II fleet boat that has not been modified, and it has been restored to its wartime appearance, inside and out. Fluckey marveled that it was "like coming home" to the *Barb*. It was Fluckey, in charge of disposing of decommissioned submarines in the late 1950s, who gave the order to relocate the *Cod* from the Philadelphia Navy Yard to the U.S. Navy Reserve Training Center in Cleveland in 1959.

12 February 1992—Legacy

GROTON, Connecticut—Eugene Fluckey was the surprise guest at a wine and cheese party hosted by the commanding officer of the Naval Submarine Base here. The admiral entertained officers-in-training with his account of the attack on Nam Kwan and the *Barb*'s narrow escape from a chasing frigate. "Fluckey spoke about calling his engineering chief to give him more speed and tie down the governors," recalled Lt. David Ratte. "Strangely, during his narrative, I could not help but think of 'Captain, I'm giving it all I've got!' from Scotty in a fictional *Star Trek* episode and how closely this resembled *Barb*'s real-life heroic escape from the enemy's clutches. That story has never left my mind. We men of today's submarine force salute Admiral Fluckey, the 'Galloping Ghost of the China Coast,' and the never-say-die legacy that heroic submariners of World War II passed to us."

11 December 1992—Sailing with the skipper I

ABOARD THE *DELTA QUEEN*—Seventy-six *Barb* shipmates and their wives joined Admiral and Mrs. Fluckey today for a four-day cruise on the Mississippi River. "Weighing anchor on a paddle wheeler is something my wife, Margaret, and I always planned to do," explained the admiral. "Then, we thought how nice it would be to return something to the men I served with, and hit upon the idea of everybody vacationing on *Delta Queen*." The river boat flew the *Barb*'s final battle flag during what the Fluckeys called "Operation Good Time," completely paid for by royalties from the admiral's book about the *Barb*'s legendary war patrols, *Thunder Below!* During the cruise, the veterans revealed that they had contributed a thousand dollars for a brass plaque permanently attached to the theater seat arm in Arleigh and Roberta Burke Memorial Theater at the United States Navy Memorial in Washington. The plaque reads:

RADM Eugene B. Fluckey USN
CO USS *Barb* (SS 220) WWII
From His Shipmates

31 May 1993—Breakfast with the Clintons

WASHINGTON, D.C.—Admiral Fluckey today was the sole representative for all the veterans of World War II at a Memorial Day ceremony at the White House and Arlington Cemetery. He and his wife enjoyed breakfast with Bill and Hillary Clinton. Gene, a great admirer of Presidents Nixon, Reagan, and the first George Bush, had visited the White House many times to meet with past presidents over security matters. Fluckey praised President Clinton for appointing David Gergen as his White House adviser despite criticism from Democrats. Gergen had advised three previous Republican presidents.

14 October 1993–1 August 1994–Limelight

NEW YORK CITY—Gene Fluckey, eighty, began a whirlwind speaking tour promoting his book before the Yale Club here. Tuck Weaver also attended the dinner, providing a "living witness to some of Admiral Fluckey's 'miracles' of warfare in World War II," as Weaver later put it. Subsequent addresses and lectures were at Old Dominion, Hampden, and Norfolk State universities near Norfolk, Virginia; the National Press Club in Washington; Submarine Group Six in Charleston, South Carolina; the Iwo Jima Survivors Convention in Wichita Falls, Texas; the Naval Academy Dolphin Club in Annapolis; Submarine Atlantic Fleet in Norfolk; the National War College in Washington; the Submarine Veterans of World War II in Ballston, Virginia; the Battleship Park Memorial in Mobile, Alabama; the Basic Submarine School in Groton, Connecticut; and the National Archives in Washington.

26 March 1994—Knighted

KANSAS CITY, Missouri—Rear Admiral and Mrs. Fluckey were inducted today into the Sovereign Military Order of St. John of Jerusalem, Knights of Malta. The order dates back to its founding in 1046 at the Vatican and was active in the Crusades of the Middle Ages. Admiral Sir Gene and Lady Margaret Fluckey are members of one of the world's oldest orders of chivalry, which uses its resources to assist the needy in the name of Christianity.

4 July 1995—Home of heroes

PUEBLO, Colorado—Wearing his Medal of Honor and a baseball cap noting his service as COMIBERLANT in Portugal, Admiral Fluckey flashed the "V" for victory sign popularized in World War II in a ceremony here today honoring sixteen recipients of the medal. Pueblo calls itself "Home of Heroes" because four Medal of Honor winners reside in the city at the eastern foot of the Rocky Mountains.

15 September 1995—Standing ovation
PEARL HARBOR, Hawaii—Gene Fluckey, one of America's most decorated living Americans, today provided introductory remarks for President Bill Clinton at the fiftieth anniversary of the Allied triumph in World War II, the most costly war in world history. The ceremony was held on the USS *Carl Vinson* (CVN 70). When visitors and dignitaries rose to their feet to applaud him, the admiral thanked them for "that standing ovation for my crew."

3 November 1995—Fluckey Hall (Georgia)
KINGS BAY, Georgia—Admiral Fluckey was the guest speaker at the dedication of Fluckey Hall at the Naval Submarine Base here. He quipped, "It puts the onus on me to keep out of trouble for the next twenty-five or more years." In a serious note, he added, "I do hope that those who study here will be imbued with some of the pioneer spirit and determination that made America great and not expect to develop knowledge without some good old-fashioned hard work and sacrifice."

14 May 1996—Sailing with the skipper II
VANCOUVER, British Columbia—Rear Admiral and Mrs. Fluckey, along with *Barb* shipmates and wives, boarded the SS *Nordham* for a seven-day cruise of the inland passage of Alaska, all of it paid for by the Fluckeys. The ship flew the *Barb*'s battle flag during the voyage.

1996—Fluckey Hall (Japan)
YOKUSUKA, Japan—Fluckey Hall, the new headquarters for U.S. Submarine Group Seven, was dedicated at the Yokusaka Naval Base with Admiral Fluckey and his wife in attendance.

18 April 1997—Celebration .
YOKOSUKA, Japan—Gene and Margaret Fluckey were guests of honor at a ball today to mark the ninety-seventh birthday of the submarine navies of Japan and the United States.

Summer 1998—Astronaut Fluckey?
WASHINGTON, D.C.—At a meeting of retired naval officers here, an elderly man approached Admiral Fluckey and said to him, "I made my

first and last ride on a submarine with you in 1944." It was Ohio Senator
John Glenn, the first American to orbit the earth. As a Marine lieutenant,
he was a passenger aboard the *Barb* off Midway during deep submergence
when a packing gland broke loose in the conning tower, thoroughly soaking the pilot. Glenn is in training to ride the Space Shuttle *Discovery* as the
first senior citizen to orbit the earth. With his trademark humor, Admiral
Fluckey asked about going along so scientists could compare a seventy-five-
year-old with an eighty-five-year-old.

1999—Long goodbye
ANNAPOLIS, Maryland—Physicians diagnosed Admiral Fluckey as suffering from Alzheimer's disease, a brain disorder common in older people
and that also afflicts former President Ronald Reagan.

3-4 April 2003—Last reunion
ANNAPOLIS, Maryland—It has been forty years since thirty-five *Barb* crewmen and officers met in Pascagoula, Mississippi, during the commissioning
of the nuclear submarine *Barb*. In the intervening years there had been six
reunions in addition to the *Delta Queen* and Alaska cruises. As shipmates
left for eternal patrol or became physically unable to travel, attendance
dropped a little at each reunion. On this occasion fourteen crewmen and
officers, their wives, and two widows came from all across the country and
met in Annapolis to exchange memories of the glory days and bid a fond
farewell to their beloved skipper. The anecdotes exchanged in many cases
were humorous sidelights that occurred during the serious business of trying to sink an enemy that was attempting to reciprocate. Admiral Fluckey
made his appearance on the second afternoon, and it was the last time most
of the attendees would see their inspirational leader.

April 2003—Message to nuclear sailors
WASHINGTON, D.C.—The *Submarine Review* this month published advice
from Rear Admiral Fluckey to young people who might follow him: "Serve
your country well. Put more into life than you expect to get out of it. Drive
yourself and lead others. Make others feel good about themselves; they will
outperform your expectations, and you will never lack for friends."

21 November 2003—Distinguished graduates
ANNAPOLIS, Maryland—The United States Naval Academy, the Brigade
of Midshipmen, and alumni this evening honored Eugene Fluckey and
Robert W. McNitt. The academy praised both men as Distinguished Grad-

uates before the entire brigade in Alumni Hall. Capt. Max Duncan, who served with both men in the *Barb* and had been a close friend of Gene for fifty-nine years, spoke for "my inspirational skipper." Duncan also honored Admiral McNitt as "the finest open sea navigator of his time," the man who correctly calculated where the sub could find shipwrecked Australian and British prisoners of war afloat in the South China Sea in 1944. Commenting on the skipper afterward, Duncan marveled, "Gene was a man of many different ideas. He used to run them by the bucket-full. All the time. Always pushing to do things differently."

7 December 2004—Gallery
GROTON, Connecticut—The Submarine Force Library and Museum today honored submariners with the opening of a Medal of Honor Gallery. Rear Admiral Fluckey, the only living recipient of the Medal of Honor for submarine service, sent a letter that was read by Neal Sever, the former *Barb* signalman who took part in sabotaging an enemy train in 1945. Sever attended the event with fellow *Barb* veterans Don Miller and John Lehman. In his letter, Admiral Fluckey praised *Barb* crewmen and thanked the sub base for creating a gallery for Navy heroes. "In the fullness of time I will depart on my last patrol. But here in the twilight of my life, please be aware that my gratitude overflows for the recognition here bestowed upon me and my *Barb* shipmates. Think Deep. Eugene Fluckey."

12 November 2005—Honors for two admirals
WASHINGTON, D.C.—The World War II Veterans Committee of the American Studies Group presented The Chester Nimitz Award for Outstanding Service during the war to Admiral Fluckey and Admiral McNitt at the committee's annual meeting at the Capitol Hill Hyatt Regency Hotel tonight. Margaret Fluckey accepted the award for an ailing Admiral Fluckey.

2006—"Standing in his light"
ANNAPOLIS, Maryland—Admiral Fluckey, suffering from severe Alzheimer's, moved permanently into the assisted living quarters at Baywoods retirement center, where he and his wife had been living in Annapolis. Paul Farace, a non-submariner and close friend of the Fluckeys in their latter years, saw him there. He summed up his feelings about the admiral and his wife. "Margaret is the perfect Navy admiral's wife. She knows how to aid him, how to protect him, and now that it is required, how to protect his image and legacy. Better that we should remember a lively, talkative, and vibrant elder warrior than to see a tiny, frail, failing man in his last

days. When the orders come for him to depart on that final, eternal patrol, I know that we will have lost a great man. He is slowly leaving us now. As someone said of those who suffer from Alzheimer's, 'They slowly fade away . . . long before their bodies.'

"I am very grateful that I had a chance to stand in his light and to help him understand that there are lots of us who think that what he and men like him did on our behalf was truly heroic."

Acknowledgments

My biography of Rear Adm. Eugene B. Fluckey came from a desire by his family and *Barb* shipmates to preserve the admiral's legacy. Barbara Bove, his daughter, contributed much to my understanding of her life with her parents, at times baring her soul in answering personal questions. Likewise, I owe much to her daughter, Gail Fritsch, who lent me a carload of boxes containing wartime letters, Navy documents, speeches, notes, and memorabilia collected by her grandfather since the 1920s. They gave me keen insights into all that had happened in his lifetime. Margaret Fluckey, the admiral's second wife, met with me on occasion in Annapolis to add context to his dynamic retirement.

Barb shipmates and those Gene served with after the war contributed their memories and comments via extensive e-mail, telephone, and snail-mail correspondence, as well as personal visits with me to help give a fuller portrait of the Navy's most decorated submarine hero. Among them, several stand out. Tuck Weaver, the *Barb*'s former battle stations officer of the deck, convinced the Naval Institute Press to go forward with this project and provided enthusiastic support and background materials. Capt. Max Duncan, former *Barb* TDC operator, provided constant help in the preparation of this manuscript, chapter by chapter, often helping me steer the course through daily e-mails. Max and his wife Trilby are close personal friends of the Fluckey family, as they have been for fifty years, and are dedicated, as Max put it, "to all things Fluckey." Adm. Robert McNitt, the former *Barb* executive officer, lent encouragement and shared wartime memories with me. Cdr. Dave Teeters, the former *Barb* electronics officer, and his wife Phyllis provided great insight into the *Barb*'s wartime patrols and life at home.

Each of these men—Max Duncan, Tuck Weaver, Robert McNitt, and Dave Teeters—went out of their way to review my manuscript and to keep me from crashing on the shoals of misinterpretation and error.

Other *Barb* veterans who helped were Don Miller, John Lehman, and Neal Sever, who convened a mini boat reunion for my benefit at John and Anne Lehman's home in Chambersburg, Pennsylvania. Max and Trilby Duncan also attended. Max facilitated a follow-up visit with Margaret Fluckey at the admiral's home in Annapolis and helped me peruse additional records and memorabilia belonging to the admiral.

Providing excellent retrospective on Admiral Fluckey's Solant Amity II voyage to Africa was Fred Sill, one of Gene's naval aides during the goodwill tour and now retired in Brazil. I also owe a debt of gratitude to those who provided useful anecdotes about the admiral's post-retirement years: Dick Pohli, Navy Cdr. Edwin V. Rahme Jr., John Fakhan, and Navy Capt. David Ratte. Also, a note of appreciation to Helen Weaver, Tuck's daughter-in-law, who translated numerous newspaper articles for me about Admiral Fluckey that appeared in Portuguese newspapers when he was commander of NATO's IBERLANT.

Reeva Hunter Mandelbaum provided insight into the last reunion of *Barb* veterans attended by Admiral Fluckey in Annapolis in April 2003. Thanks also goes to Gary LaValley, archivist at the Nimitz Library at the Naval Academy, who expeditiously retrieved information I needed, as he has done in the past. Also, a tip of the hat to Barry Zerbe at the National Archives in College Park, Maryland; the Bucks County Free Library system for help in tracking down nonfiction sources on World War II and its aftermath; the David Library of the American Revolution in Washington Crossing, Bucks County; and Carol Bifulco and Jessica Schultheis, production editors for this book. Tom Cutler, my editor at the Naval Institute Press, provided consistent support and, like Admiral Fluckey, believes in the power of persistence in overcoming adversity, signing off on his e-mails, "DGUTS"— "Don't Give Up The Ship."

Finally, deep appreciation and love to my wife Mary Anne and daughter Genevieve. For nearly twenty years, they've shared my adventure with the Silent Service through three nonfiction books. Unlike her many friends, Genevieve understands a "boat" to be a steel vessel that travels beneath the waves. She can vaguely recall trips as a toddler to the World War II museum sub *Becuna* docked in Philadelphia to study its inner mechanisms. Meanwhile, Mary Anne has proven to be my best editor, with a greater understanding of human dynamics than I can ever hope to attain. Many times she pulled me back on track when I veered too far away on some meaningless tangent or drew the wrong conclusions.

Bibliographic Essay

Rear Admiral Fluckey collected thousands of letters, official documents, and photographs over his lifetime and they provided the underpinning for this book. This was augmented by letters, telephone calls, videotapes, and e-mails provided to the author by members of Admiral Fluckey's immediate family, surviving *Barb* officers and men, and acquaintances, many of whom consented to face-to-face interviews. Following are additional sources and observations by the author.

PROLOGUE: THE BOMB: Admiral Fluckey's personal records refer to the bombing of NATO headquarters in Portugal numerous times. However, attempts to obtain more information through NATO sources were unsuccessful. Historical information about Portugal, NATO, and background on the Salazar regime came from Portuguese newspaper clippings and Reg Grant, *NATO* (New York: Franklin Watts, 2001); Ettagale Blauer and Jason Laure, *Portugal* (New York: Scholastic Press, 2002); *NATO Handbook* (Brussels: NATO Office of Information and Press, 1995); and NATO's online library (www.nato.int/docu/comm/49-95/c681115a.htm).

PART ONE: Most of the material for this section came from Fluckey family memorabilia and the admiral's own reflections.

NORTH BEACH: Historical information about North Beach, Maryland, came from www.ci.north-beach.md.us/history.html. Likewise, biographical background on Gene Fluckey's childhood hero, Rear Adm. Adolphus

Staton, came from the Arlington National Cemetery Web site, www. arling toncemetery.net/adlophus.htm. A history of the Boy Scouts of America came from www.troop97.net.

20-20: Historical background on the Naval Academy comes from my previous book, *Slade Cutter: Submarine Warrior* (Annapolis, Md.: Naval Institute Press, 2003). Gene Fluckey's determination to overcome nearsightedness at the academy is drawn from the admiral's personal papers and his magazine article "AYE! The Eyes Have It" (*Shipmate,* July 1994).

OVER AND UNDER: An excellent history of Long Beach in its drive to become a major port came from www.cms.longbeach.gov. As is the case for official information on all naval vessels, past and present, the Naval Historical Center is a treasure trove of information at www.history.navy.mil. Background on war planning and the buildup of the U.S. Fleet in the Pacific is treated in Robert W. Love Jr., *History of the U.S. Navy,* vols. 1 and 2 (Harrisburg, Pa.: Stackpole Books, 1992). The break-in of the Japanese consulate in New York City by the FBI and the Office of Naval Intelligence in 1922 that resulted in the theft of Japan's naval code is detailed in *History of the U.S. Navy* as well. In researching causes and treatment of diabetes in connection with Marjorie Fluckey's long battle with the disease, I found the Joslin Diabetes Center's Web site very useful, at www.joslin.org.

SUBMERSIBLES: My description of sub training comes from Admiral Fluckey's letters to his family and my two previous books, *Slade Cutter* and *Back From The Deep* (Annapolis, Md.: Naval Institute Press, 1994). The history of S-42 comes from the Naval Historical Center.

WAR FISH: The consummate troubles of the V-class submarines including the *Bonita* are covered in Clay Blair Jr., *Silent Victory: The U.S. Submarine War against Japan* (Annapolis, Md.: Naval Institute Press, 1975). Deck logs of the various submarines containing hour-by-hour notes of World War II subs, including *Bonita* (V-3), are available for review at the National Archives' research center in College Park, Maryland.

THE BOAT FROM SCOTLAND: The official war patrol records of the submarine *Barb* prior to Eugene Fluckey coming aboard provide the basis for this chapter, as well as the author's interview with Admiral McNitt and his oral history on file at the Nimitz Library at the Naval Academy. The invasion of North Africa in Operation Torch from a submarine point of view came from a Web site devoted to the first war patrol of USS *Gunnel* (SS-253), which participated in the invasion with the *Barb*. That Web site is www.jmlavelle.com.

PART TWO: The author consulted a number of primary sources in addition to Admiral Fluckey's own records and the recollections of spouses and veterans of the USS *Barb* for Part 2. Of great value were *Silent Victory* and *History of the U.S. Navy,* as mentioned above; the official war patrol reports of the *Barb,* reprinted by J. T. McDaniel, ed. (Riverdale, Ga.: Riverdale Books, 2005); Theodore Roscoe, *United States Submarine Operations in World War II* (Annapolis, Md.: Naval Institute Press, 1949), considered by submariners as the "bible" of the undersea war; and Admiral Eugene B. Fluckey, *Thunder Below!* (Chicago: University of Illinois Press, 1992), which covers the seventh through twelfth war patrols of the *Barb*. Additional notes regarding Part 2 are as follows.

RIFT: The so-called skipper problem in the early days of the war in which older submarine captains were criticized for a lack of aggressiveness plus the notorious torpedo malfunctions are fully explored in *Silent Victory* and *United States Submarine Operations in World War II.*

KITO: The capture of a Japanese sailor is described in *Navy Times, They Fought Under the Sea* (Harrisburg, Pa.: Stackpole Books, 1962).

LOST: Admiral McNitt's oral history on file at the Nimitz Library at the Naval Academy provides insight into how the former executive officer on the *Barb*'s ninth war patrol was able to find Australian prisoners of war adrift in the South China Sea. A more detailed account of Admiral McNitt's remarkable ability as a ship's navigator is covered in the admiral's article, "The First Watch," which appeared in *Proceedings* (January 1959, pp. 49–53), and "The Submarine Navigator—Some of His Methods," in *Proceedings* (May 1949, pp. 566–71). Transcripts of interviews conducted by author Clair Blair Jr. with Australian and British prisoners rescued by the *Barb* that were in Admiral Fluckey's personal records also were useful. The declassified report of POW experiences recorded by naval interrogators on the USS *Fulton* on 30 September 1944 provided great detail, as did the transcript of a remarkable speech that Neville Thams, one of the Australian prisoners rescued by the *Barb,* delivered on 19 March 1980 before the Broadbeach Lions Club in Southport, Queensland, Australia.

CHAOS: The construction of the Navy base in Majuro and other bases in the Pacific can be found at www.microworks.net/pacific/bases/btnb_online/majuro.htm.

SECRET HARBOR: Controversy over whether Capt. Fluckey received help from spies in the successful attack on Nam Kwan Harbor during the boat's eleventh war patrol is discussed in Capt. Emil Levine, USNR (Ret.), "Who Helped the Barb?" in *Naval History* (U.S. Naval Institute, June 2001, pp. 44–47). Additional narrative on the attack comes from Capt. Walter Karig, USNR, and Lt. Cdr. Frank A. Manson, USN, "The Hairbreadth Escapes of the Barb," *Saturday Evening Post* (22 October 1949). Captain Fluckey's warfighting leadership techniques and innovations are discussed in Lt. Nathan D. Luther's essay "Bureaucracy," *Proceedings* (February 2006).

MOM CHUNG: Information about Mom Chung is drawn from my earlier book, *Slade Cutter,* with additional sourcing from Judy Tzu-Chun Wu, *Dr. Mom Chung of the Fair Haired Bastards: The Life of a Wartime Celebrity* (Berkeley: University of California Press, 2005).

GRADUATION: The sabotage of the troop train by crewmen of the *Barb* on the boat's twelfth war patrol is recounted in Lt. John Strohmeyer, "The *Barb* Strikes" (publisher unknown), and "The Hairbreadth Escapes of the *Barb*" (previously cited). The American military believed troop trains moved at night to avoid attack.

PART THREE: Most of the material for this section comes from personal records of Admiral Fluckey and reflections of those who knew or worked with him. Additional sources are as follows.

NIMITZ: The rivalry between the Army and Navy during World War II and its aftermath are discussed in Dean C. Allard, "Interservice Differences in the United States, 1945–1950: A Naval Perspective," *Aerospace Power Journal* (Winter 1989). An excellent mini-biography of Fleet Adm. Chester William Nimitz is available through the Naval Historical Center at www.history.navy.mil/faqs/faq36-4.htm. Admiral Fluckey wrote of the Nimitzes' visit to his home with humorous consequences in Fluckey's "The Nimitzes Call," *Naval History* (Spring 1988). Additional reflections by Admiral Fluckey when he was Nimitz's aide can be found in Admiral Nimitz's oral history on file at the Nimitz Library; Admiral Fluckey contributed his recollections to that history in an interview by John T. Mason Jr. in 1971 in Portugal.

THE FLUCKEY FACTOR and FLAG OFFICER: Vice Adm. William R. Smedberg's oral history, vol. 2, on file at the Nimitz Library, covers the fund drive to build a football stadium at the academy and Captain Fluckey's involvement in that drive (pp. 527–34).

BOOMERS: Admiral Fluckey's daring swim in twenty-foot waves to the submarine *Plunger* to evaluate SubRoc missile tests is recounted in detail in "Admiral—by Choice—Is All Wet," *Honolulu Advertiser* (25 March 1965, p. A-9).

SINTRA: A summation of the threat to NATO posed by the Russian military came from NATO's online library found at www.nato.int/docu/com/49-95/c68115a.htm. Additional information came from Adm. Elmo R. Zumwalt Jr., "Where Russian Threat Keeps Growing," *U.S. News & World Report* (13 September 1971, pp. 72–77). The history of NATO's IBERLANT headquarters is found at www.jc-lisb.nato.int/history.htm.

EPILOGUE: IN HIS LIGHT: The Revolution of the Carnations is detailed in Blauer and Laure's *Portugal* (previously cited).

USS *Barb* Muster Rolls

Eighth War Patrol
Polar Circuit in Sea of Okhotsk—
21 May–9 July 1944 (49 days)

LCDR. Eugene B. FLUCKEY
LCDR. Robert W. McNITT
LT. James G. LANIER
LT. Jay A. EASTON
LT. Paul H. MONROE
LT. John R. POST
LT. Everett P. WEAVER
LTJG. Richard H. GIBSON
LTJG. David R. TEETERS

BENTLEY, Warren T. SC1
BLUTH, Paul D. QM3
BOCHENKO, Henry S. RM2
BRENDLE, Louis J. CFC
BROOCKS, William R. QM2
BYERS, Clarence J. TM3
CAMPBELL, Fred I. MoMM1
DAVIS, Ezra A. A. EM1
DITTMEYER, Jack L. RM1
DONNELLY, William E. CPhM

DOUGHERTY, Charles SC2
DURBIN, Troy MoMM2
EPPS, James O. EM1
FOSTER, Alyin B. GM3
GREENHALGH, Irving TM2
HINSON, Edward E. CRM
HOFFERBER, Edward H. QM2
HOGAN, John E. EM2
HOUSTON, Traville S. MoMM2
HUDGENS, Thomas J. CMoMM
JACKSON, Elmer J. CMoMM
JERNIGAN, Charles B. MoMM2
JOHNSON, Charles MoMM3
KERRIGAN, John C. RM2
KOESTER, Glen L. EM2
KOSINSKI, Julian MoMM3
LAMUTH, William C. EM2
LANGSTON, Claude MoMM3
LAUGHTER, Wade V. TM2
LEGO, Herman F. CY
LEHMAN, John H. RT2
LEIER, Ralph G. MoMM2
LIBBY, Frank W. CEM
LINDBERG, Wallace RM2

MAHER, Timothy P. RT1
MALAN, Stephen CCS
MARKUSON, John MoMM1
McCLOUD, Dean TM3
MILLER, Donald L. TM2
MULRY, Raymond D. EM2
MURPHY, Buell M. GM2
NOLL, Thomas P. CMoMM
NOVAK, Emil L. F1c
PENNA, Jesse L. MoMM2
PETERSON, Howard MoMM1
PETRASUNAS, Joseph GM2
PITTS, Morris C. EM2
POWELL, Henry J. TM3
RAGLAND, Paul F. Ck3
RICHARD, James E. MoMM2
ROARK, Rufus W. TM2
ROMASZEWSKJ, Anthony MoMM2
RYAN, Thomas J. MoMM1
SALANTAI, Joe A. TM2
SAUNDERS, Paul G. CGM
SAVAGE, Russell T. Y3c
SHANKLES, Ellis P. QM2
SHOARD, Sydney A. TM2
SIMPKINS, Cullen MoMM2
SMITH, Gaines W. TM1
SPENCER, Clarence MoMM2
STARKS, Frank E. CMoMM
STOWE, Carroll D. EM1
TOMCZYK, Charles A. TM1
TURNAGE, Sam M. MoMM1
VOGELEI, James P. SC2
WEARSCH, Norman MoMM2
WELLS, Robert W. TM3
WELLS, Stanfield McN. SM1
WELSH, Wesley A. EM1
WHITEHEAD, Gordon MoMM2
WIERSKI, Casmire TM2
WILLIAMS, Owen FC3
WILSON, Randall RM2
ZAMARIA, Joseph MoMM3

Ninth War Patrol
South China Sea and Luzon
Straits—4 August–3 October 1944
(59 days)

CAPT. Edwin R. SWINBURNE,
   Wolf Pack Commander
LCDR. Eugene B. FLUCKEY
LCDR. Robert W. McNITT
LCDR. Daniel S. BAUGHMAN PC
LT. James G. LANIER
LT. Max C. DUNCAN
LT. Paul H. MONROE
LT. Everett P. WEAVER
LTJG. Richard H. GIBSON
LTJG. David R. TEETERS

BENTLEY, Warren T. SC2
BLUTH, Paul D. QM2
BOCHENKO, Henry S. RM2
BOWDEN, Dallas G. EM1
BROOCKS, William R. QM2
BYERS, Clarence J. TM3
DAVIS, Ezra A. A. EM1
DONNELLY, William E. CPhM
DOUGHERTY, Charles SC2
DURBIN, Troy M. MoMM2
ELLIMAN, Russell R. Bkr3
EPPS, James O. EM1
FANNIN, William M. S1c
GREENHHALGH, Irving TM2
HANSLEY, John C. FC1
HIGGINS, John H. QM1
HINSON, Edward E. CRM
HOUSTON, Traville S. MoMM2
HUDGENS, Thomas J. CMoMM
JACKSON, Elmer J. Ck3
JOHNSON, Charles MoMM3
KERRIGAN, John C. RM2
KIRK, Travis G. S1c
KLINGLESMITH, Edward TM3

KOESTER, Glen L. EM2
KOSINSKI, Julian MoMM3
LAMUTH, William C. EM3
LANGSTON, Claude TM2
LARSEN, Norman EM3
LAUGHTER, Wade V. TM2
LEGO, Herman F. CY
LEHMAN, John H. RT2
LINDBERG, Wallace RM3
MAHER, Timothy P. RT3
MARKUSON, John RT1
MAXWELL, Richard S. TM2
McDOLE, Frederick EM1
McKEE, Edward L. MoMM3
McNALLY, Raymond D. Y2c
MILLER, Donald. L. TM2
MULRY, Raymond D. EM2
MURPHY, Buell M. GM2
NOLL, Thomas J. CMoMM
NOVAK, Emil L. F1c
PENNA, Jesse L. MoMM2
PETERSON, Howard MoMM1
PETRASUNAS, Joseph GM2
PITTS, Morris C. EM2
POWELL, Henry J. TM3
PRICE, Walter W. EM3
RAGLAND, Paul F. Ck3
RICHARD, James E. MoMM2
ROARK, Rufus W. TM2
RYAN, Thomas J. MoMM1
SALANTAI, Joe A. TM2
SAUNDERS, Paul G. CGM
SEVER, Neal Francis SM2
SHANKLES, Bills P. QM2
SHERMAN, Forrest H. EM1
SHOARD, Sydney A. TM2
SIMPKINS, Cullen MoMM2
SPENCER, Clarence MoMM2
SWEARINGEN, Charles EM3
TOMCZYK, Charles TM1
TURNAGE, Sam M. MoMM1

WEARSCH, Norman MoMM2
WELLS, Robert W. TM3
WHITEHEAD, Gordon MoMM2
WHITT, William F. MoMM1
WILLIAMS, Franklin CMoMM
WILSON, Randall RM2
ZAMARIA, Joseph MoMM3

Tenth War Patrol
East China Sea—27 October–25
November 1944 (29 days)

CDR. Eugene B. FLUCKEY
LT. James G. LANIER
LT. Max C. DUNCAN
LT. Paul H. MONROE
LT. Everett P. WEAVER
LTJG. Richard H. GIBSON
LTJG. David R. TEETERS
LTJG. Thomas M. KING
LTJG. Lawrence J. SHEFFIELD

ARTHUR, John J. TM2
BENTLEY, Warren T. SC2
BLUTH, Paul D. QM2
BOCHENKO, Henry S. RM2
BOWDEN, Dallas G. EM1
BROOCKS, William R. QM2
BURNETT, Michael FC3
CHAPMAN, Paul A. S1c
CUSTER, Russell A. MoMM3
DONNELLY, William E. CPhM
DURBIN, Troy M. MoMM2
ELLIMAN, Russell R. Bkr3
EPPS, James O. EM1
FANNIS, William M. S1c
FLAHERTY, Thomas J. S1c
HANSLEY, John C. FC1
HATFIELD, Billy R. EM3
HIGGINS, John H. QM1
HINSON, Edward E. CRM

HOUSTON, Traville S. MoMM2
HUDGENS, Thomas J. CMoMM
JOHNSON, Charles MoMMl
JONES, William L. StM2
KERRIGAN, John C. RM2
KIRK, Travis G. S1c
KLINGLESMITH, Edward TM3
KOESTER, Glen L. EM2
LANGSTON, Claude MoMM3
LARSEN, Norman EM3
LAUGHTER, Wade V. TM2
LEGO, Herman F. CY
LEHMAN, John H. RT2
LINDBERG, Wallace RM2
MAKER, Timothy P. RT1
MARKUSON, John MoMMl
MAXWELL, Richard S. TM2
McDOLE, Frederick EM1
McKEE, Edward L. MoMM3
McNALLY, Raymond D. Y2c
MILLER, Donald L. TM2
MULRY, Raymond D. EM2
MURPHY, Buell M. GM2
NOLL, Thomas J. CMoMM
NOVAK, Emil F1c
PENNA, Jesse L. MoMM2
PETERSON, Howard MoMM1
PETRASUNAS, Joseph GM2
PHILLIPS, Robert C. SC3
PITTS, Morris C. EM2
POWELL, Henry J. TM3
PRICE, Walter W. EM3
RAGLAND, Paul F. CK3
RICHARD, James E. MoMM2
ROARK, Rufus W. TM2
RYAN, Thomas J. MoMM1
SAUNDERS, Paul G. CGM
SCHMITT, Rudolph H. MoMM1
SEVER, Neal F. SM2
SHANKLES, Ellis P. QM2

SHERMAN, Forrest H. EM1
SHOARD, Sydney A. TM2
SIMEK, George L. F1c
SIMPKINS, Cullen MoMM2
SPENCER, Clarence MoMM2
SWEARINGEN, Charles EM3
TURNAGE, Sam M. MoMM1
WEARSCH, Norman MoMM2
WELLS, Robert TM3
W. WHITE, James A. TM3
WHITEHEAD, Gordon MoMM2
WHITT, William MoMM1
WILLIAMS, Franklin CMoMM
WILSON, Randall RM2
ZAMARIA, Joseph MoMM3

Eleventh War Patrol
East China Sea and Taiwan
(Formosa)—19 December–
15 February 1945 (56 days)

CDR. Eugene B. FLUCKEY
LT. James T. WEBSTER
LT. Max C. DUNCAN
LT. Paul H. MONROE
LT. Richard H. GIBSON
LT. William H. WALKER
LTJG. David R. TEETERS
LTJG. Thomas M. KING
LTJG. Lawrence J. SHEFFIELD

ALLEN, Fred W. EM1
ARTHUR, John J. TM2
BENTLEY, Warren T. SC2
BLUTH, Paul D. QM2
BOCHENKO Henry S. RM2
BOWDEN, Dallas G. EM1
BROOCKS, William R. QM2
BRUNTON, Howard A. F1c
BURNETT, Michael FC3

CHAPMAN, Paul S1c
COLE, David F. StM2
CUSTER, Russell A. MoMM3
DELAMATER, John T. RM2
DONNELLY, William E. CPhM
DURBIN, Troy M. MoMM2
EDWARDS, Mason L. MoMM2
ELLIMAN, Russell R. Bkr3
EPPS, James O. EM1
FANNIN, William M. S1c
FLAHERTY, Thomas J. S1c
HANSLEY, John C. FC1
HATFIELD, Billy R. EM3
HAZELWOOD, Emmit MoMM3
HIGGINS, John H. QM1
HINSON, Edward H. CRM
HOUSTON, Traville S. MoMM2
HUDGENS, Thomas J. CMoMM
HUTCHINSON, Alden MoMM1
JOHNSON, Charles MoMM1
KIRK, Travis G. S1c
KLINGLESMITH, Edward TM3
KOESTER, Glen L. EM2
LARSEN, Norman EM3
LAUGHTER, Wade V. TM2
LEGO, Herman F. CY
LEHMAN, John H. *RT2*
LINDBERG, Wallace RM2
MAHER, Timothy P. RT1
MARKUSON, John MoMM1
MAXWELL, Richard S. TM2
McDOLE, Frederick EM1
McKEE, Edward L. MoMM3
MILLER, Donald L. TM2
MULRY, Raymond D. EM2
NEWLAND, Lawrence SC1
NOLL, Thomas J. CMoMM
NOVAK, Emil L. F1c
PARKER, Todd D. TM1
PENNA, Jesse L. MoMM2

PETERSON, Howard MoMM1
PETRASUNAS, Joseph GM2
PHILLIPS, Robert C. SC3
POWELL, Henry J. TM3
PRICE, Walter W. Ck3
RAGLAND, Paul F. MoMM2
RICHARD, James E. TM2
ROARK, Rufus W. MoMM1
RYAN, Thomas J. CGM
SAUNDERS, Paul G. MoMM1
SCHMITT, Rudolph SM2
SEVER, Neal F. SM2
SHANKLES, Ellis P. QM2
SHERMAN, Forrest H. EM1
SHOARD, Sydney A. TM2
SIMEK, George L. F1c
SIMPKINS, Cullen MoMM2
SPENCER, Clarence MoMM2
SWEARINGEN, Charles EM3
TAGUE, Robert H. S1c
WEARSCH, Norman MoMM2
WELLS, Robert W. TM3
WHITE, James A. TM3
WHITEHEAD, Gordon MoMM2
WHITT, William F. MoMM1
WILLIAMS, Franklin CMoMM
WILSON, Randall RM2
ZAMARIA, Joseph MoMM3

Twelfth War Patrol
Empire Area (Okhotsk Sea)—
8 June–2 August 1945 (54 days)

CDR. Eugene B. FLUCKEY
LT. James T. WEBSTER
LT. Max C. DUNCAN
LT. William M. WALKER
LTJG. David R. TEETERS
LTJG. Charles W. HILL
LTJG. Thomas M. KING

LTJG. Lawrence J. SHEFFIELD
ENS. William MASEK Jr.

BENTLEY, Warren T. SC2
BLUTH, Paul D. QM3
BOCHENKO, Henry S. RM2
BROOKS, William R. QM2
BRUNTON, Howard A. F1c
BURNETT, Joseph H. S1c
BURNETT, Michael FC3
CHAPMAN, Paul A. S1c
COLE, David F. StM2
CUSTER, Russell A. MoMM2
DELAMATER, John T. RM2
DURBIN, Troy M. MoMM2
EDWARDS, Mason L. MoMM2
EPPS, James O. EM1
FLAHERTY, Thomas J. S1c
GIERHART, Frank W. CRM
HANSLEY, John C. FC1
HATFIELD, Billy R. EM3
HAZELWOOD, Emmit MoMM3
HIGGINS, John H. QM1
HILL, Leonard L. F1c
HUTCHINSON, Alden MoMM1
JOHNSON, Charles MoMM1
KIRK, Travis G. S1c
KLINGLESMITH, Edward TM3
KOESTER, Glen L. EM2
LARSEN, Norman EM3
LAYMAN, Cecil M. PhM1
LINDBERG, Wallace RM2
LUNDE, Everard Y3c
MAKER, Timothy P. RT1
MARKUSON, John MoMM1
MAXWELL, Richard S. TM2
MCCARTHY, James A. F1c
McDOLE, Frederick EM1
McKEE, Edward L. MoMM1
MILLER, Donald L. TM2

MULRY, Raymond D. EM2
NEWLAND, Lawrence SC1
NOLL, Thomas J. CMoMM
PARKER, Todd D. TM1
PENNA, Jesse L. MoMM2
PETRASUNAS, Joseph GM2
PHILLIPS, Robert C. SC3
POWELL, Henry J. TM3
PRICE, Walter W. EM3
RAGLAND, Paul F. Ck3
RICHARD, James E. MoMM2
ROARK, Rufus W. TM2
RYAN, Thomas J. MoMM1
SAUNDERS, Paul G. CGM
SCHILKE, Edwin E. RM3
SCHMITT, Rudolph MoMM1
SEVER, Neal F. SM2
SHANKLES, Ellis P. QM2
SHERMAN, Forrest EM1
SHOARD, Sydney A. TM2
SIMEK, George L. F1c
SIMPKINS, Cullen MoMM2
SINGER, Robert L. PhoM1
SPENCER, Clarence MoMM2
SWEARINGEN, Charles EM3
TAGUE, Robert H. S1c
TURNAGE, Sam M. MoMM1
WADE, Gordon L. CEM
WEARSCH, Norman MoMM2
WEAVER, Henry A. EM3
WELLS, Robert W. TM3
WHITE, James A. TM3
WHITT, William F. MoMM1
WILBY, Theodore SC3
WILLIAMS, Franklin CMoMM
WILLIAMS, Owen FC3
WILSON, Randall RM2
WOOD, Arthur R. MoMM3
ZAMARIA, Joseph MoMM3

Index

About the Author

Carl LaVO, a native of California and graduate of the University of Florida, is the author of *Back from the Deep: The Strange Story of the Sister Subs Squalus and Sculpin* and *Slade Cutter: Submarine Warrior,* both published by the Naval Institute Press. He has contributed stories to *Proceedings* and *Naval History,* periodicals published by the institute, as well as to a variety of popular magazines. He appeared on the History Channel in 2001 in the four-part series *Silent Service* and the series *Man, Moment and Machine* in 2004. He resides in Bucks County, Pennsylvania, with his wife Mary Anne, a photojournalist. They have a daughter, Genevieve, who is a studio artist and graphics designer.

LaVO is an experienced scuba diver who has explored many of the water-filled caverns and subterranean rivers of Florida, exceeding depths of two hundred feet. A childhood interest in the atomic submarine *Nautilus* and the book *Twenty Thousand Leagues Under the Sea* by Jules Verne gave him a lifelong curiosity about the Silent Service and underseas exploration. In high school he was co-founder of the Merced Explorers, which mapped many of the limestone caves of the Sierra Nevada Mountains.

LaVO is assistant managing editor of the daily and Sunday *Bucks County Courier Times* newspaper based in Levittown, Pennsylvania, and is an award-winning journalist.